Dear Rosie,
 Thank you for everything
 all of us and for bei...
 you can be.

   All my love always,
      Kate x Francis
         2006

THE BEST I CAN BE

ALLANA ARNOT
THE BEST I CAN BE

MACMILLAN
Pan Macmillan Australia

All reasonable attempts have been made by the author to obtain permission to quote from material known to be copyright, any copyright holders who believe their copyright to have been breached are invited to contact Pan Macmillan.

First published 1998 in Macmillan by Pan Macmillan Australia Pty Limited
St Martins Tower, 31 Market Street, Sydney

Copyright © Allana Arnot 1998

All rights reserved. No part of this book may be reproduced or transmitted in any form or by any means, electronic or mechanical, including photocopying, recording or by any information storage and retrieval system, without prior permission in writing from the publisher.

National Library of Australia
Cataloguing-in-Publication data:

Arnot, Allana.
The best I can be.

ISBN 0 7329 0969 4.

1. Arnot, Allana. 2. Physically handicapped – Australia – Biography. 3. Aircraft accident victims – Australia – Biography. 4. Air pilots – Australia – Biography. 5. Women air pilots – Australia – Biography. I. Title.

362.43092

Typeset in 12/16.5 Sabon by Midland Typesetters
Printed in Australia by McPherson's Printing Group

This book is dedicated to the memory of my friends:

Laurie Smith
Peter Whitehurst
Allan Hannah
Janine Watson
Robert Holmes
Lace Maxwell

Acknowledgments

Firstly, I wish to thank Amanda Hemmings for her support and encouragement as I was writing my book. Pan Macmillan for giving me the opportunity to tell my story. My editor, Carolyn Beaumont for guiding me through the writing process and sharing her knowledge and talent with me.

My thanks to the staff of Curtis Aviation who were most helpful with my research. I am very grateful to Kevin Waller who provided technical information regarding the coronial inquest into the two aeroplane crashes referred to in my book. And to David Dent from Dent Aviation for his professional advice and assistance. Thanks to Jenny Wickham for the use of her fantastic photographs and Jamie Campbell, Grant Shoreland and Jim Wickham for their help with my research and their wonderful friendship.

To my brother Derek, my sister Leanne, her husband

John, and their children Scott, Troy and Deneile. I thank you with all my heart for your never ending love and support.

Most importantly, I wish to thank my mum and dad. You have always been there when I've needed you. You have been with me through my darkest times, providing the strength I've needed to keep fighting and striving. When I decided to write my book you allowed me to use your holiday house for three months so I could begin. Then you welcomed me back home to the mountains where I finished my book. You have relived many emotions with me and endured the many demands that come with writing. I thank you for making this possible.

I was given life thirty-one years ago and it was almost taken away from me in December 1990. Since then every day is a gift. I thank God for my second chance.

Hold fast to dreams
For if dreams die,
Life is a broken-winged bird
That cannot fly.
— LANGSTON HUGHES

Contents

Preface 1
1 Carefree Childhood 7
2 Up, Up and Away 24
3 Give Me Wings 50
4 Life and Love with Nigel 72
5 The Day My Life Changed Forever 96
6 The Pain of Recovery 124
7 New Year – New Strength 148
8 One Step at a Time 167
9 The Long Road Ahead 188
10 Fighting for Me 214
11 Tragedy Again 233
12 Taking on Goliath 255
13 A New Beginning 274
14 My Greatest Adventure 295
15 Going Home 321

Preface

Ring! – Ring! – Ring! – I reach over, fumbling with the phone. A perky voice on the other end is singing 'wake up, wake up, you sleepy head – wake up, wake up, get out of bed.' I lie staring at the ceiling for a moment, smiling. Those recorded wake-up calls are always a bit over the top. But I don't need that much motivation to get up because today is the biggest day of my life. I sit up on the side of the bed, I can see the bright blue ocean from my hotel room window and all the way up North Wollongong Beach. Gentle waves roll in, lapping onto the white sands of the familiar coastline that has been my guide for the past six and a half weeks. Twenty-one thousand kilometres I've travelled around the whole of Australia. And today I'll make it home.

Local reporters are coming to pick me up at 8.30 to drive me to the airport, where my little helicopter sits waiting for the final leg of our epic journey. My clothes are laid out ready although the thought of wearing those jeans again is almost unbearable. I swear I'll burn them when I get home. With the limited luggage space and enormous amount of support equipment I needed, all I could fit in were two changes of clothes.

Almost 7 a.m. and I'd better get a move on. I reach down, picking my calipers off the floor and proceed to attach them to my lower legs. I fasten the straps that sit just below my knees and make sure my ankles and feet are placed snugly inside the braces. Look at my poor, wasted legs lying outstretched on the bed, so lifeless and numb. I pick up my shoes and carefully slide each foot in, feeling with my fingers to make sure all my toes are sitting straight. I usually hate this ritual and find the paraphernalia I have to wear every day cumbersome and a great bother. I hate the identity it gives me, but somehow it doesn't matter this morning. For all the labels that have been placed on me over the past six years – disabled, handicapped, paraplegic, crippled, and so they go on – now it doesn't matter because today I'm a survivor, a fighter, and today I'm an achiever. I notice the collection of newspaper articles on the coffee table. I have been saving them over the past few months. Some of the headlines read, 'Allana, the flying miracle', 'Paraplegic crash victim shows who's the boss', 'A flight back from hell'. It feels good to be me today, not because of all the media attention or recognition, but because of all the events that have brought me to this point in my life. It feels good to know that, despite all the barriers that were put in my way, I stepped around them. Every time I fell on my ass, I picked myself up and climbed the mountain I had created for myself. Today I'll reach the peak.

Preface

The phone rings again.

'Reporters from the *Illawarra Mercury* are here to pick you up, Mrs Arnot.'

'I'll be right down'.

'Hi, Allana, I'm Louise Turk, I'll be writing your story for our newspaper.' Louise has a relaxed approach and I feel instantly comfortable with her. She conducts her interview with me while Kirk Gilmour, the photographer, drives us to Albion Park Airport just south of Wollongong. I have become accustomed to the traditional questions reporters tend to ask as we talk about the plane crash that left me paraplegic, about my struggle to conquer the fear of flying, and particularly about the past six weeks. The twenty-five minute drive has given us time to complete the interview which is fortunate because, as we drive into the airfield, camera crews are also arriving. My small two-seat helicopter, named Echo Lima Foxtrot – ELF for short, is parked on a grass area not far away, still with her blades tied down and covers on, just the way I left her yesterday. A small group of onlookers are standing along the fence, curious to know what all the fuss is about.

It's 9 a.m. and although I have over an hour before becoming airborne, I'm keen to get the helicopter packed, pre-flighted and ready to go. Cameramen and photographers poke around taking close-up shots as I check the fuel and oil then complete my list of inspections around the blades and airframe.

'Everything is ready to go,' I announce.

Kirk is lying on the grass in front of the helicopter. 'Just come forward a bit, Allana, just a bit more, that's a great shot. Now look up a bit, perfect!' This continues for a few minutes until Kirk is satisfied he has the shot he wants for the newspaper.

My friend, Bruce Tarrant, from Westpac Rescue Helicopter Services arrives and is talking to the television reporters. It's nice to see a familiar face. The Westpac crew almost feel like part of my family. Not only did they save my life after the plane crash seven years ago, but some of their helicopter pilots have helped train me to fly.

The reporters from Prime and Win TV introduce themselves and they set up the cameras for the first interview. 'So how does it feel to be almost home after such a great adventure, Allana?' The questions continue and I answer them as best I can. The mood is electric and I guess everyone can feel my excitement as I joke around and join in light-hearted conversation while the second camera crew sets up.

'We're ready,' comes the call. I excuse myself from the group and walk over to meet the second reporter. The poor man is suffering a dreadful bout of hay fever but composes himself, taking his position with his back to the camera. The interview is going well until I see a stream of tears flowing down his face. I lose my concentration and start to laugh.

'Are you okay?' I ask.

'It's this damn hay fever,' he says. Again he wipes his eyes, stands straight-faced and repeats the question. I hesitate with the answer, only to bust into laughter again as more tears flow. I take a step forward and put my arm around him saying, 'I know it's a really emotional story, so just let it all out.' Everyone watching is also laughing as I struggle to complete the interview.

Preface

It's 9.30 a.m. That's good. I have half an hour to go, which gives me time for quiet reflection as I again walk around my helicopter making sure she is ready for the short flight home. Some of the media crew and onlookers stand by ELF amazed that this tiny machine, which looks more like a toy, has taken me around the country. Away from the cameras, they ask a barrage of questions that are on a more personal level. What made you want to fly in the first place? Who was it that inspired you to fly? Does anyone else in your family fly? Were you always this adventurous? Did you dream of flying helicopters as a child? My head is spinning, they probably wouldn't believe me if I told them my whole story.

There've been so many things that have happened in my life to bring me to this spot on this day. The line of questions makes me smile and think about a particular day when I was just six years old.

Chapter 1

Carefree Childhood

It was a typical summer's day and my father was busy in the backyard, smoothing out the top layer of a big square concrete slab. Dad was always doing something terribly important, inventing or building something of great worth. I watched with interest for a while from the second-storey verandah of our home, imagining what it could possibly be that had taken his attention for the past two days. The platform looked enormous and took up most of the back garden.

The day was heating up, cicadas sang their high-pitched song with its rhythmic beat. 'Mum, I'm going to the Coombers' house for a swim,' I called out.

'Have you asked if it's all right with Mrs Coomber?' Mum said.

'Yes, she knows I'm coming, I won't be late home.' My friend Daralyn had the most incredible in-ground pool at her house. It was lined with little blue tiles extending into a wall that rose up over a metre on two sides, where ugly-faced gargoyles with poised lips spat little fountains into the water. It was so luxurious I would never turn down the offer for a swim.

Mrs Coomber met me at the door. She was always bubbly. There were some other friends already there. 'Come in, Allana, what have you been doing today?' she asked

'Oh, not much, just helping my Dad build the helipad!'

'A helipad ... for a helicopter?' she questioned.

My reply was quite confident and matter of fact. 'Yes, that's right!'

These little fibs were common with me but I must admit, this was a doozy. Mrs Coomber delights in telling this story today and we both reflect on the irony of it now that I am a commercial helicopter pilot. Oh, and by the way, I really did believe that a helicopter was going to land on our pad – that was until the carport went up over the top of it. Anything is possible in the fanciful eyes of a child.

I don't recall having any desire to become a pilot and fly an aeroplane or a helicopter when I was little. But ever since I can remember, I've had flying dreams. Not of flying a machine, but clear and precise dreams where I take a few steps forward, flap my arms up and down, and before I know it I'm flying high above the trees. I usually take off from the back verandah at home and soar all over the countryside. It's terribly disappointing to wake up.

Home to me will always be the foothills of the Blue Mountains where I grew up. Mum and Dad are still living in the same house they built when they were first married. It was one of the first in the new estate of Lapstone, and almost the entire street was filled with young families so there were plenty of children around to play with. Often in the evenings there would be ten or so kids playing cricket in the street. I loved to join in. My brother, Derek, who was four years older than me, was usually playing as well, although he would roll his eyes in embarrassment when he saw his little sister coming. We didn't get on very well as kids, but I guess that's a common thing with brothers and sisters. Derek had a favourite trick to play on me. He would present me with a stick of paspalum and ask me to put it between my teeth like a Spanish dancer would do with a rose. Then he would pull the blunt end, shredding all the sticky black seeds through my teeth and into my mouth. Derek would roar with laughter as I stood spitting out sticky grass bits, somewhat humiliated, but at least satisfied that I had received his attention and provided for his amusement. I fell for that trick many times.

Derek was a tease but I think he was just relieving all the built-up frustration from being subjected to the same practical jokes and stirring from our sister, Leanne, who was ten years older than me. Poor Derek was completely defenceless against her unrelenting taunts, and I guess it was only natural, being the next in line, that I was Derek's target.

Whenever I was hurt or fell over, though, he was the first to run over to help and his concern was genuine. I remember we were racing each other home from the park one day, just on dusk, and we took different tracks down either side of a house. The local council had been preparing to lay huge concrete pipes along the pathway I was heading for and the pipes were stacked ready to be dug into the ground the next day. I could see Derek just ahead of me as our race continued. I could never beat him but I always tried my best. I scooted past the pipes, but the council workers had run a rope line to keep people away from the site. It was getting dark and I couldn't see the rope, so I collected it at chest height, catapulting me backwards, headfirst into the pipes, knocking me out cold. Derek was frantic. He had turned around in time to see it all happen and he ran back, trying to get me to come around. When I didn't, he ran home screaming for Mum. They both found me staggering down the middle of the road in a complete daze a few minutes later. I was very sick for about two weeks suffering severe concussion, and I was looked after by my doting brother.

Even as a little girl I'd squeeze the most out of life. I was extremely imaginative, adventurous and outgoing – a true individual, exuding confidence in everything I did, never afraid to climb the highest tree, welcoming any challenge and always the first to accept a dare. I remember how I used to scale the fence instead of using the gate in our backyard that led into a park. On a few occasions, I got hooked up and was left dangling until Mum heard my faint calls for help, or realised I'd been missing for too long and would come to rescue me. I must have been exhausting, and I seemed to have permanent scabbed knees, bumps and bruises.

My grandfather on my mother's side had lived with us for a year or so when I was four, going on five. He was a softly spoken man. We had a special bond and we were like two peas in a pod. One afternoon I was running down our steep driveway, bringing in some milk bottles, when I stumbled and fell onto the ground, smashing the glass and cutting a deep gash into my finger. Grandad was horrified. All he could do was bandage me up as best he could and wait for Mum to come home shortly after. When she walked in the door, she found us both in quite a mess with me sobbing into Grandad's embrace. It turned out I had cut all the tendons and had to have a few stitches. I was ultimately left with one very droopy finger.

When the exciting time came for my first day at school, I was almost jumping out of my skin to get there. I couldn't wait to meet my teacher and all the kids. Grandad watched proudly as Mum made such a fuss over me. I wanted to look my best and as I stood in the bathroom brushing my teeth, I decided that my already short and wispy hair needed a bit of a trim. I found Mum's good scissors in a box where she kept all the tools for cutting Dad's hair, then I took hold of my fringe and cut it straight across. Mum walked in just at the right time to see it happen. Half horrified and half amused, she spent the next ten minutes cleaning it up. I thought I looked beautiful though and, after waving goodbye to Grandad, I bounded in the school gate, dragging Mum along, ready for all this 'learning stuff'.

After school, Grandad would help me write the alphabet and sometimes read stories to me. He used to call me his 'bluebird of happiness' and he'd often make up stories about the bluebirds. I don't remember all the stories but they were always symbolic of hope, happiness and everything good. Grandad had a little ceramic bluebird in a trinket cabinet, which I used to love to play with, and with it I'd act out the stories. Although some of my memories of those days are a little fractured, I well remember how I loved my Grandad so much, and I can recall the last time I saw him as if it were yesterday.

Grandad had moved back to his home in Wagga Wagga and our family had gone to stay with him and Gran on a week's holiday that came to an end all too quickly. I was never very brave at goodbyes and I remember waving to him through the back window of our car as we drove off. I had little puddles of tears collecting in the creases of the red parka I was wearing. I think I knew it would be the last time I would see him.

Grandad died soon after and although I didn't really know what death was, I knew it was something final and I would never see him again. Mum decided it was best I didn't go to the funeral, but a few months later we went to visit Gran and Mum took me to the gravesite. I didn't understand why Grandad had been put in the ground, and I couldn't comprehend death at all. That afternoon Gran gave me the little ceramic bluebird to keep. Even today it makes me feel close to my grandfather. Mum keeps it in pride of place on the mantelpiece at home and every birthday she makes sure I have a little bluebird on my birthday cake or in a present somewhere.

Mum's sister and her family also lived in Wagga Wagga and Mum's brother and his family lived in Woomera, South Australia, at this time. Although there were great distances between the three families we were extremely close and on many occasions we managed to be together for special family functions, weddings, funerals, christenings. There seemed to be so many of us together at one time. It was noisy, often raucous, and I loved every minute of it. Lynda and Janine are two of my cousins. We're the same age, only three months separating the three of us. Because of this, we've grown up almost like sisters and we still keep tabs on each other. Lynda loved horse riding as a child and had her own pony named Polly. Janine was a more studious type and an avid reader.

My extended family on my father's side lived around the Sydney area although these cousins were all much older than I was and we didn't see as much of them. I was very close to my grandparents (on my father's side). Grandma and Pa Thomson were born in Scotland and although they had moved to Australia as young adults, they never shook their broad Scottish accents.

Weekends were a relaxing time for me, often spent at family picnics, pottering around the house or playing with my friends. Sometimes we'd get up to all sorts of mischief and, looking back on some of the things we did, they were downright dangerous. There was a train station about five minutes' walk from home, and at one end of the track there was a cutting in the rocks where the train would snake through. There were usually two or three of us egging each other on to run through the tunnel that was only wide enough to allow the train to pass. Strategically along the passage, there were safety refuges cut into the rock, and once or twice we had to dart into the nearest one, holding onto the safety bars as a train screeched past. This was one of the dumbest things I ever did, but at that very young age I felt ten feet tall and bullet proof. I could push the limit because nothing bad could ever possibly happen to me!

On warm summer mornings, my favourite place to go was into the bush. There was a natural gully just at the end of our street and if ever I had a special place, that was it. The forever changing beauty was enchanting, drawing me into it time and again. Sometimes hours would pass while I lost myself in its tranquil charm.

Along a steep ledge there was a series of caves. Sometimes I'd climb up the rock face and then sneak my way along the sheer ridge so I could venture inside for a closer inspection. One time I found what remained of a small fire in one of the largest caves. There were also some candles and empty tin cans lying around. I remember feeling disappointed that somebody else had been in this place.

After a rain shower, waterfalls would flow along the rocks, changing my natural playground again. The string of little pools not only provided relief from the summer heat, they created even more interesting things to see and discover. Sometimes a few friends would come along and we'd trek down to the pools armed with ice-cream containers on a hunt for tadpoles. Slippery little things they are, but I always managed to get a few and would take them home to present to Mum.

'Look what I caught!' I would say. Mum always showed a great deal of interest despite her cringing expression.

Mum and Dad had a caravan at a permanent site in Sussex Inlet, which is on the New South Wales coast, south of Sydney. This was our usual holiday destination. We have been going there since I was about five. It was our home away from home. In the caravan next to ours were Bill and Gloria Quinn, whose children had grown up, and who would let me play with their little dog, Suzy.

Bill was a real character. 'I'm going to marry you one day, Bill!' I used to tell him.

He and Dad were keen fishermen and would go off for the day in their boats while Mum took us kids to the beach or swimming in Swan Lake not far away. In the summer time, the town would hold weekend fishing competitions. There'd be many boats out and people would catch beautiful big fish in the river. At the end of the weekend, there would be a presentation night where prizes were awarded for catches in several categories. My Dad won an Esky one year for a prize flathead.

When I was a bit older, Dad would take me out on the river to go fishing with him, and sometimes my Uncle Pete would come along in his own boat. Uncle Pete and Aunty Marion weren't really related, but they were such close friends of Mum and Dad's that I always called them Uncle and Aunty.

I would scream out whenever I caught a fish. 'Look what I caught, Uncle Pete,' holding it up for him to see.

'Good one, Lani,' he'd always call back.

On the nights when the prawns were running, the river would be lit up like fairyland with dozens of people floating their lanterns on the water. The lanterns would reflect the prawns' eyes, and then they'd be scooped up. There were huge pots of boiling water on the bank where Mum and I would watch as Dad brought in his catch, and we would cook up the prawns right there and then. They were great days.

Dad and Uncle Pete were prawning one night, whispering to each other as the idea was to keep really quiet and not scare the prawns away. As Mum and I waited on the bank, we suddenly heard two almighty screams. We could see the two men wading back to shore in a frenzied panic. Later we laughed when they told the tale of an over-friendly eel, 'as big as a boa constrictor', chasing them out of the water.

On Saturday mornings at Sussex Inlet, there was a chook raffle held outside the old corner store at the caravan park. There was a chocolate wheel and all you had to do was buy a ticket for twenty cents and hope your number came up. One day, Mum, Dad and Derek were getting our boat ready to motor to a spot further upstream where we were going to have a picnic. In the meantime, I wandered over to the crowd that had gathered for the raffle and paid the man my twenty cents. Mum and Dad noticed that I was missing. I could hear them calling for me but I ignored them, mingling amongst the people watching the wheel finally whizzing around.

'Number twenty-seven,' the man announced.

'I won, I won,' I called out, pushing my way to the front to collect my frozen number seventeen chook. Mum loves to tell the story of my gangly little legs running as fast as they could towards her, while I was screaming out, 'Look Mum, I won a chicken!'

Sussex Inlet was great fun. There was always a huge bonfire at the caravan park on Cracker Night, Easter bonnet parades at Easter, and Santa making an appearance for

Carefree Childhood

Christmas. When I was about eleven, Mum and Dad bought a block of land just up the road from the caravan park and Dad built a two-bedroom holiday cottage that the whole family still uses during summer. It's fitting that this is the quiet haven I've chosen to retreat to while I write my book.

All in all, my young years were filled with happy memories although the most difficult times for me as a child were a result of a medical condition, which I had been born with, called kidney reflux. As a result, I was often stricken with kidney infections that were not only painful but made me very ill.

Treatment and testing for this ailment began at a very young age, about three years old. I can vividly remember being subjected to horrible tests in various clinics and I was permanently taking medications to control the attacks of infection.

I was five years old when I was first required to be hospitalised for more testing. It was very frightening. Mum and Dad took me on the train to Sydney and then we boarded a bus that took us to Prince Henry Hospital, located on the coast south of the city. The hospital grounds were spread out and, as we walked along the road to the Children's Ward, we passed separate single-storey white buildings. The Children's Ward was down a hill and looked a lot taller than the others. Its dark brickwork made it even more menacing.

Mum and Dad stayed with me until late in the afternoon, making sure I was settled in while a nurse took my temperature and explained to me that, in the morning, I'd go to theatre and be given a little needle that'd feel just like a mosquito bite. This would make me go fast asleep, and when I woke up I'd be taken back to the ward and Mum and Dad would be waiting for me.

The only theatre I had heard of was a picture theatre, so I didn't really understand where I was going. I'd had plenty of needles in the past, too, which had felt nothing like a mosquito bite. Despite this attempt to prepare me for tomorrow's ordeal, I was terrified. I cried when Mum and Dad had to go home and leave me, but after a while I was encouraged by one of the nurses to explore my new surroundings where I would be staying for three days.

The ward was one long room with beds down each side, strategically separated in places by dividing walls. There were some closed-in rooms but my bed was in the main part of the ward. As I walked down the cold white floor, I noticed bright and colourful cartoon characters painted onto most of the walls. At the end of the room was a doorway leading into a private room with a large window at the end. I felt drawn towards it. The window was opened slightly and as I came nearer, I caught the scent of the fresh sea air interrupting the clinical hospital smell.

From here, I could see down to a grassy field and the wild ocean pounding onto the rocks at the shore. The blue water sparkled and went forever into the distance. This is where I liked to spend my time while I was in hospital. These visits were always traumatic. I'd have to endure them every three to six months at first, then each year until I was almost a teenager. Prince Henry became a very familiar place to me.

★

As I reached my teenage years and started high school, my rebellious side came out. I was in most of the higher-graded classes, but was considered somewhat disruptive and was often asked to leave the room in the middle of a lesson. This was usually in English, of all subjects. The restraints of having to sit for forty minutes in a class, then move to another room and sit through another forty minutes, bored me terribly. My school reports always said things like, 'Allana could do much better if she applied herself'.

Many times I used to wag school with friends and we often spent the day swimming in the Nepean River. Sometimes Derek would catch me and rush home to tell Mum. He was very concerned for my safety and well-being. But at the time, I just saw him as a dobber. Mum laughs about this now, and wonders how I finally became educated. 'You were never at school,' she says.

When I was almost fifteen, I started dating a guy named Tim Honess, who was a year older than me and in the form above. Tim was slightly eccentric, almost a hippy, however less herbal and more neurotic than some. My attraction towards him is something I still have trouble analysing, but initially it was his uniqueness that captured my imagination. His personality was often childlike and there was something about him that made him appear very vulnerable. Tim had a gift for music and I'd go so far as to say he was bordering on genius. He could hear a piece of music, pick up a guitar and start to play it, or touch a keyboard and do the same.

As our relationship progressed, Tim became more possessive and obsessed with me, to the point where we couldn't go out to restaurants or movies or do any normal things young couples do because inevitably Tim would get into a fight. He didn't like other guys looking at me. And so began a chapter in my life that would last more than four years.

When I left school at fifteen, I enrolled in a twelve-month technical college course doing secretarial studies. The first week was a nightmare as Tim came to terms with me spending each day at a place outside his control. One day I went to his house for lunch, intending to return to tech for my afternoon lessons. But he couldn't bear to let me go back and so he barricaded me in the bathroom for the afternoon. I don't know why I tolerated these events, but I was very young and stupid. Things eased off gradually and Tim became used to me attending college. I eventually graduated from the course. How, I'll never know!

I was nineteen when I finally came to my senses and decided to end the relationship. As you could imagine, it was a devastating scene. Tim plummeted downhill, according to the reports I received from our friends. However, I disciplined myself to stay away from him. It wasn't until three months later that he turned up on our doorstep. Mum, Dad and I were shocked at how much weight he'd lost, in fact his entire appearance had changed so dramatically he was almost unrecognisable. Tim seemed quite rational though and we spent an hour or so talking sensibly about the past months. We agreed to remain friends and started to spend more time together. This was a very bad move!

It became apparent that Tim's weight loss was a result of him continuously indulging in drug use, mainly amphetamines (speed). He told me he'd turned to them to help him cope with our split. Over the next few weeks, his demeanour changed again and he blamed his new drug problem on me. Somehow he convinced me that I was responsible and completely to blame, and I believed him. From here, Tim kept telling me it was my duty to help him stop the drugs because I had caused his problems. I didn't know what to do, but I did try to be a supportive friend, which didn't really help because after a period of a few months nothing had changed.

'Just stop, walk away from the drugs, you don't need them,' I kept saying to him.

Tim's reply was, 'I can't stop, you don't know how addictive the drugs are, you have to try it to understand.'

This continued, as he methodically assured me I had no credibility to be telling him to stop the drugs, until I tried them myself. So I did. But still nothing changed with Tim. He wouldn't listen to me, even though I had done as he asked. 'Once isn't enough,' he started to say. Looking back on this part of my life, not only am I ashamed, but I am extremely embarrassed to realise how weak I was. It was an episode that took place, and it is part of the many facets of my life that have made me who I am today. My story would not be complete if I didn't include this, although it is very difficult for me to write about it.

For three months I allowed myself to be dragged down into the gutter. Now we were both taking drugs. My own weight also plummeted and my health suffered terribly. At one stage, I hadn't had any sleep or eaten for about four days. I looked at myself in the mirror and didn't recognise the person looking back at me. I was under Tim's control again, and I knew I had to walk away from him for good. His problems were his to sort out, but if I didn't take action immediately, I knew the drugs would eventually kill me.

The end was frightening and violent! I drove to Tim's house where he still lived with his parents. We were outside talking, and I told him I didn't think I was helping him and that he couldn't see me anymore. I was still sitting in my car with the door open and, before I knew what was happening, he began a frenzied attack, kicking me. I reached for the door while also trying to fend off his blows but, before I could close it, he grabbed the back of my jumper and dragged me out over the grass and up a small flight of concrete stairs. I was trying to gasp for air as the woollen collar cut into my neck. Tim opened the front door and threw me inside, demanding that I apologise to his mother. I didn't know what I was apologising for, but I wasn't going to argue with him, so I stumbled into the kitchen where she was standing and spluttered out some nonsensical blurb before making my escape while his parents tried to calm him down.

Tim continued to stalk me for almost a year. And after that he would call me every now and again, usually every six months. But, by then, it was only to ask for money to buy drugs.

Tim was found dead by his parents in their home, where he was residing, in 1997. Various reports say the cause of death was a drug overdose. Either way, the Tim I knew had died in my heart years before, and on hearing the report it came as no surprise. It was only a matter of time. I always knew that. I still cried for him, his life was such a waste. Behind the tough facade, Tim had a gentle soul. But despite this, his incredible talent for music and the love and support from his wonderful family, Tim believed the world owed him something and he lived his life with a huge chip on his shoulder. It's sad that he didn't get the chance to share his gift – Tim had the world at his feet but he just couldn't see it.

Chapter 2

Up, Up and Away

It was 1987, the year of Mum's fiftieth birthday. I could never have imagined such a celebration would set off a chain of events that would alter my life forever.

I'm afraid to say that my family had never made a great effort to mark Mum's birthdays and make them special for her. In fact there were times when she'd have to remind us that it was her birthday. It was Leanne's suggestion to make up for those years, given this was her fiftieth. We would throw her a surprise party. We had about two months to make the arrangements and between Dad, Derek, Leanne and me, the plans went into full swing. We decided on a function room at a leisure centre that usually hosted exhibitions, car shows and the like. We made up a guest list of fifty people and held many secret discussions over the next few weeks. We were very excited. Everything was on track and running smoothly. Mum didn't have a clue.

I was having dinner with Mum and Dad one night.

Mum was particularly quiet and then she unexpectedly announced, 'I am going to have a birthday party!' Dad and I looked at each other astonished, not knowing what to say. We both thought someone must have let the cat out of the bag until she added, 'For the first time, I am going to celebrate my birthday in style. The invitations are all ready to go, it's going to be a great party.'

'What a wonderful idea,' was the only reply I could muster without choking on my mouthful of lamb cutlet. The next day all our guests had to be contacted. Derek, Leanne and I shared the list and phoned them to report this new development. They simply had to go along with it until we could work out what to do. Fortunately Mum's invitations put her party two weeks after ours, so we just let her continue making the arrangements for her second celebration.

The day before the big event, my Gran arrived in secret from Wagga Wagga and was hiding out at Leanne and her husband John's house, along with my Uncle Richard and Aunty Bev who had driven across from Mt Gambier where they now lived. Our plan was coming together, but it was so difficult acting normally at home because I felt so tensely excited.

The big day arrived. At lunch time I went down to the function centre with a few helpers to decorate the room. Derek met me there to make sure everything was running on schedule. On the wall, we hung a huge banner that we'd had an artist paint for us. It read Happy Birthday, May in huge bright yellow and red letters. Streamers and balloons hung from the ceiling and fresh flower arrangements were centred on each table. Late in the afternoon, the caterers arrived to prepare the food. We'd agreed on a smorgasbord with a selection of hot and cold dishes. The three-piece band we'd hired for the night was setting up, so I went back home to get ready. I told Mum I was going out for the night with some friends. Mum thought she was getting ready to go to dinner with Uncle Pete and Aunty Marion at a restaurant in Blacktown.

'Have a good time, Mum, don't wait up,' I said, kissing her goodbye.

As the final hour's countdown started, the guests began arriving. We had already briefed the caretaker of the centre that the guest of honour would think she was coming to see a boat exhibition with Dad on their way to dinner. We even had signs saying Boat Show on display at the door. The band was warming up and Derek stood pacing across the entrance like an expectant father waiting for the big arrival. 'Here they come' was whispered like an echo through the hall. Everyone stood quietly, only the occasional whisper and 'shhh' could be heard.

Dad parked the car. 'Come on, Pete, I want to show you this boat quickly, then we'll go to the restaurant.' Mum was slightly annoyed at this inconvenient diversion. After all, they did have a restaurant booking. She had to be strongly encouraged to venture inside to see the boat. The caretaker was waiting behind the reception desk looking very official.

Dad greeted him with, 'Hi, mate, we're here for the boat show.'

'Well, we're about to close for the night. But I suppose I can give you a few minutes. Come this way.' As the caretaker opened the door for them, Mum was directed in first to explosive screams of 'SURPRISE'. The look on her face was priceless. She was completely stunned, unable to say a word. The band flew into 'Happy Birthday to you ...' right on cue. It was a total surprise.

Our friends and family enjoyed a fantastic night. During the speeches, Mum informed her guests that the party she had planned was cancelled. As she said, 'Who could top this?' And I was pleased that she looked a little bit embarrassed.

My job was to present Mum with a joint gift from the four of us. A lot of thought went into choosing something perfect and memorable. Mum is so outgoing. She will give anything a try and she's sometimes a bit of a dare-devil. I remember when Derek and I were little, Mum and Dad sometimes took us to fun parks. Mum would always come with us on the roller-coaster and other scary rides. On a recent trip to Thailand, Mum and Dad were in the crowd watching working elephants show their skills. A volunteer was invited to come forward from the audience to help display how gentle and disciplined the animals were. Mum enthusiastically stepped up much to Dad's horror, and she happily followed the instructions to lie flat on the ground, remaining very still while the elephant stepped right over the top of her. 'I hoped he was well coordinated' is all she said later.

You can understand then why we were unanimous in our choice of a gift. We wanted something that would reflect Mum's personality – a ride in a hot-air balloon.

You could see her excitement at the prospect of her

pending adventure. At the end of the night, we were exhausted but ecstatically happy to have celebrated Mum's fiftieth birthday with such a fantastic occasion.

A month had passed, it was early Sunday morning, about 2 a.m. when I arrived home. I had spent Saturday night dancing with friends at Panthers Leagues Club at Penrith. It seemed that I had only just put my head down and fallen asleep, when Mum was gently shaking my shoulder, trying to wake me.

'Come on, Allana, get up, we're all going ballooning.' My Aunty Heather – Mum's sister – and Uncle Mervyn had driven up from Wagga Wagga to watch, and Uncle Pete, my old fishing buddy, was so taken with the idea of flying in a balloon that he had bought himself a place in the basket as well. Everyone was getting ready to go.

'What's the time?'

'It's 3.45 a.m. Come on, get up!'

'I'm too tired. You go and have a good time.'

'No, it won't be the same if you don't come.'

I realised she wasn't going to let up so I dragged myself out of bed. 'Where do we have to go, again?'

'Camden Airport'

'I'm too tired to drive to Camden, wherever that is.'

'Well, you can go along with Leanne and John.'

Yes, the whole gang was going to be there to see Mum safely into the air. We were to meet at Camden Airport after Mum and Uncle Pete had gone to a special briefing at Balloon Aloft's headquarters.

Driving into the airport at 5 a.m., a ridiculous hour for

a Sunday morning, everything was very quiet. There was nobody around. The air was still and it had a crispness about it. There were little patches of fog nestling in the valleys along the river. I was captured for a moment by the beauty around me. There were several large hangars, each closed. When we stopped the car, I could see something strange resting against one of the buildings and I went for a closer look. It was a hovercraft. Very old and broken down, it obviously hadn't been run for a long time. I looked around, fantasising about the old aeroplanes that were probably stored in the hangars, imagining old Tiger Moths, the only aeroplane I knew the name of, playing among the puffy clouds that were starting to develop above the hills in the distance. Dancing around in my head were visions of the old barnstorming days, when audacious young men dressed in jodhpurs and brown leather flying jackets pushed the boundaries of a new, third-dimensional world, pioneering their way in rattly old flying machines. My own anticipation and excitement was growing by the second, knowing I'd be seeing and touching a real life hot-air balloon this morning. Until now, the only ones I'd seen were in picture books and on television. Just imagine how incredible they must have seemed in the early days of flying balloons when the Montgolfier brothers were first sending people into the air way back in 1783.

The tranquil silence of the morning was broken by the rumble of the Balloon Aloft company trailer entering the airfield with a small convoy of vehicles following. They came to a stop outside the amenities block not far from where I was standing. The main vehicle was an old converted ambulance, which I hoped was not an omen. My wild imagination again! The door opened and people started piling out one after another, about fifteen of them. I saw Mum and Uncle Pete in there too. I was surprised to learn that the morning's flight required only one crew and one pilot. The pilot was a tall thin man named Jim Murray. Wearing a big cowboy hat, he looked just the part. He had the biggest, happiest smile and he was very friendly, making everyone feel relaxed. The crew chief was a young guy named Laurie Smith who also went out of his way to make us feel like an important part of the morning's proceedings.

Laurie drove the vehicle onto a grass area near the runway and we followed on foot. The first job was to drag the balloon basket off the trailer. It was huge and could carry eight passengers. Everyone helped. The balloon itself was stored in a big canvas bag. Once attached to the basket, we dragged the bag along the ground, feeding the balloon out like a big sausage. The group was split in two and given positions down each side of the fabric. Next we dragged both sides out to expose the brightly coloured canopy of red, white and blue stripes now taking form. The material was only thin ripstock nylon. I couldn't imagine that this flimsy web was going to hold my mum and eight other people up in the air.

The mood was uplifting. We could see our balloon taking shape, and being able to help made the experience even more special. Jim explained to us that every balloon has a name and that ours was known as Bojangles.

Now we were ready to inflate the balloon. Uncle Pete

and Derek were selected to hold the mouth open. This was a critical job because the flame from the burner would be passing very close to them. A big fan was initially used to inflate the nylon envelope. I stood back in awe as Bojangles began to fill with air, as if the balloon were rising out of the ground. The sheer size of the balloon was breathtaking. Jim lit the burners and began heating the air inside. The balloon waffled around the ground then slowly rose like a friendly giant waking from a long sleep. Laurie and two other people were being dragged along the ground from a rope that was attached to the very tip of the balloon. They were there to control Bojangles' inflation so she wouldn't rise off the ground too quickly. I laughed out loud. It looked so funny, like a scene out of The Three Stooges. They certainly didn't look like they had any control at all.

Everyone rushed to the basket. As the big round canopy settled into position above us, Jim asked us to put our weight on the sides so he wouldn't take off while his passengers were getting in. Mum and Uncle Pete established their position inside the basket with the other passengers and, with a few short bursts of flame, they were up, up and away. I was screaming 'Bon voyage' and waving frantically, but before long they had drifted too far away to hear me calling.

Laurie was keen to leave the launch site now. He explained that the balloon would drift along with the wind and we would chase it to its final landing spot.

'Where will that be?' I asked.

'Wherever it ends up,' was a reasonable reply, I thought.

I hadn't really noticed until then that Laurie was paying me a lot of attention, much to the amusement of my family. He asked if I would like to travel with him in the chase vehicle while we tracked Bojangles. He was really cute, so I jumped at the chance. Our little convoy with Derek, Leanne and John, Aunty Heather and Uncle Mervyn included, trundled down the road keeping Bojangles in sight. As we chattered, Laurie told me ballooning was only a part-time job and that he was a commercial pilot, one day hoping to get a job with an airline. He was also a keen skydiver. I was suitably impressed that this 24-year-old had achieved so much and was living such an exciting life. Although I was only nineteen-years-old, Laurie didn't seem that much older than me. But his life was so different from mine. I had never met a real life pilot before so when he asked what I did for a living, 'legal secretary' sounded incredibly humdrum. My working week consisted of typing, answering the phone and running around town doing errands for my boss – boring!

Jim kept in constant contact with Laurie by radio and, after flying for an hour, he picked out a suitable paddock to land the balloon, not far from where we were. We arrived first and we watched as the balloon gently bounced back onto mother earth. Mum's face was still poking up over the basket, her big smile proving she had enjoyed every minute of her flight.

After packing everything away, Jim and Laurie offered me a ride back to their headquarters where the group would meet for a champagne breakfast. I was keen to learn more about ballooning and Jim obliged with his hilarious adventure stories. Jim had stopped outside the amenities block at the airport earlier that morning and made all his passengers use the facilities because one day he'd had a passenger who desperately had to use the bathroom midway through the flight. Jim landed next to a farmhouse and the lady jumped out of the basket, ran across to the homestead and knocked on the door, asking the elderly couple who were still in their pyjamas if she could use their toilet. Another morning, Jim was floating low across a field that led straight to a home where he and his passengers could see a naked lady standing in the window. She stayed there, looking straight at them, unaware that they could see her until one of the men in the basket waved. You could imagine how embarrassed she must have been.

As we pulled into Balloon Aloft's base, Jim asked me if I would like to come and help out again the next weekend.

That week went so slowly. I had given Laurie my phone number at work and he rang me on Friday to make sure I was still coming along.

'Are you kidding, I can't wait,' I told him. In fact I ended up helping out on the Saturday and Sunday flights. Laurie and I worked together. He showed me how all the cables and controls on the balloon worked, and he explained how to track it during the flight. We packed Bojangles up together at the end and I helped him with the champagne breakfast. Laurie and I didn't stop talking the whole time, while Jim looked on with an approving twinkle in his eye. The three of us were becoming quite a team, and I was becoming hooked on the idea of ballooning – and Laurie as well.

'It looks like I might have a spare slot in the basket next

weekend, Allana, I think you should come for a ride,' Jim said.

I couldn't believe it. The anticipation that week was almost unbearable.

Saturday morning was perfect, still as still. There was a bit of fog around that made the atmosphere strange and eerie. I climbed aboard joining the other seven passengers, then Jim gave Bojangles a few short bursts of flame. I was both excited and apprehensive.

I had never flown before, apart from in a Jumbo when I went on a family holiday to America. But that had been eight years earlier when I was eleven years old. I remember that flight clearly. The air hostesses were very friendly and had handed Derek and me a packet of playing cards to keep us amused. The start of the engines had given me an awful fright, making me sit bolt upright, gripping white knuckles onto the armrests. The entire aircraft had seemed to creak and groan as we taxied along. I was quite terrified, not knowing what to expect. Then we came to a complete stop, the anticipation making me feel even more anxious.

'This is it,' Mum had said, placing her reassuring hand on mine. The low drone of the engine built quickly into a roar. I could feel my body being pushed hard against the back of the seat as I watched the airport buildings pass by the window, going faster and faster. The nose of the aeroplane had begun to rise. I directed my attention forwards and I noticed I was looking uphill and the walls of the cabin were flexing quite considerably.

'Yahoo!' Derek had said. 'Look, we're off the ground.'

The tall surrounding office buildings were way below us now. It felt strange looking down at them from high above. We were soon headed straight out over the ocean for the very long flight, direct to Hawaii ...

'Everybody ready?' Jim asked his passengers in the balloon. Up we went, ever so gently. There was no sensation at all to indicate we were rising into the air. It was as if the balloon had stayed perfectly still and the earth was dropping down away from us. I was amazed how stable the basket felt underfoot and, as we climbed higher, you could see from horizon to horizon. There I was, suspended over the world, looking down to the Camden Valley. It was the most beautiful sight I had ever seen. I looked up and was able to see inside the colourful ball that contained nothing but hot air. I found it difficult to comprehend that this balloon was carrying us a thousand feet over the land.

Apart from the occasional burst of flame required to keep us buoyant, it was quiet and peaceful up there. I had my body wedged in the corner of the basket with my arms folded on the padded suede rim, oblivious to the people around me. This was my world as I'd never seen it before. Flying so high above it made me feel invincible, yet vulnerable at the same time. Look at the tiny trees and miniature cows scattered in that field. Look how the river winds all around the airport, and how the township of Camden is like a toy village, complete with church and steeple on the top of the hill. The warmth of the sun touched my face as it finally emerged to hover low in the distance, allowing my world to at last awaken.

Sometimes we flew up high, which was so exhilarating it made me feel at one with all I surveyed. And sometimes we flew low, even skimming the tops of the trees where I saw a family of birds hopping from branch to branch. On the other side was a paddock leading to a farmhouse, and an old man and an old lady were standing on their back verandah.

'Good morning!' they called out, as we floated by.

'It is a beautiful morning,' I called back with an enthusiastic giggle. How blessed I felt to venture into this new dimension – the sky – where there were no boundaries, no restrictions. All I felt were peace and freedom, my head resting on my arm as I gazed dreamily out.

'Are you enjoying yourself, Allana?' Jim called out to me.

'Oh, Jim, this is the highlight of my whole life,' I answered.

Jim had a good site picked out ahead and he asked everyone to brace themselves against the basket as we came into land. It wasn't necessary though, because we kissed the ground so gently you couldn't even feel it. What a morning! Something had been awoken in me, something I could never turn my back on, ever again – a need to fly. But the day wasn't over yet.

After packing up the balloon and finishing the chores ready for tomorrow's flight, Laurie told me he would be taking some friends flying that afternoon and he asked if I would like to go along. I still couldn't imagine he was going to fly an aeroplane all by himself, but feeling like an experienced aviator all of a sudden, I accepted. We met Laurie's friends, Jamie and Jeannie, back at Camden Airport at about lunchtime and wandered over to the aeroplane Laurie had hired. It was a Cessna 172 called the Yerranderie Silver Ghost. Strange name for an aeroplane, I thought, but I climbed into the back seat with Jeannie feeling confident and very spoilt.

'Where are we going?' I asked Laurie.

'Let's fly over to Wilton Parachuting Centre. We can land there and have some lunch.' How decadent, if only my mum and dad could see me now.

Laurie had already walked around the outside of the aeroplane checking the wings, controls, wheels and oil. He made his way into the pilot seat next to Jamie and put on his seatbelt and headset.

'Is everybody comfortable?' he asked, before reaching over and turning the key to the master switch.

The engine fired up immediately. It was very noisy in the cabin as I didn't have a headset to wear. Jeannie and I had to yell so we could hear each other. She was as excited as I was. With a quick burst of power, Laurie directed the aeroplane forwards along the taxiway. There were a few corners to negotiate and I noticed Laurie didn't even have his hands on the steering wheel. I wondered how he was controlling our direction, until I looked down and noticed he was using the pedals on the floor to turn left and right. We turned into an area where a sign said, Run-up bay. Laurie stopped the aircraft, then pushed the throttle in. I could feel the aeroplane wanting to leap forwards. It would have, too, if Laurie hadn't had his feet firmly on the brakes. He turned the key alternately onto two different positions, which changed the pitch of the engine. Then he pulled the throttle back, putting it into idle.

'Everything is in order,' he announced. As we headed towards the main runway, Laurie picked up a microphone from the top left-hand corner of the cockpit and was talking, presumably, to the tower although I couldn't hear what he was saying. I concentrated hard, analysing everything Laurie did, especially during the take-off. We ran onto the runway and stopped, looking towards the enormous strip of bitumen that had a broken white line running down the centre. Laurie pushed the throttle all the way in and we began to build up speed. Then he pulled back gently on the steering wheel and we lifted off the ground. The earth fell away and we were off. I watched in awe as Laurie flew us around that day, he was so efficient and so confident. There were many buttons to push and levers to pull and he did it all. I want to be able to do that too one day, I thought.

The flight to Wilton took about half an hour, although I don't think we flew directly there. It took me a few minutes to become orientated but I could see the Sydney skyline standing prominently on the horizon and I worked out roughly where we were. The countryside below us consisted mainly of rolling green fields. I was amazed to see so many dams. They looked like giant mirrors sitting flat amongst the contours of the Camden Valley. A tiny matchbox car travelled along a dirt road, leaving a dusty cloud trailing behind. Everything looked so small, especially the dirt strip at the drop zone Laurie pointed to. Surely we're not going to put down there! We made a straight-in approach to land. Laurie made it look so easy, popping us down effortlessly.

Laurie had a lot of friends at Wilton, and he sometimes flew the jump plane for them. We sat out on the grass in the sun, eating our lunch and watching groups of brightly coloured parachutes floating down to land in front of us.

'I'm going to do some jumps next weekend, you should come out and watch,' suggested Laurie. It looked terrifying, but Laurie jumping out of a plane was something I had to see.

Back at Camden Airport, Laurie made sure the Silver Ghost was tied down and locked up before walking me to my car. I was leaning against the driver's side door playing nervously with my keys. We'd been getting on so well, I knew it was only a matter of time before our friendship would develop into something more intense. I didn't have to wait too long, although I didn't think Laurie was the romantic type. He took a step forward and planted me with a passionate kiss. It took me by surprise. He leaned back, staring straight into my eyes. I tried to talk but all I could do was blurt out something silly that I'm sure didn't make any sense. He smiled and put both arms around me, holding on tight.

'You feel so good,' he whispered.

I could not believe it was happening.

Our romance blossomed. When Laurie was parachuting, I would go along and watch. I was becoming a regular face at Wilton and I made a lot of friends there.

'When are you going to do a jump, Al?' they started asking. Al was my new name at Wilton, courtesy of Laurie who got sick of stumbling over the pronunciation of Allana.

We spent all our spare time on weekends together over

the next month. Laurie even took me flying into the mountains one day. We flew over a huge lake called Lake Burragorang, all the way to the Three Sisters rock formation at Katoomba, then back to Camden. It was spectacular.

My working week was becoming increasingly mundane. Being stuck inside an office all day was suffocating me. Sometimes I'd stare out the window that overlooked a park, aching to be outside in the fresh air. I was unsettled, yearning for my weekends to arrive. There was a balloon festival coming up and bookings for the balloon flights at Camden were increasing.

The opportunity was presented to me by Peter Vizzard and Judy Lynne, who own Balloon Aloft, to take on a part-time position with the company. Initially I would assist Judy at the festival and then take on regular flight crew and promotional work. My pay would be determined by the balloon flight bookings so I would have to give up the security of a set wage. There were a lot of issues to consider. My future was never going to be in a legal office, but my long-term dream had always been to become a real estate salesperson. I was nineteen and I had a long time to pursue that dream. I had spoken to some local real estate agents who agreed I should be at least twenty before pursuing my career. In the meantime, I felt a little bit of adventure would do me good so I accepted Peter and Judy's offer, resigning from my secretarial job.

Speaking of adventure, the time had come for my first parachute jump. I didn't tell Laurie and I booked in to do the course on a day I knew he wasn't going to be jumping so it would be a complete surprise. Laurie had introduced me to aviation. But my growing passion for flying activities was independent of my feelings for Laurie. I wanted to jump out of an aeroplane because it was a challenge I could set myself – I had to achieve it on my own. I had never thought of myself as a daredevil. However, the element of danger associated with parachute jumping was very seductive.

Training started early. There were seven in my class and during the morning we sat learning all we needed to know for the jump. Some of the lessons were conducted on a blackboard, then we were shown over the parachuting equipment and, most importantly, the reserve chute. The reserve was a separate kit and was worn around the waist with the pack sitting on the stomach area. We learned what to do if the main parachute failed to open or only opened partially. Our instructions were to undo the secured reserve pack and drag out the bundle of silky nylon with both hands, then throw it away from the body, shaking it around so the air would catch it and it would inflate. In the meantime, the earth below would be getting pretty close, I thought. There seemed to be so much to do in a very short period of time. I went through this drill over and over to ensure the procedure would be automatic, just in case my main should fail.

After lunch we had practice runs jumping out of a mock-up aeroplane. It was a pretend metal fuselage sitting almost a metre off the ground. One by one we went through the exercise repeatedly. I climbed inside, bracing myself in the open doorway. My instructor counted to three, then I launched myself out onto the ground with my arms and legs stretched like a star and my head tilted back looking up into the sky. I screamed out, 'one – one thousand, two – one thousand, three – one thousand.' I felt pretty silly but we all had to do it.

There were only two more phases of our course left. First, the instructor took us over to a cross laid out on the ground, which we were supposed to aim to land on. He began to explain how we could locate the drop zone from the air.

'As you can see we are right next to the freeway ...' my attention was interrupted momentarily. I could see a little aeroplane flying onto the dirt strip just near us. It was Laurie in the Silver Ghost. The instructor knew I didn't want Laurie to know about my jump so he huddled the group together trying to keep me out of sight. Laurie even came over for a chat, while I cowered down behind them. How he didn't see me I'll never know, and luckily he didn't stay for too long before flying back to Camden.

The last thing we needed to learn was how to impact the ground properly to avoid breaking an ankle. The entire class lined up along a platform raised one and a half metres. Our instructor jumped off first, showing us the correct method to land. The important thing to remember is that once your feet hit the ground, you bend at the knees and roll. We each took it in turns to practise over and over until we got it right. At the end, I was covered in dirt.

It was late – 5 p.m. in the afternoon – by the time we donned our gear and piled into the aeroplane. The tension and anticipation had mounted during the day although, surprisingly, nobody got cold feet. Each student had his or her own reason for doing the jump. However, the class had developed a comradeship and we would make the jump as a group. Nobody wanted to let the team down. All the instructors were very motivating, but they made it clear to us that if anyone froze up there and couldn't take the plunge, they wouldn't be forced to do so. They would just land with the aeroplane. How embarrassing that would be!

'Don't forget, everyone, when you leave the aircraft, I want to see your arms and legs stretched out, your head back, and I want to hear you counting one – one thousand, two – one thousand, three – one thousand.' More last minute instructions were being yelled out, but we had been trained well and I was confident about the jump. The parachute was connected to a static line inside the aeroplane. This would open the canopy. All I had to do was jump – easy! The back seats had been taken out of the aeroplane so we could all fit in with our heavy, cumbersome parachutes. The door had also been taken off. When we became airborne, the wind blew all around the cabin. It was very cold and noisy. I was furthest from the open void with my back against the pilot's seat, looking out over a sea of heads towards the doorway where I could just sight the ground way below as the pilot began a slow turn to the right. I was wondering what made me want to do this and, as the minutes passed, my nerves got the better of me. Just keep calm, nothing's going to go wrong, I kept telling myself, although I wasn't totally convinced.

We had reached our designated altitude and the first student, who was a young guy, got into position. I could see the terror in his face and felt pleased I wasn't going first. Without much fuss he leapt out. One minute he was there, the next he was gone. The instructor watched outside for a moment then turned to us giving the thumbs up, indicating his parachute had opened. I watched each one of my new friends go through the motions. I felt their fear each time and the relief when their chute opened. I hated going last and by now I was thinking it would have been better to have gone first. It would be all over by now.

My turn! I shuffled forward towards the door, getting into position just as we had been shown in training. The wind was beating into me fiercely, pushing me back inside the aeroplane. It was so cold. I managed to peep outside, looking down to the miniature world below. The realisation of what I was about to do struck me like a lightning bolt. My old humdrum world in an office, behind a desk, didn't seem so bad. Through sheer terror my whole body was numb. I looked down again. Of all the demented things I could do in my life, I have chosen to jump out of an aeroplane, I thought.

'Are you ready! – Al, are you ready?' The instructor had to yell so I could hear him. I looked up to see his reassuring face.

'I think so,' I shouted back, lifting myself up and bracing myself in the doorway. The pilot powered the engine back, reducing the pounding wind slightly.

'After three!'

I gave the thumbs up and gathered every bit of nerve I had in my body. I really didn't want to let the team down but more importantly, I couldn't let myself down.

'One – two – three.' I launched myself out and was swept away from the aeroplane, falling, falling. I was screaming. 'One – one thousand, two – one thousand, three – one thousand.' I remembered seeing the aeroplane disappear, but after that I experienced complete sensory overload. Spiralling down, out of control, I didn't have a clue what I was doing. Wind, noise, arms, legs, breathe . . . I forgot to breathe. I took a deep breath, filling my lungs to capacity. This sparked my conscious being again as I realised I was kicking my legs about and grabbing for air with my arms. My subconscious was obviously thinking now is a good time to swim. I remembered my instructor's words and stretched my arms and legs out straight as I continued to hurtle towards the earth. My heart was beating fast, adrenalin pumping through every blood vessel, the wind rushing past made it hard to catch my breath . . . falling, falling. I could hear the rustling sound of my chute unfolding, whipping me upright as it was caught by the wind. I felt the impact grab me in the crutch as my harness restrained me hard against the force of the inflation. I was so relieved to look up and see the big round canopy towering over me. I reached up to take hold of the steering toggles, but the lines were twisted. Remembering what I was taught in class, I kicked my legs about and that soon twisted my body right around, almost three hundred and sixty degrees, freeing the lines.

'YAHOO, YAHOO, YIPPEE, I DID IT, YAHOO, I DID IT,' I was screaming.

The elation I felt was magnified by an incredible burst of adrenalin. It was unlike anything else I had ever experienced. This could certainly be an addictive feeling.

The earth below looked so small, laid out like a patchwork quilt. The setting sun still hovered over the horizon,

The Best I Can Be

casting a brilliant orange haze across the land. The parachuting centre was easy to pick out, it was right next to the freeway. The runway and the big cross that was my target were easy to see. It seemed to take ages as I slowly floated down, steering myself around the sky as free as a bird. I could see three other students still under canopy some distance below me and I noticed some of them had already landed.

The ground was coming closer and closer and suddenly I felt like it was rushing up to meet me. I was about fifty metres off the ground.

'Knees together, knees together!' An instructor was yelling at me from the ground as I came hurtling in, aiming straight for the clubhouse, knowing if I hit it I would hurt myself or, at best, get stuck on the roof.

'Right, right, right!' he demanded.

I pulled the right handle, veering me away towards the open field. I didn't make the target and my landing was far from graceful, more a crash into the ground than a landing. I remembered to bend at the knees and roll. However, it still knocked the wind out of me. Then, to make matters worse, I didn't collapse the parachute quickly enough before a gust of wind caught it and dragged me along the ground for about ten metres. By the time I was able to stop it, just before hitting a fence, I had dirt in my eyes, in my mouth and up my nose.

I picked myself up, dusted myself off and looked towards the class who had gathered, all laughing at my exciting arrival.

'Yahoo!' I screamed out to them.

I picked up the bundle of fabric lying on the ground and began to walk back to the clubhouse to join the rest of the group. This had been the most unbelievably exhilarating experience of my entire life, leaving me feeling as though I could take on the world. The class members were given certificates for having completed their first jumps and a few of us arranged to come back the next weekend to do it again.

I couldn't wait to tell Laurie about my first jump. I hadn't told Mum and Dad either so I left the others who were still celebrating. Laurie met me outside his house and was amazed when I showed him my certificate.

'But I flew out to Wilton today,' he said. We both laughed when I told him how I had hidden behind the others.

Driving home, I couldn't stop thinking about my new life. Ballooning, flying and now parachuting, it was hard to believe that it had all started only six weeks earlier. My old life had been left so far behind me. It was as if I were sprouting wings, discovering a whole new world that I could never have imagined was mine to take. But I was taking it by the hand, and running with it as fast as I could. I had the ability to do things I had never thought possible. I was learning all about balloons and flying. Some of it was technical, but I was enjoying every little bit. I was discovering the adventurous me, this person with such a zest for new experiences. I was approaching life with a sense of urgency, as if I were making up for lost time.

Mum and Dad were sitting in the lounge room watching television when I finally made it home.

'What did you get up to today?' Mum asked. They

looked forward to hearing about my flying adventures and were thrilled to see me so happy with my new life.

But their response when I answered, 'I jumped out of an aeroplane today,' was that of typically protective parents.

'YOU WHAT!'

I had their undivided attention as I told them all about my exciting day which, I'm sure, left them thinking, 'What next?'

After work the next Saturday, I rushed back to Wilton to jump again. Laurie came along this time. He didn't jump that day, but stood watching, amused as I came tearing onto the ground, way off course again. The big round army parachutes that were used for training at the time were very hard to steer. Laurie told me about a parachuting weekend coming up at a place called Rylstone. There was going to be an Australian formation skydiving record attempt so we made plans to go along. In the meantime, I clocked up another four jumps using the more manoeuvrable square parachutes.

It was late evening by the time we left for the drive to Rylstone. We had to arrange our gear to camp out at the airfield and wait for Jamie and Jeannie who were coming along as well. Jamie, like me, had done only a few jumps and we both hoped there'd be a chance to do some more over the weekend. Laurie and I drove up in his car while the other two drove ahead. It was a long trip and I was tired, half dozing off to sleep. Some time had passed and I woke with a fright to hear the sounds of rough gravel beneath us. We had run off the road. I looked across and Laurie was fast asleep. 'Wake up, Laurie!' I yelled, hitting him in the chest. He woke, startled, pushing his foot on the brake

'Oh shit, I did it again,' he said. It wasn't the first time he had fallen asleep at the wheel. I stayed very alert for the rest of the trip.

The weekend was fantastic. Jamie and I did another few jumps despite some persistent rain and the odd hangover. Laurie even flew the plane during one of the loads. It felt weird seeing his smiling face before plunging into the open air. After I landed and had gathered up my parachute, I noticed another student screaming in downwind at a great rate of knots. His instructor was desperately yelling at him from the ground. He didn't respond and he hit the dirt with a thud. I don't think it would have mattered if he had remembered to bend at the knees and roll or not, because he hit with such force that it broke his ankle. It was somewhat gruesome. Jeannie and I bundled him into the back of a ute and drove him to the local hospital to have the ankle set in plaster.

Laurie also had a close call during one of his jumps when his parachute only partially opened. Jamie and I watched from the ground as he spiralled slowly down then cut away, free falling for about another hundred feet. My heart was in my mouth before we could see the reserve parachute inflate and could hear Laurie's screams of delight at cheating death. This sounds a bit morbid, I know, but skydivers are a pretty wild bunch.

Chapter 3

Give Me Wings

Laurie began studying for his senior commercial pilot's licence. The course was very intense so we didn't get to see as much of each other. I understood this was his career. He'd already put in years of hard work to gain hundreds of hours flying, not to mention the horrendous cost. His dedication could only be admired and, unlike a lot of young pilots, he'd worked and paid for all his training on his own. Laurie had eased off the balloon crewing work, which I was still doing on a part-time basis. The good bookings were an indication that hot-air ballooning, all around Australia, was growing more popular daily.

There were other companies who flew passenger balloons out of Camden. Most of the balloons carried eight passengers and flew two one-hour hops during the morning. The industry was so healthy in 1988 that we were flying almost seven days a week. I used to start work at 4.30 a.m. and finish at 11.00 a.m. which left the rest of the day free.

After packing away the balloon one morning, I dropped into Camden Flying Club to get some information on learning to fly. It was inevitable and, working seven days a week, I felt I could afford to start taking lessons. The instructor on duty introduced himself as Ross Whittle and said that I should go on a Trial Instructional Flight, TIF for short, to see if I liked flying before I committed to the cost of lessons.

'Can we do that now?' I asked.

Ross checked his bookings.

'I'm free till after lunch, so now is good.'

We went into a small briefing room where he showed me how each of the controls on the aeroplane worked. The rudder pedals on the floor were used to steer the aircraft on the ground – I knew that – and in the air they controlled the yaw. The steering control was a wheel that could turn left or right, operating the ailerons located outboard and at the trailing edge of both wings. This rolled the aeroplane in the direction the wheel was turned. The wheel could also be pushed in or out, moving the elevator on the tail – push forward to make the aeroplane go down, pull back to go up. Ross explained we'd be learning how to climb, descend and turn during our thirty-minute flight.

It all made reasonable sense to me. I had only flown in a light aircraft with Laurie a few times, but it was enough to make the controls in the cockpit familiar. After walking around the aeroplane, a Cessna 152, to complete the pre-flight checks, we jumped on board. Ross talked me through the start up and I was soon taxiing towards the run-up bay for take-off on runway 06. We stopped to complete our precautionary checks just as Laurie had always done, and then headed for the runway.

'I'll talk you through the take-off,' Ross said.

'You're going to let me do it by myself?' I questioned.

'You'll be fine,' he said.

It was exciting. I really wanted to do well.

'Foxtrot Mike Gold, clear for take-off.' The command came from the tower.

'Okay, push the throttle all the way in – that's good, now keep the aeroplane straight with the pedals. Keep glancing down at the airspeed indicator. When it hits sixty knots, ease back on the elevator – forty knots, fifty knots, sixty knots, easing back now – excellent! Now maintain sixty-five knots until we climb to five hundred feet then we're going to turn.'

I looked out my window and could see we were still over the runway and climbing steadily. Up ahead, the nose sat high against the blue sky. It felt so right. I don't know why, it just did. I looked towards Ross with a Cheshire cat grin from ear to ear.

'I'm ready to learn to fly now,' I said.

'We're almost at five hundred feet.' He pointed to the altimeter. 'We're going to make a left-hand turn.'

Ross talked me through the turn, then we flew north of Camden to a designated training area where we continued our lesson, climbing and descending. I flew the whole time, although I was only doing what Ross told me to do, even to the very end.

The main runway was directly ahead and becoming uncomfortably close. I hoped Ross didn't expect me to land this thing, I thought. At the last minute, he did take over and land the aeroplane, much to my relief.

My first lesson had come to an end all too quickly. Back at the Aero Club, Ross and I worked out a plan for me to take two one-hour lessons a week. Each hour would cost ninety dollars, which I felt I could handle. I told Ross I wanted to work towards a commercial licence. I had fire in my belly and I was rearing to go. I chose not to tell Mum and Dad. They were still coming to terms with me jumping out of aeroplanes.

My whole world revolved around aviation. There were even a few days where I would balloon in the morning, go skydiving after lunch, then rush back to Camden for an evening flying lesson. One of those times I arrived at the airport at about 4.30 p.m.

'Les Paul is going to fly with you today, Allana,' Ross explained. Les was the chief flying instructor and I guessed he was checking on my progress. I made sure to do my best, trying to demonstrate my competence during the short flight.

Once on the ground, Les asked me to stop in the run-up bay. He gave me some tips on a few minor details, then undid his seat belt and climbed out.

'You're ready to fly on your own now,' he said. 'Just do a couple of circuits then taxi back here and pick me up.'

My heart started pounding. I was very nervous, but ready nevertheless.

'Camden tower, Foxtrot Mike Golf is taxiing solo for circuits. Received, Charlie.'

Ready at the holding point, I called over the radio, 'Foxtrot Mike Golf is ready.'

'Foxtrot Mike Golf, clear for take-off.'

I lined up on the centre line and pushed the throttle all the way forward – forty knots, fifty knots, sixty knots – easing back on the elevator. I'm doing it, I'm really doing it. My little aeroplane leapt off the ground. It felt so light with only one person on board. I looked across to the empty seat beside me and started to laugh. Never in a million years did I think I'd be flying a plane all by myself. I suddenly remembered when Mum was teaching me to drive a car. It had been only a year earlier. I'd get so stressed. Once I had stalled in the middle of a crossroad and got out of the car, demanding Mum take over and drive us home. She got out also and we had an argument across the bonnet because she stood defiant and insisted I get back in the car and continue my lesson. She had won and perseverance paid off because I did finally get my driver's licence – and here I was flying a plane.

The sun was getting low over the mountain range. There were no clouds in the sky or a ripple in the air. The horizon was a blaze of blue and pink. God had certainly turned it on for me this evening. Sometimes I think he does this on purpose. Many times in my life I've turned to God for help and received an instant response. And sometimes nature has provided me with magical moments that can only be a gift from God.

After three circuits, I landed and taxied in.

'Congratulations,' said the man in the control tower.

'Thanks very much,' I replied.

It had been a perfect day. I raced home that night to tell Mum and Dad about my flight. They were sitting in their usual positions in the lounge room.

'I flew an aeroplane all by myself today,' I announced.
Their reaction was predictable.
'You did what?'
This time however they weren't so surprised and, once again, they sat attentively listening as I told them all about it.

My lessons continued but I had to take on a second job, waitressing at night, to help pay for them. The restaurant was open twenty-four hours and my shift usually ended at 2 a.m. Then I'd go straight to work at Camden. In the meantime, Laurie had been applying for full-time flying jobs. He was finally offered a position flying a bank run. Unfortunately, it was based at Tamworth. I knew he had to take the job, but it was sad for me to see him go. We had been so close and I loved him dearly. But Laurie was a free spirit and deep down I knew he wasn't ready for a commitment to me or anyone else. Laurie had given me my wings and now I was flying on my own. We did keep in touch and saw each other when he came home some weekends, which I always looked forward to.

One weekend Laurie came back to do some skydiving at Wilton. On the Sunday during his last jump, his parachute suffered a severe malfunction and, despite trying to correct the problem, he was forced to pull his reserve chute. Fortunately it opened, bringing him back to earth safely.

'Cheated death once again,' I could imagine him saying. I didn't get to see him, but I was told that Laurie's near miss made for some serious celebrating by our friends at the pub that night. Laurie had a flight the next day so he'd left to drive all the way back to Tamworth. It was some time in the early hours of the morning. He had almost made it home – there were only five kilometres to go to the township of Tamworth – when he fell asleep at the wheel, drove straight into a tree and was killed instantly.

I didn't find out about the crash until I rang the Balloon Aloft's office at lunch time to get the details for the next day's flight. Robyn, the secretary, answered the phone, assuming I knew.

'I'm so sorry to hear the sad news about Laurie,' she said.

My heart sank. 'What news?' I asked.

As the devastating story unfolded, I stood holding the phone to my ear, oblivious to any emotion. Robyn's words were clearly heard, but they simply couldn't be true. I put the phone down, my only sensation was to feel cold all over and, before I could make sense of what Robyn had said, my legs buckled from beneath me and I fell into a crumpled mess on the floor. I cried for hours wondering, why Laurie? He was so full of life. How cruel for it to be taken from him so young. I waited by the phone, hoping someone would ring to tell me there was a mistake. It wasn't true, Laurie was alive. This was the first time I'd been touched by death with a full comprehension of what it meant. I could remember what I'd felt when my grandfather had died. Bewildered loss. This time all I had was a hollow feeling.

A group of us drove to the funeral in Tamworth where Laurie was laid to rest. Jim and I sat together in the church. I couldn't help but remember that first day we took Mum ballooning, that first time I had met Laurie. He was so full of life. I didn't want to believe he was gone. He had been my inspiration. I will never forget the short time we spent together. You woke something special in me, Laurie. I wonder if you ever knew.

That afternoon Jim and I had to drive back to the Hunter Valley for a flight the next morning. We talked non-stop about the adventures the three of us had shared. It helped us both to be able to talk about him.

Over the next few months I continued struggling to come to terms with Laurie's death. I hadn't been back to Wilton parachuting, or sat in an aeroplane since his funeral. I had no desire to fly and my own ambition to work towards a commercial pilot's licence seemed pointless. I lost the fire. Ballooning bookings were still up though and there were even a few short promotional trips with the GIO balloon that I crewed for in Queensland and around New South Wales. But most of the flights I was working on were still in Camden.

It was spring, we had a cold snap and the morning was freezing. There was a thick fog over the valley, a pea souper, as Jim and I would call it. My hands were numb from the cold, my fingers felt as though they were going to snap off. Jim and I crouched beside each other, attaching the balloon wires onto the basket as it lay on its side on the crispy grass. 'I can't feel my hands,' I said to Jim, steam billowing from my mouth with every breath. He laughed as he also struggled to undo the metal attachments that hold the balloon in place.

'It's going to take a while for the fog to lift,' said Jim. I looked towards the hangars that were hidden behind the white haze.

'We'll just sit it out,' I answered, still straining to see the big green buildings. There are a few weather conditions that stop the balloon flying. One is high winds because the balloon travels at the same speed as the wind and fast landings can be dangerous. Another is fog, because the pilot can't see where he's going until he's above it and eventually he would have to descend back down through it to land.

Through the fog I could see a figure coming closer. It was a man on a push bike. He had a dog bounding alongside him – a golden retriever pup. The man was dressed in jeans with a big fur-lined brown leather jacket and a white scarf around his neck. I could see he had a moustache and his blond hair was slightly long and wavy.

'Good grief, it's Biggles,' I said to Jim.

He laughed. 'That's Nigel,' he said.

As Nigel came closer, I saw that he had the most brilliant blue, piercing eyes and a day's shadow that made his rugged appearance very attractive. He had a boyish face and I estimated he was about thirty. Nigel stood back watching while I selected a few men from our group of passengers to help me drag the balloon out along the ground. I continued my work, discreetly glancing towards him every now and again. He was certainly captivating. Our balloon was ready to inflate but the fog still hadn't lifted. I walked over to Jim who was talking with Nigel and introduced myself.

'Nigel's going to take a Tiger Moth up and fly around the balloon once we get airborne,' Jim said.

'So you're a pilot then?' I questioned.

'Yes, I am. I've seen you flying at the Aero Club, haven't I?'

'Yes, but I haven't flown for a while.'

We continued to chat while Jim entertained our passengers. Nigel was softly spoken and he told me that he had a business on the airfield restoring old aeroplanes. He even offered to take me up in a Tiger Moth one day.

'The fog is lifting, let's get going,' Jim called out to me.

'Can I help with anything?' Nigel asked me.

'Yes, you can. Go to the very top of the balloon where you'll find a rope, follow it out to the end and I'll meet you there,' I explained as I ran back towards the basket.

Jim started up the fan and Bojangles came to life. The rigging inside the balloon was twisted so Jim and I walked in to sort out a mass of tangled control lines.

'Is he married?' I asked.

'Separated,' Jim replied with a smirk on his face.

'Girlfriend?' I continued to enquire.

'Yes,' said Jim

'Bugger, bugger, bugger, that'd be right.'

We were ready to go and Nigel was standing at the end of the crown line. I ran up, quickly explaining that we had to hold the balloon down with the rope as hard as we could while Jim fired the burners and Bojangles began to rise. The grass was covered with dew, which made us skate along the ground slipping and sliding, laughing hysterically along with our audience. I remembered watching Laurie on the crown line that first day. It always looked hilarious. I helped the last passengers into the basket and noticed Nigel disappearing towards the hangars, dog in tow. Oh, well, so much for that, I thought.

The Best I Can Be

The morning was still. Jim climbed to about one thousand feet and hovered over the airfield. He wasn't going anywhere. 'It's going to be an easy chase this morning,' I said to Jim over the radio.

At that moment I could hear the popping of an engine struggling to kick over, coughing and spluttering in the distance until it finally fired up. A black Tiger Moth taxied along towards the grass runway, weaving like a snake beside me. It lined up and powered on down the strip, lifting about a foot off the ground. It was so close that I could see it was Nigel with his long scarf trailing. He was wearing a black leather helmet and flying goggles and he gave a quick wave as he passed the small group of spectators I still had with me. I looked up with envy as he danced and played, looping and rolling, twisting and turning, a short distance away from Bojangles.

After packing the balloon away, we returned to a beautiful old house on the airfield that was owned by a lovely lady named Phoebe Macarthur Onslow. She had been providing our champagne breakfasts for the past week. I was surprised to see Nigel walking into the front garden with a woman who was obviously his girlfriend. They sat with us and joined in with breakfast. Later in the day, I found out that Nigel had moved into a room in Phoebe's house only a few days earlier.

The weeks went by and every morning as we set up the balloon, Nigel would ride his bike out onto the airfield and help. Most times he would race off and drag the Tiger Moth out of his hangar and put on a show, usually thrilling the balloon passengers by looping the loop right next to them.

A few times he flew away but I could see him in the distance playing around the clouds.

Jim and I had worked sixty days straight and a welcome break was coming up.

'Come down on your day off and we'll go flying,' Nigel suggested.

'I would like that a lot.'

We planned to be airborne at sunrise which was fine with me. My body clock would have me awake at that time anyway.

There was a slight breeze blowing that morning. The valley was crystal clear with no fog, but big patches of cumulus clouds hung over the field. I drove down to the hangars where Nigel had the black Tiger Moth out ready to go. He helped me up onto the wing, showing me where I could step before I climbed into the front cockpit.

The instrument panel was very basic, still as it had been in the 1940s. The controls were manipulated through wires that were exposed down the side of the fuselage. The aircraft, except for the aluminium engine cowl, was covered with fabric, which had then been layered with a paint-like substance called dope. I was sitting up in the open air with only a small screen to protect me from the wind, and feeling slightly vulnerable. Nigel helped me with the harness that ran over both my shoulders and across my lap.

'Make sure the straps are tight and secure. We don't want you falling out when we go upside down.' That was not reassuring. I tugged on the belts, making sure they were fastened properly, then put my helmet and goggles on, feeling very much like Eve Tossar flying with Patrick

O'Malley in *High Road to China*. This was one of my favourite adventure movies in which these two had flown in old fabric-covered bi-planes against the stunning backdrop of China.

The Tiger Moth was unlike anything I had experienced. It had a tail skid instead of a nose wheel which caused the front of the aeroplane to sit up high, making forward visibility almost impossible. Nigel weaved the plane from side to side as we taxied along purely to see where he was going. We lined up on the grass strip which I had never used before.

'Are you ready?' Nigel's voice came through my headset.

I raised my arm and gave the thumbs up. Before I knew it, we were airborne and flying over the river at the end of the runway. About a dozen water birds scattered into the air as we passed overhead, climbing, climbing.

An intricate maze of towering white clouds suspended above became our destination. A playground of weird shapes, tunnels and canyons was looming ahead. As we moved closer, the sheer size of each swelling cloud formation made me feel that Nigel was taking me to another world. The clouds were so close now you could almost touch them. I felt like a tiny black mosquito, flying along beside the biggest mountain in the world.

'There's a hole, let's fly through it,' Nigel screamed as he pulled us around hard to the right.

The sun disappeared and we vanished deep into the cavern. Its walls were so defined it was hard to believe they weren't solid. We soon punched out into another ravine and followed its steep and twisting turns until it delivered us back into the clear blue sky. A lone puffy cloud sat before us like a giant cotton ball.

'Hold on! We're going to loop around that cloud.'

We dived down, picking up speed, passing underneath, then Nigel pulled back on the elevator bringing the nose up. I could feel my body being pushed into my seat as my world tipped upside down. I looked up to see the top of a white ball of fluff and the earth below it. Gravity made my shoulders press hard against the strain of my harness. There was nothing between me and the valley beneath us. My head was poking up in the open air and I imagined how I would have fallen straight out of the aeroplane if it weren't for my seat belt. Nigel made sure to hang us inverted for only a few seconds, but it had seemed much longer. Then down the other side we flew, hurtling towards the ground.

'Yahoo, yahoo, that was so great,' I screamed as we levelled out and continued back in through another set of mountainous white clouds. It's another world up there. It almost felt as though we'd stepped straight into a child's fantasy where heavenly structures, inspired by myths and legends, were formed like castles suspended in mid air. I remembered how, as a little girl, I'd lie on the grass with my cousins, Janine and Lynda. We'd stare into the sky, making images come to life with our imagination – dragons, serpents and fortresses. And here in the clouds, I had ventured back to my childhood fantasy. It made me feel like I was in a dream, that I had wandered into a scene where any minute Jack might appear at the top of the beanstalk.

The urge to jump overboard and bounce around on the billowy forms was overwhelming. My whole being was filled with awe. The sensation was one of boundless freedom and it made me laugh uncontrollably. I felt privileged to be one of so few to experience this. It's difficult to describe the feeling it gives you. A friend once summed it up saying, 'It's as if your soul is singing.'

When we flew back, we parked outside the hangar Nigel was renting. The large doors were slightly ajar, enough for me to see part of an aeroplane inside. It looked different to anything else I had seen. We rolled open the doors together and before me was the most beautiful old plane. It had a highly polished metal fuselage that was so shiny I could see my reflection. The wings and tail were yellow with red, white and blue military markings.

'It's gorgeous, Nigel, what is it?' I asked.

'It's a Ryan PT-22, it's my baby,' he replied proudly, wiping a mark off the wing with a rag. Nigel explained that he had bought her as a wreck. He had found her outside Los Angeles at a farm where she was being used to prop up a chicken shed. He'd shipped her back to Australia and spent two years restoring her. I was very impressed. Inside there was also a white Tiger Moth that had a few pieces missing.

'I don't own this one. I'm restoring it for a client who lives in Wollongong. It's nearly finished. I'll be delivering it during the week,' Nigel explained.

I spent most of that day helping Nigel work on the Tiger, not that I could do much, but I did manage to become covered in grease and oil. We talked a lot about flying and about each other.

After work most days I would visit Nigel, just to sit and chat while he worked. He was so charming, he had me captivated. The white Tiger Moth had gone to its new home in Wollongong but it still required some final adjustments to the rigging.

'Why don't you come with me, we can have lunch on the beach,' Nigel asked.

I was keen to go. We packed the necessary tools into Nigel's ute for the short drive. I knew we were only mates but I couldn't help the way I was feeling. If only he'd touch me. I wished he'd just kiss me. These silly schoolgirl thoughts were making me dizzy as I tried not to blush every time he looked at me.

The rigging was completed after an hour and we made our way to the beach. It was a beautiful warm day, not a cloud in the sky.

'Let's walk on the rocks,' I suggested. I was crouched down peering into a rock pool when Nigel grabbed me around the waist pretending to push me in. I got such a fright I was screaming and laughing, at the same time grabbing hold of his arm so I wouldn't fall in. He held me for a moment longer than he needed to. As we stood up together, he stared at me with 'that look' that reveals when an attraction is shared. We continued our walk along the beach, mucking around and teasing each other, almost like we were trying to read each other's intentions. On our way home, Nigel asked if he could take me out for dinner.

I couldn't believe it. 'I'll have to go home and get cleaned up first, but I'd love to,' I answered.

Mum and Dad were home. I burst in the door running around frantically, trying to get myself ready.

'What's going on?' Mum asked.

'Oh, Mum, he asked me out!'

'Who asked you out?'

'You don't know him but he's gorgeous – oh, my God, oh, my God, what am I going to wear – oh, my God, I'll have to iron something. I've got an hour to get ready. I can't do it.'

Mum is always terrific in a crisis. 'Calm down and go and have a shower. I'll get your clothes ready,' she said in a soothing voice.

I'm not sensational but that'll do, I thought, as I kissed Mum and Dad goodbye and bolted out the door.

Nigel took me to a small intimate restaurant for a candlelit dinner with all the trimmings. We were both relaxed and had almost finished our bottle of wine. Our hands sat close together on the table, his moving gradually towards mine, and he started playing with my fingers.

My heart was pounding. 'Is this for real?' I asked Nigel. Needless to say it was.

After dinner, we drove back to Phoebe's and strolled hand in hand into her back garden. There was a full moon shining, reflecting off the tranquil water of the Nepean River that ran behind the house. The air was as still as still, and only the occasional frog croaking down by the river broke the comfortable silence. Nigel wrapped me in his strong arms. I had never felt so safe than at that moment. He took my head in his hands and kissed me with a tenderness that sparked a warmth I didn't want ever to let go. I was a goner, and from that moment we were inseparable.

A few days later, Nigel had the chance to speak with his girlfriend, explaining his feelings for me and calling off their relationship. The happy outcome was that they were able to remain great friends to this day.

Nigel had two children, Michael, who was four years old and Kylie, who was then seven. They were living with their mother in Camden. I hadn't give it much thought when he'd first told me about them weeks earlier. It was difficult for me to picture Nige as a dad, but he brought them both out to the balloon one morning when he had them on a weekend access visit. I'll never forget Kylie's angelic baby face and her little bobbed haircut. She was wearing a pretty blue dress that reflected her eyes. They were just like Nigel's. In fact, she mirrored so many of his features it was uncanny. Kylie held her Dad's hand, snuggling into him the whole morning. She was so shy and obviously Daddy's girl. Michael on the other hand, although only four, was effervescent and confident. He also had Nigel's eyes and his snow-white hair was gelled and sticking up in the spiky style. He looked like he'd just walked off an Anne Geddes children's poster.

It made me feel awkward watching the three of them together. I felt like an outsider. Up until then it had just been Nigel and me. But this weekend we were going to be four. I had never been the maternal type and was never really good with kids. What am I going to say to them? How are we going to entertain them? Am I supposed to be just Nigel's friend? Do they know we are in love? I hadn't anticipated this dilemma, and suddenly our simple young love had outside issues to consider. I fumbled through that weekend trying to create a happy family atmosphere as best I could, but at twenty-years-old, I don't think I had the maturity to cope or the foresight to anticipate problems that might occur in the future.

After taking the children home, Nigel and I had a chance to talk. His divorce would be finalised in six months and he had accepted the fact that he could only be a part-time dad on a fortnightly basis.

I never imagined myself with children. A ready made part-time family seemed daunting. But I hung in there. When the children stayed with Nigel for the weekend, we made sure we went on normal family outings, often bushwalking or seeing a movie. Sometimes they'd come and help with the balloon. There were many hard times, a result of Nigel and his former wife adjusting to two separate lives and sharing responsibilities with the children. I often got caught up in all the emotion and tried not to let it affect us. But sometimes it did put a strain on our relationship.

The summer of 1988 and Australia's Bicentennial year: The hot-air ballooning community planned to celebrate the two-hundredth anniversary of the arrival of the First Fleet in Australia with a balloon race across the country from Perth to Sydney. It was an international event with eighty-eight competitors. The object of the competition was to fly a task each morning, accumulating points, then the convoy of participants would drive to the next town to do it all again.

Each task basically required the pilot to navigate his balloon, using the varying wind currents, to a target. He would drop a sandbag as close to it as he could get. The pilot who scored the closest hit was awarded the most points. The event was a fly, drive, party, fly, drive, party expedition through Central Australia that would take seventeen days to complete. Jim was one of the first pilots to register for the race. He and his wife, Raewin, had their own private balloon that they planned to use and they asked if Nigel and I would crew for them.

Everybody met at the Burswood Casino in Perth to sign on and a black tie ball was planned to launch the race. Jim's balloon, Mercury, was silver with a red, white and blue band around the middle so I had a silver ball gown made with a big red, white and blue sash that tied around my waist.

Logistically the coordination of a thousand people, to be relocated and accommodated each day, should have been quite an ordeal. But to the organisers' credit, the process went like clockwork. Each town put on a party to welcome us. Sometimes crews were billeted out to families or slept in caravans.

These types of events inevitably attract eccentrics, and our close friend and balloon pilot, Aden Wicks, was no exception. Aden and his crew dressed each day in 1788 regalia either as Captain Arthur Phillip's officers or as convicts. Every morning as the sun came up, Aden and his crew would raise the Australian flag on a pole attached to their chase vehicle, then complete the ceremony with a gun salute. One morning the crew arranged for the local police to be close by and arrest Aden for letting off a firearm without a permit. Aden was last seen being handcuffed and driven to the police lock-up, trying to explain to the officer that he was using blanks. He really did think the race was over for him, until he was rescued by his smug and overjoyed team.

Bad weather hampered us some days, making it impossible to fly. And there were hairy moments when some of the balloons tried to land in high winds resulting in a few bruises and the odd broken bone. One time Nigel and I were tracking another competitor's balloon that was travelling directly along a fence. We were doing about sixty kilometres an hour and keeping up. Suddenly the other balloon began to descend, hitting the fence. All I saw was the basket spinning around and a woman's body being thrown out. She was very lucky because I believe she suffered only a broken ankle.

Another day the task was to fly to an oval in the middle of Broken Hill where a cherry picker was extended into the air. On the top was a silver ingot donated by one of the mines. The idea was to fly down and grab the prize. We'd driven to a site about ten kilometres away from the oval. But just as Jim began to heat the air inside the balloon it broke its tether attached to the car trailer. A metal ring at the end of the rope flew off and hit Jim in the head.

The balloon dragged along the ground for about twenty metres. Fortunately it was undamaged. We took Jim straight to hospital to have the large bump on his head checked. Apart from minor concussion, he was okay.

Despite these incidents, Nigel and I were sharing a wonderful experience. It was a great opportunity to see Australia. Whenever possible, we took advantage of our limited spare time to play tourist, stopping to see the Twelve Apostles on our way to Sydney. We had also been wine tasting in the Barossa Valley, and we'd ridden push bikes around the Dubbo Zoo.

The Mercury team didn't place after the scores were tallied. At the presentation night in Sydney, Nigel and I agreed we'd had a great time, but we were exhausted. And we were suffering from an overdose of hot-air balloons.

Chapter 4

Life and Love with Nigel

Some might say Nigel and I had a whirlwind romance. It had only been six months since our first date, but we had spent every free moment together and we were seen by our friends as the perfect couple. We felt we were too. Our individual hopes and dreams for the future had merged together and talk of marriage was in the air. We had even discussed this with Mum and Dad, who were ecstatic with the idea of Nigel becoming their son-in-law. Life with Nigel was never going to be dull. I knew that all too well. He craved adventure even more obsessively than I did and sometimes it was difficult to keep up with him. However, we really were a great match and our marriage was inevitable.

We stumbled upon a beautiful engagement ring one day while we were out shopping for a gift for Nigel's son, Michael. It was the nicest ring we'd seen and, after some negotiating with the jeweller, we decided to buy it. I had to have the setting lowered slightly so it didn't look too overwhelming on my tiny hand. I couldn't wait to pick it up, but Nigel had made the arrangements for the alteration and I had no idea when it would be ready. I wasn't expecting the full traditional proposal at all, but Nigel went the whole way. He took me back to our first restaurant, even making sure we were seated at the same table. I felt very special that night and was very flattered that he'd taken the time to make the evening so perfect. After we'd eaten and were suitably relaxed – and giggly, thanks to a special bottle of chardonnay – Nigel got on his knees right at the table.

'I love you with all my heart. You make me complete, and I want to spend the rest of my life with you. Will you marry me?' he asked.

How could a girl resist? I almost choked on the lump in my throat before I was able to speak. I looked into Nigel's eyes, pausing with my response. The depth of my love for this man frightened me. I couldn't imagine life without him. I wanted us to grow old together. I wanted to share my whole world with him.

'Of course, I'll marry you, darling,' I answered. We were so happy and in love. Life couldn't have been better.

Given our plans for the future, I felt it was time to pursue my interest in real estate. I had waited two years. But now, at the age of twenty-one, the time was right. Nigel and I were planning a wedding and we hoped one day to buy a house. It was time for me to settle into a secure job and a regular wage. Ballooning had been a wonderful adventure, but I needed to look at a serious career.

Nigel and I were in the office at the hangar discussing our

future when the phone rang. I left him deep in conversation and wandered back out to the aeroplanes. He was talking for ages before he hung up and walked over to me.

'How would you like to go to America?' he asked.

'I don't understand, who was that on the phone?'

'It was George Markey. He's in the US working on his Ultrabat project. He needs a hand,' Nigel replied.

I had met George a few times. He had designed and built an aerobatic aeroplane that he had named the Ultrabat. It was very odd looking. The first prototype had been built in Australia. Its registration, VH-ANT, was appropriate because it was so tiny. Most people on the airfield called it the angry mosquito because of its high-pitched screech as it manoeuvred through the air. The test pilot, Allan Hannah, who had been working with George, was a friend of ours. He was a young Air Force pilot more used to flying F-18s and Caribous. Allan had originally told us about George in America building the second prototype, and he'd planned to join him there in a few months' time to test fly and display the Ultrabat at an air show in Oshkosh.

'When does he want you there?' I asked Nigel.

'I can leave as soon as I arrange a passport and have my visa approved,' he answered.

Plans had to be made immediately if we were to go. At the time, neither of us had any commitments to keep us in Australia. My working life was in limbo and I knew real estate was something I could pursue at any time.

'Let's go for it,' Nigel said. The decision was made within minutes, which sent us into a frenzy, knowing there were many arrangements we had to make quickly. Neither of us had a passport so the first thing we did was race to the post office and submit our applications.

Just over a week later, Nigel flew out. There were a few things I needed to tie up before I could meet him there. It was also a chance for Nigel to assess the conditions in which we would be living. The place, called Mojave, is in the middle of the desert. We hadn't been given a great deal of information and we didn't know what to expect. If Nigel found the situation unacceptable, he could make a hasty retreat before I left Australia. This wasn't necessary though. I made my way across after Nigel gave the okay and he picked me up from Los Angeles airport soon after.

The project took three months to complete before the Ultrabat debuted in Oshkosh. During that time, Nigel worked incredibly long hours helping build the aeroplane. He wasn't a licensed aircraft engineer, however he'd been working on planes for so long and had developed so many varied skills that George knew he would be invaluable, especially since the job was behind schedule. George also knew Nigel was a hard worker and there was a lot of pressure to complete the aircraft in time for the show. The Ultrabat was a composite-built aircraft and most of the work Nigel did was with fibreglass. This was a change from his usual work with fabric-covered planes. There wasn't much I could do to help but I was pleased to be involved, even if it was sanding back moulded components or making the boys cups of tea.

Mojave is not much more than a truck stop and a huge airport located about two hours' drive from Los Angeles. We made it our home and established some great friendships during our stay there. Allan joined us in the final two weeks to complete the test flying. Then, four days before the air show, the three of us packed the aeroplane in a specially built trailer and drove across the US to Oshkosh, Massachusetts. It took three days. We rotated the driving duties and only stopped once to grab some sleep in a motel. Allan was great company, and this journey firmed our already strong friendship.

Some of the countryside we drove through was unbelievable. I was amazed how quickly the scenery changed from flat plains to rugged mountains. But it was extremely tiring, a very long drive.

'We should be in Oshkosh in about half an hour,' Nigel said. We all commented on how inactive the sky was.

'By this time, I expected the air to be swarming with aeroplanes,' Allan said.

Oshkosh Airshow was opening the next day. It was the biggest air show in the world and we expected there would be hundreds of planes flying in. We didn't have to wait long. As we rounded the next corner, we could hear the deep drone of a powerful radial engine. Just to our left was a yellow Harvard – a large warbird – flying extremely low and tracking beside the road. Allan's eyes lit up and Nigel, who was behind the wheel, strained to keep an eye on the plane and drive at the same time. Before long, there were different types of aircraft flying in all directions.

We had made it on time. The show was due to open the next day and would run for a week. I know Nigel was relieved to have made the deadline, but he'd been working so intensely all he wanted to do was rest. We stayed for the first two days of the show then made our way back to Australia. We didn't ring Mum and Dad to tell them to expect us. We just arrived on their doorstep at seven one morning. This was the first time I'd been away from home and outside their protection, so you could imagine the reception we received.

Nigel moved out of Phoebe's house soon after and was living at my parents' home. His room was way, way down the opposite end of the house from mine. I wonder if Mum and Dad ever heard the floorboards creaking when we snuck around during the night? Derek also moved back home for a few months following his return from a year in Europe. It was certainly a full house.

My childhood dream had come true now. I was working as a real estate salesperson in the Lower Blue Mountains and loving every minute of it. I had never been in a sales job before, but there wasn't much to it. I was operating under the proprietor's licence so I wasn't required to take in an official course. All my training was done on the job. The most important attribute I think one needs to sell a house is a genuine desire to help people, which is what I found most satisfying. Nigel continued with his work restoring aeroplanes, which was a business he hoped to build up and one day expand to include buying and selling them. We were happy with our work and life was very good.

I returned to the real estate agency one day after two days' break. There had been a few new houses listed while I was off. So, during the morning, I took the chance to familiarise myself with them. I pulled up in front of a run-down, overgrown home in Glenbrook, only five minutes from

Mum and Dad's. My information sheet said that it was vacant. As I walked down the gravel driveway, I noticed a family of rosellas feeding in a tree full of berries right next to me. The house was nestled in a valley surrounded by natural bush. There was a high paling fence, only about one and a half metres in front of the house, that ran along the entire length, its depressing chocolate brown paint faded and peeling. The front door had partly rotted at the base, due to dampness. It scraped and creaked as I pushed it open. The first thing I noticed inside was a foul musty smell, the odour of wild animal. I went in to a large living area with dark green carpet. The timber ceiling had dropped in places and had waves all along it. Some of the walls were bowed as well. The kitchen was galley style and had dirty dishes still in the sink as if the occupants had left some weeks or months earlier in a great hurry. As I made my way through the rest of the house, I observed walls that didn't meet, floor surfaces that were uneven in places, and there was a different carpet in every room.

I opened the back door and walked onto a small decking that was a bit wobbly and would need to be pulled down. The outlook was magnificent, a private bushland with a natural rocky creek that ran through the backyard. I could hear the soothing trickle of water and noticed a little waterfall feeding into a small rock pool. The block backed onto another road that you couldn't see because of the natural leafy screen. It was beautiful.

When I returned to the office, I needed to write an advertisement to put in our sales window. You guessed it: Renovator's Delight.

That night I told Nigel about the old house. Being a builder by trade, he would be interested to hear all about this disastrous structural nightmare. Nigel was keen to see it for himself and the next day after work we went for a look.

'Oh, my God, look what they've done here! – Oh, no, look at that!' he kept saying as he wandered through. We were there for an hour and Nigel had become quiet. Then, walking back down the stairway that lead to a loft overlooking the main bedroom, he said: 'It's calling me, Lan.'

'What are you talking about?'

'The house. It can be fixed up. We can really do something with this.'

'You're not kidding, are you!'

'I know it looks really bad, but it's mainly cosmetic. Let's buy it.'

Over the next week, Nigel and I went back to the house several times. We even showed it to Mum and Dad who couldn't see the reason for our enthusiasm, which was growing by the day. We negotiated with the owner backwards and forwards a few times until we agreed on a price. It was ours. The settlement date was scheduled for a week after our wedding so we arranged to move in after the honeymoon.

Our wedding day was the fairytale every girl dreams about. I had tried on many dresses over the six months leading up to the day. Mum came with me each time and she would often get choked up to see me standing as a bride in front of her. I ended up having my dress made. It was raw silk with lace and pearls embroidered over the bodice and skirt. Mum and Dad paid for it and gave it to me as my twenty-first birthday present. I loved that idea. Leanne was my bridesmaid and her daughter, Deniele, was the flowergirl.

Mum woke me on my wedding day with a cup of tea for what was supposed to be a relaxing morning, although between going to the hairdressers, the make-up artist arriving and getting dressed, I had begun to get stressed. The sky was overcast and light drizzle was falling, but I wasn't too worried about the weather. I'm told that it brings good luck. It did ease off slightly just as I arrived at the gorgeous old sandstone church we'd chosen in Cobbitty near Camden.

All in all, the day went like clockwork. I managed not to be paranoid about everything being perfect. I just wanted to enjoy a memorable day with our friends. After the service, we all went to the reception centre where there were drinks served in the garden. To our delight, our friends Steve Curtis and his father, Bob, surprised us by doing a fly past low over the reception centre in two Tiger Moths. It made our wedding very special and it was fitting that one of the Moths was the black Tiger Nigel had first taken me flying in. At the end of the night, we said goodbye to everyone amongst many hugs and tears, then drove to Leura in the Blue Mountains for the night. I stayed in my wedding dress until we arrived at the resort. I wanted to be a bride for as long as possible.

The next day we began our drive to Shute Harbour in Queensland where we'd hired a yacht for ten days. It took us three days to get there. We agreed next time we'd fly. The weather was perfect. An instructor took us out for a quick crash course in handling the boat before we sailed off into the sunset. We managed to find a small protected cove to anchor in for the night.

Gentle water lapping onto the hull woke us to a stunning morning. The Whitsunday Islands were mirrored in the clear blue ocean that was home to a pod of dolphins and a resident turtle that swam up to the boat to greet us as we indulged in a breakfast of fresh tropical fruit. This was paradise and the perfect honeymoon. There were two other boats just near us which had also sought shelter in our cove during the night.

'Let's sail to a more private spot today, Lan.' Nigel already had the map out. 'Let's aim for Thomas Island. We won't make it there today, but we should get most of the way.'

Thomas Island looked to be the most southern island in the Whitsunday group. We were both ready to play Robinson Crusoe so we upped anchor and sailed through the day. Some sections through the open sea were quite rough and waves crashed over the bow

'This is great,' I yelled out. It was exhilarating, not to mention a lot of hard work, and in the evening we enjoyed a well-earned rest, nestled into a pretty bay.

Again we sailed on, leaving as the sun poked up over the horizon. Nigel and I worked like a well-oiled machine and, although we didn't have much experience on the water, we handled the old girl pretty well. With Thomas Island up ahead, the wind was becoming gusty, but we could see a sheltered spot and pulled down the sails, motoring in slowly.

'I want to get in as close as I can, Lan.'

I was leaning over the bow watching the coral on the ocean floor, directing Nigel who was steering from behind.

'Nice view,' he said. All I was wearing was a G-string and nothing else.

'Concentrate on what you're doing,' I called back.

Crunch! Our vessel came to a sudden stop as we hit the bottom.

'That'll do,' I called, laughing at the situation. Nigel reversed out a bit further and we dropped the anchor.

It was mid afternoon, which gave us time to jump into the metal dinghy we were towing and go and explore our island. There was not a soul around. This was the peaceful solitude we'd wanted. Standing on solid ground, my whole body felt strange. The sand beneath my feet was moving up and down like the motion of the boat and my balance was upset, making it hard to walk in a straight line. How bizarre, I thought. But Nigel was having the exact same problem. I hadn't noticed either that we were both very sunburnt despite soaking ourselves in sunscreen. It was a relief to be relaxing on the beach with the refreshing water dancing around my toes.

During the night, the wind swung around bringing the sea to life. Wave after wave rolled in, rocking us backwards and forwards, backwards and forwards, as we tried to sleep in our bunk below in the cabin.

'I've got to go up on deck, Nige, or I'm going to be sick.'

'Good idea.'

The fresh air helped but our motion sickness took hold again.

'Let's get off the boat for a while and settle our stomachs,' Nigel suggested.

Our brilliant starlit sky had been covered over by menacing black clouds. Without moonlight, the night was so dark you couldn't see your hand in front of your face. However, the darkness was interrupted with the occasional flash of lightning. We gathered some bedding, a tarpaulin and a milk crate full of supplies, including a torch, and bundled them into the dinghy to motor to the shore.

'I feel much better, Nige. I couldn't stand that rocking much longer. Do you think it's going to rain?'

'No, the storm is going around us.'

We prepared a fire that helped to light up the beach so we could see. Our Robinson Crusoe adventure had turned into a scene out of Gilligan's Island. We made a bed on the sand, covered by the tarp, and settled in for some sleep.

An hour or so passed before the heavens opened. Just a few drops at first, then down it came. Our protective cover began leaking and soon we were soaked to the skin.

'This is ridiculous. We'll have to go back to the boat,' I said.

Nigel agreed. He grabbed the torch and we walked down to the dinghy.

'Where is it?' I asked.

'I'm sure we tied it up right here,' Nigel shone the torch along the breaking surf. 'Oh no, here's the rope.' It was still attached to the tree and it ran all the way into the water. As the tide had come in and the surf had come up, our little boat had gone down. It had sunk.

'We need something to help bail the water out,' Nigel

yelled. I ran back with the torch, fumbling through the crate of supplies. All I could find was an empty Meadow Lea tub and a foam cup. I was giggling uncontrollably as I ran down to Nigel who was now in the water and trying to drag the boat up onto the shore.

'Will this do?' I asked, holding the containers out for him to see.

He wasn't impressed.

'Come in and help me.'

We were both in the water up to our necks and after much straining, grunting and swearing, we managed to beach the boat and tip most of the water out, bailing the rest by hand.

We loaded the soaked blankets and other material in and lined up ready to push into the breaking waves. Nigel lifted me into the boat first, then jumped in and began frantically pulling the starter cable trying to get the engine to kick over. Another wave pounded, rocking us violently.

'Hurry up, Nigel, or we are going to tip over.'

Another set of breakers bigger than the first were looming offshore. 'There's another wave coming – hurry up.'

The engine fired as the wave hit. We powered through, away from the breakers, only to realise we hadn't left a light on in the yacht and we were blinded by the darkness. Nigel killed the engine and we listened . . . tink – tink – tink – tink. It was the rigging tapping gently on the mast. We headed towards the sound.

It was a long night. We didn't really get any sleep and we ended up lying on the upper deck until dawn. It was a relief to see the sun come up. We were both not only seasick, but also suffering sunstroke and we needed to make it back to civilisation in a hurry. We didn't have the energy to hoist the sails so we motored all the way back to Shute Harbour which took most of the day. The rent-a-yacht company arranged for us to see a doctor so we could claim our travel insurance in case we didn't return to finish our ten-day sailing trip.

In the surgery, the young female doctor asked us both to stand up straight and close our eyes. Nigel and I began rocking from side to side and eventually we fell over. We couldn't walk in a straight line or pass any of the other minuscule tasks she set.

'Well, you two are land lovers for the rest of your holiday. I suggest you find a nice resort and rest,' the doctor said. And that is exactly what we did. We found a comfortable hotel on the mainland and settled in for a week of recovery.

'The first thing we need to do is open up all the windows and try to get rid of that horrible smell.'

It was old, dirty and dilapidated, but it was our first home. We spent the week cleaning and scrubbing before we could move in. We didn't really have any furniture, but there was an old lounge, dining table, two single beds and a fridge left behind by the previous owners. They all cleaned up okay, even the fridge, which was disgusting. It took a whole day to make it presentable. It was fun playing house despite the continual surprises from rats, mice, oh, and the possums – we finally discovered what the smell was.

All my family came to help on the weekend, armed with machetes and handsaws to join in a working bee to clear the dense vegetation that had overtaken the backyard. Our task was monumental. Friends dropped in over those two days, all saying we must be crazy to take on a house as bad as this.

Mum came over for lunch a few days later. We were sitting in the dining room admiring the parrots perched in a tree just outside the window. Nigel can't usually sit still for too long and he was getting agitated.

'I can't stand that wall,' he announced, indicating the white-painted brickwork that was almost a metre high, segregating the dining room and a walkway to the back door. 'Pass me that hammer, Lan.'

Nigel tapped the corner brick without much force and it fell into his hand. His eyes lit up, and the second one broke away just as easily. Within half an hour, the entire wall was gone and Mum and I were left sitting covered in dust and completely dumbfounded.

'That's much better,' he said, satisfied with a job well done.

It seemed that everything we touched was about to crumble or fall down. I remember one night inspecting a built-in cabinet that had open shelves in the top section and a closed cupboard below. I had a nice vase that I thought might go well sitting on the shelf to help brighten the place up. As I sat the vase down, the whole structure wobbled slightly.

'Look at this,' I called to Nigel. I pushed it on one side and the cabinet moved. I picked up my vase, luckily, because

Nigel gave the cabinet a decent shove and it crumbled into a pile of timber at our feet. We laughed a lot at those silly situations because there were so many of them.

The entire living area was one big room. The walls and ceiling were lined with timber panelling that was stained from smoke that had billowed from the open fireplace located in the centre. It made the place dark and dismal. We didn't have much money so we decided to pull all the timber lining down, sand it back and use it again. It took a few nights to pull it down, which exposed the original ceiling underneath. It was a mess, water stained and rotten in parts. It also had to come down. Nigel and the children completed the job while I was at work one day, thankfully, because they found dead rats, possum nests and other disgusting things. He had also decided to pull up the carpet that was so encrusted with dirt. It was the middle of winter and the mountains can get very cold. We had no heating in the house and now we were looking up into the rafters and the tiles lining the roof.

After work each evening, we would get stuck into sanding and de-nailing all the panels, often under the watchful eye of Mister Possum, who looked on from his perch in the ceiling. We managed to get much work done that winter because it was one of the only ways to keep warm. Our 'it's not that bad' renovating project was growing by the day. The roof had sagged over the living area and had to be propped up and re-beamed. The roof itself was lined with three different styles of tiles that would one day need to be replaced. There were also large gaps along the gables, allowing free access to our resident family of possums who decided to make a new nest directly above our bed.

You could almost set your watch by it. At two every morning they would pounce onto the roof, stomping across the tiles. In the stillness of the night, they sounded like a herd of elephants wearing army boots. In they came, shuffling between the tiles and the raked timber ceiling in our bedroom to settle right above our heads, bumping and scratching for hours, keeping us awake. It got too much for Nigel one night. He climbed up onto the roof at 4 a.m., frenziedly tearing tiles away trying to get to Mister Percy Possum. I could hear the commotion and ran outside.

'What are you doing?' I called out in a whisper, trying not to wake the neighbours.

'I can't stand these bloody possums, they've got to go.'

Allan was staying with us at the time and he was stumbling out of his room, wondering what all the fuss was about. I met him in the living room as Percy came bounding along the rafters above our heads.

'He's in here, Nige.'

I will never forget the look of determination on Nigel's face as he ran into the room armed with a broom, and in one motion lunged at Percy, knocking him onto the ground. I screamed and jumped onto a chair while the two men cornered Percy under the lounge, eventually scooting him out the door. Percy jumped back onto the roof with Nigel in hot pursuit. Their game of chasing went from one side to another and ended with Percy suspended in the air at the very top of our tall TV antenna, being attacked by a flock of swallows he'd disturbed. I walked onto the driveway and looked up at the stand off between them, a ridiculous scene illuminated by the brilliant full moon that was also watching on.

'Now look what you've done. I don't understand what you're trying to do. Are you trying to catch him?'

'No, I just want him to stay off my roof.'

'Maybe if you ask him nicely.'

'That's not funny, Lan.'

'Well, he's not going to come down with you standing there. Come inside, I'll put the kettle on.'

Nigel kept watch from the ground. Feeling the coast was clear, our frightened little friend made his way back onto the roof, heading towards the open hole where about ten tiles had been removed. Nigel rallied Allan and, arming me with the broom and directing me to stand station in front of the antenna, they tried to encourage the possum off the roof. But instead, he came bounding straight towards me, despite the fact that I was waving the broom around like a mad woman. I screamed and jumped out of the way at the last minute. I'm sure all the neighbours were awake by now as again our furry friend found refuge on top of the aerial.

That day, I had possum traps placed in the roof and, once the possums were captured, I had them relocated. Every time we had new residents move in, we would trap them and have them taken away into the bush. I loved the wildlife around the house but not inside. One night we heard rats in a cavity in the wall, chewing constantly on the timbers. This went on night after night, despite laying baits and traps, until one night Nigel got out of bed and quite calmly destroyed the wall with a sledge hammer. It was going to be moved anyway, otherwise it would have been a radical solution. The water rats did get the message, though. They didn't come back.

Allan was based in Victoria at the time, but often when he was on leave from the air force he came to stay with us, always interested to see the improvements we had made. Allan was a keen aerobatic pilot and a very good one. He had come first in the advanced category in the previous Australian Championships. He was also our partner in a small aeroplane called a Citabria. It was able to do basic aerobatics, but the three of us had discussed selling it and upgrading to a high performance aircraft called a Pitts Special.

Nigel had dabbled in aerobatics, but was in no way a professional. However, we thought it would be a good investment and we wanted to help Allan in his sport. The boys found a suitable single-seat aircraft in Queensland, VH-IOO, owned by a girl named Bonnie who lived in Darwin. They flew up to have a look. It was pretty tired, but basically a good machine, and after a bit of negotiating, we bought it. Nigel spent long hours every day restoring Oscar, which was the name we gave it, ready for Allan to fly at the Nationals. They were both so proud of their baby when it debuted at Griffith that year. Its shiny new paintwork even boasted sponsorship logos that Allan had secured from Westfield Shoppingtowns. This was Allan's first year flying in the highest class, the Unlimited, and he proudly claimed fourth place.

Another friend of ours, Peter Whitehurst, came out to watch some of the competition as well. He was interested in flying aerobatics and was trying to arrange a partnership with some local pilots to buy a two-seater Pitts Special. Pete was a young instructor and a really easy-going bloke. His relaxed manner made him a brilliant instructor whose reputation was well known. He had been based at Camden for only a short time but he quickly became a close friend.

Peter was my motivation to start flying again. I decided to use our old Citabria, which was now on line at the flying school Peter worked for. It was a tail dragger, which meant it had a tail wheel instead of the nose wheel that I was used to. The tail wheel was much more difficult to handle. Many times Peter calmly took over the controls while I careered off course, trying to keep her straight as we hurtled down the runway. Once in the air, he'd give me gentle instructions while never changing the pitch in his voice.

'Just lift your right wing up a bit – that's it. Watch your air speed – good.'

I progressed quickly and was flying solo again before long.

In the meantime, Nigel and I took a quick trip back to America for the purpose of locating several aircraft for a client of ours who was starting up his own flying school. We had been building our business up to include buying and selling aircraft. This proved reasonably lucrative and was something we agreed would be a large part of our future. While we were in the States, we also chased up a few Pitts Specials for Peter and finally found a perfect specimen in Seattle. It was crated up and shipped back to Australia. Our airfield at Camden was turning into a real aerobatic hub.

Christmas 1990 was closing in fast. Peter, Allan, Nigel and I were discussing taking the aeroplanes to Hamilton

Island. Nigel and Allan would fly the Pitts Specials, and Peter and I would take the Citabria and complete my flying training on the way. We agreed it was a tremendous idea and were geared to leave on Boxing Day. Allan made sure our accommodation bookings were secured and we made plans to do joy flights off the island to help pay for the trip.

Early Friday morning, 21 December, 1990. Allan had been with us for a few days helping Nigel get the aeroplanes ready for our journey north. The boys were leaving for Camden as I put the lead on Ben ready for our run before breakfast. The golden retriever pup Nigel had had when we first met had gone missing about six months later, never to be seen again. So a month after our wedding, we bought another just like him and named him Ben. Allan was always perplexed at my motivation to gear up at this time every day and, with pooch by my side, dash off up the road and into the bush. A few days earlier, there had been steady rain falling and he was convinced that I was a complete nutter when still I warmed up at the front of the house, grabbed Ben, and took off.

'You're mad,' he called out.

'It's invigorating, Al, you should try it some day,' I called back from the top of the driveway.

This particular morning was clear and fresh. The start of the mountain track was about five minutes away. Ben knew that once we reached a big tree that marked the boundary into the bush, I would stop and take his lead off and he could explore to his heart's content, always keeping me in sight. Sometimes I forgot to stop, but he would come to a halt anyway, jerking me back, reminding me of our routine.

It felt good that day, pushing my body until a healthy sweat ran down my back. We traversed down a rock ledge into a small valley, and then up the other side. The muscles in my legs were burning as I gasped in the crisp morning air, absorbing the essence of my bush surroundings with every breath. There is nothing like being at one with nature to make you feel alive.

Today was my last day at work before two weeks' holiday so I spent the morning tying up a few loose ends. My boss, Brian McKay, had arranged to relax with me and the rest of the staff at 2 p.m. for a few Christmas drinks. It was a real family affair working at The Professionals Real Estate at Glenbrook. Brian's daughter, Alicia, was also on the sales team. She was my age, we worked extremely well together and were good friends. Brian's sister-in-law, Carolyn, was in charge of property management and occasionally his wife, Dianne, or another of their six kids would help out in the office.

Alicia and I were talking that afternoon about our plans for the holidays and for 1991. She had been accepted into university and would take on full-time studies next year doing a Bachelor of Arts degree, majoring in applied communications. As for me, I said, 'I love my work here. I am happy with what I am doing. I don't expect 1991 to hold too many changes for me.'

I left the office at four to do some shopping then headed home at six. Headlining the news on the radio in my car: 'There are grave fears for two occupants of an aeroplane that left from Camden Airport late this afternoon on a training flight and didn't return.' My heart always skips a few beats when I hear about flying mishaps in the hope that it's not Nigel or any of my friends. I raced home to call Nigel, thankful to hear his voice. He told me there was an Air League camp on and it was one of their planes that was still missing despite a search and rescue that was in progress. The Air League is similar to the boy scouts but boys and girls can join and the focus is on learning about flying. Recruits are encouraged from the age of nine to ninety, according to their advertisement.

Nigel and Allan arrived home at seven and told me there was still no sign of the missing plane. The aviation industry in Australia is very close-knit and although we didn't know the people who were missing (a young instructor and his female student) we were very concerned for them. The three of us discussed several theories, but felt they had probably flown out to the telephone box. This location was known to be a favourite with local pilots. The telephone box was located about twenty minutes away from Camden by air. It was a small island where someone had deposited an old red telephone box right in the centre. It was bizarre, serving no real purpose, but worth a look from the air. In the sameness of the Burragorang Valley area, the telephone box on its barren podium stood out like a beacon.

At 10 p.m. the phone rang. It was Robert Holmes who was one of the organisers of the Air League camp. Robert wanted to speak with Allan and asked if he could be at Camden Airport early the next morning to coordinate the search. Any other volunteers were also requested to attend, especially pilots with local knowledge.

Allan put the phone down and paused for a moment,

then said, 'I need to be at the airport early, guys, to organise this search and rescue. But I want to be ready for it, so I think I'll go now. Can you two come down early tomorrow? We need all the help we can get.'

Nigel and I agreed to be there.

Chapter 5

The Day My Life Changed Forever

Saturday, 22 December, 1990. Nigel and I were very quiet during the thirty-minute drive to Camden Airport. I couldn't help thinking about the two missing people, wondering if they were injured or if they were even alive. The picture of them injured in the bush wouldn't escape me. A news report over the car radio confirmed that poor weather conditions had delayed the search, and this bad news made our mood even more sombre. To try to lighten the moment, I asked Nigel if he had any suggestions for the many Christmas gifts we still had to purchase. As with most years, our Christmas shopping was done at the last minute and this year was no exception. We were able to decide on a few presents and planned to finish the shopping late in the day.

We arrived at Camden Airport at 8 a.m. There were a few police cars in the car park. Air League students who were attending the camp were wandering around aimlessly. The airport had been closed to all aircraft traffic excluding official search planes and, given the weather was clearer, the search was in full swing.

There was an aeroplane taxiing towards the fuel bowsers. We could see that Peter Whitehurst and Allan were sitting at the controls. Nigel parked the car and we walked over to meet them.

'Any news?' we inquired.

'There is still no sign of them,' Peter explained.

Another aircraft taxied in. It was a Cessna 210 VH-PLD. The pilot was a local instructor named Steve Curtis whom we knew well. Steve parked near the control tower and also greeted us with the news that nothing had been found. We headed into the tower where most of the activity was centred, hoping for encouraging news.

From the control room, you can see in every direction. I stood at the window, staring towards the mountain range where the missing plane was expected to be. The area west of Camden is terrain so extremely hostile that most pilots refer to it as tiger country. Certainly the last place you would want to try to land a plane. In fact, where you would land in this part of the Burragorang Valley in an emergency was the subject of many discussions between local pilots. Some would say, head for the water (Lake Burragorang) if you can make it. Some would say, put down into the trees. Wherever these people were, it was going to be like finding a needle in a haystack. But we simply had to find them.

Peter and Allan had almost an hour before they were scheduled for another flight so the four of us went to get some breakfast at Phoebe's. Allan's authoritative role in the search and rescue was one he took very seriously. His air force discipline and training was evident by the official way he was conducting himself. So when he asked if I would help by being an observer on his next flight, I was only too happy to oblige. After breakfast, Peter and Allan went to prepare the aircraft which was VH-PLD, the six-seater Cessna 210 that Steve had flown earlier. Nigel and I went to find my headset.

'I'll get some work done in the hangar and we'll do the shopping after you get back,' Nigel said as we walked along the tarmac, hand in hand. I was the last one to arrive at the plane where a group of people had already gathered and were waiting by the door.

A log was taken of all the names of those who would be on board VH-PLD, beginning with Peter Whitehurst, pilot in command and Allan Hannah, co-pilot. Janine Watson was next to log on. We had met each other before, at a party, but I didn't know her very well. We chattered briefly while we waited to board the plane and both observed that the day was heating up. It was going to be a hot and uncomfortable flight. Robert Holmes was the next observer. He had a senior role in the Air League so I knew it was one of his planes that was missing and I understood why he was even more anxious than the rest of us. Robert was a regular pilot at Camden Airport and, although I only knew him to say hullo in passing, he always impressed me as being quietly spoken and a true gentleman. A young student pilot then gave his name to the officials. He had been attending the Air League camp and was very concerned for his friends. Steven Doggert was his name. He was only nineteen or twenty, I guessed.

Allan checked the official's list after I had given my name. Peter was briefed on our search area. It was to be the area 'Charlie' that was marked on the map the official handed him. The observers' briefing was delivered by Allan who told us to look out for anything reflecting in the distance or any debris seen through the trees etc.

'Okay, let's get going,' Allan gestured towards us.

I quickly made my way into the back left-hand seat. Steven sat next to me. Janine sat in front of me with Robert to her right. Peter was in front of Janine with Allan to his right. Everyone strapped in and we were off. Our poor aeroplane laboured during the take-off, due to a full load of fuel and passengers plus the heat of the day.

The dramatic events of the past eighteen hours had been building to what we all hoped would be a happy outcome. Never had I felt such tension, though that was shared by the whole community of Camden Airport. As each hour passed, the chances of finding the two occupants of VH-BUO alive were diminishing. Allan had informed us during our briefing that the two young people we were looking for were Andrew Patterson, aged nineteen, and Angeline Neale, aged eighteen. To know their names made me feel a connection with them, especially Angeline. I fully comprehended the seriousness of their probable fate, knowing they had to have crashed or landed soon after 4.40 p.m. yesterday, which was the time they had left Camden Airport. There was a chance they could have survived an emergency landing if they'd had engine problems, but to be possibly injured and lost out in the dense bush in this heat would be any pilot's worst nightmare.

I was thinking about Angeline's mum and dad and how worried they must be about their daughter. I'd hate my parents to be going through such an agonising time of simply not knowing. It would be especially sad for her family being three days before Christmas. I couldn't help putting myself in Angeline's position and imagining the repercussions if it were me out there. How devastated Derek and Leanne would be, not to mention my darling Nigel and Mum and Dad.

I knew if it were me missing, I'd be relying on volunteer pilots and observers to try to find me. I was thinking of all these things, which made me focused and completely committed to the task ahead. We had to do whatever we could to find Andrew and Angeline.

Once at our preferred height of what looked like one thousand feet over the ground, we began flying a zig-zag pattern that took us over open fields, then into the rugged mountainous terrain in the Burragorang Valley, and back to the open fields again. To observe the green paddocks required nothing more than careful scanning. There were numerous farmhouses and plenty of roads scattered in this area. If VH-BUO had had had an engine failure out here, there were plenty of places to land and help was only a short walk away. Even if the plane had struck a tree or had run into a fence, Andrew and Angeline probably would have been found by a friendly farmer. Because of this, it was highly unlikely they would be here. But we made sure to leave no stone unturned and we covered this section of our search area with just as much devotion as we would in the thick bush.

The Day My Life Changed Forever

The hammering unrelenting sound from the engine of our Cessna 210 was so loud it began to give me a headache. I put my headset on to cut the noise considerably.

In many sections of the bush below, the tall leafy foliage was so lush and thick that it created a natural screen, hiding the valley floor. I knew there was a chance we'd fly over the top of the wreckage and not even see it. This realisation was frustrating. What if Andrew and Angeline could hear us fly overhead and then keep going into the distance? All we could do was our best - to keep looking out.

'I can see something through the trees.' Steven yelled out. He pointed down to the right. Peter spotted the debris, putting the aeroplane into a steep descent. Oh, please let it be them, and let them be all right, I prayed. Once we were established a few hundred feet over the site, it was clear the debris was the remains of a wrecked car. Although we felt deflated, the brief excitement had motivated us to keep looking even harder. In these areas, the bush canopy was at its thickest. It was a strain to try to see through it, but we continued on, hoping and praying that we would find them.

Almost an hour had passed. We had reached Lake Burrogorang for the third time and were turning to continue our zig-zag pattern. I scanned the water's edge intensely, thinking that if they'd crashed and survived, the most likely place to head for would be the water. Sometimes my mind played tricks on me and a large rock or the trunk of a fallen tree would look like a human figure. But it was only wishful thinking. There was no sign of wreckage, or people. Then I noticed the fuel gauge was below half and I knew we'd be heading back to Camden Airport soon. I also knew none of the other rescue parties had found anything or we'd have been contacted by radio.

To be returning without a result made me feel as though we had failed, although we all needed a break. The sound of the engine was mesmerising and the intense concentration required for observation was draining. It was also becoming oppressively hot and I felt very dehydrated.

We had flown another few minutes and were over a valley as we continued to focus on the dense canopy of trees below. Without warning, the drone of the engine was shattered by an enormous BANG. Almost like an explosion, it sounded like metal going through metal. It gave me such a fright, my heart started thumping heavily and a cold sweat swamped my body. I didn't know if we had hit something or what was going on. I sat forward in my seat and focused my attention towards Peter and Allan, who turned to each other with looks of shocked disbelief.

Instantly the engine began running rough, shaking the entire aircraft. I couldn't believe what was happening. We each knew VH-PLD had suffered some kind of catastrophic engine failure. But we were so shocked, all we could do was sit in a dazed silence. Within seconds, oil was spraying from the engine bay onto the windscreen. The dirty brown fluid spread quickly upwards making it difficult to see ahead of us. Although I had complete faith in Peter and Allan, being stuck at the back of the aeroplane, unable to hear any conversation or contribute to it was very frustrating. Although I had my headset on, there was no outlet to plug it in. Peter calmly and professionally started his emergency checks while Allan took control of the radio. It was 12.41 p.m.

The Day My Life Changed Forever

'Mayday ... Mayday ... Mayday ... Sydney ... Papa Lima Delta ... Papa Lima Delta ... Papa Lima Delta ... located approximately five miles west-south-west of Oakdale with a partial engine failure. Tracking to the Oaks. POB 6.'

I remembered my flight training for emergencies and discussions about engine failures in this hostile area, and how it was the worst possible place for an engine failure to occur. And here it was being played out for real. I just couldn't believe it was happening.

Approximately thirty seconds had passed and the oil continued to cover the windscreen. We all knew nothing could be done and we were going to have to land – somewhere. All eyes were directed outside, hoping in vain to find a cleared area suitable for a safe landing although we knew it was almost impossible.

Allan radioed again. 'Sydney ... Papa Lima Delta ... Update on that. We're ... ah ... negative oil pressure and the engine failing. We're in the Kangaroo Point area, presently located in the valley ... ah ... just to the west of Tumbledown Mountain through two thousand on descent.'

Forty-four seconds later, Allan continued, 'We're over a road at this stage to the south of the weathered area and a suitable paddock to the north where it would be best to land.'

Janine and I had spotted a small grassy field below, just to our left. It wasn't an extremely large area but it was the only grassy patch we could see. Then I heard her say, 'No, Peter, there are power wires!'

Now there was nowhere to land. The helpless feeling

was overwhelming, although our efforts to find a clearing continued. Peter turned the aircraft to the right, tracking up a valley, although how he could see where he was going I don't know as the windscreen was now covered with oil. I guessed he was mainly looking out through the side windows. The failing engine was deafening and vibrating so violently that I wondered if PLD would hold together. Our situation was desperate. The small metal hull of our aeroplane was dwarfed by the mountains around us. The only way was down into the valley floor and that's where we were headed. Peter and Allan were talking to each other through the radio intercom, but I couldn't hear what they were saying. My thoughts at this time were random and irrational – I have all my Christmas shopping to finish – I wonder what Mum and Dad are doing – This is only a dream – It can't be happening. It would be just moments, and we were going to crash land into the trees.

We had lost most of our height when the engine gave in. 'South from Tumbledown Mountain ... I say again ... south of Tumbledown Mountain ... through one thousand feet descending. Engine stopped.'

Heavily wooded mountains towered over us on either side and the trees below were getting bigger and bigger. I knew it wouldn't be long before we hit them, although I fought my conscious awareness of our plight, trying to convince myself I was stuck in a bad dream and soon I'd wake up and be safely back in my home.

Steven placed his hand on my shoulder and asked, 'Are you okay?'

The Day My Life Changed Forever

'I think I am,' I replied. There was still no panic from anyone. The disbelief was shared amongst the six of us, although we sat with silent dignity and full comprehension of our fragile fate.

Peter turned around in his seat and looked at each of us as he yelled, 'Make sure you are strapped in tight, this is it.'

I took my headset off and placed it on the floor at my feet as he began slowing the aircraft down. We all checked our seat belts. The basic belt across my lap seemed inadequate for the magnitude of our imminent disaster. The last radio call Allan made was at 12.44.02 p.m. – just over three minutes from the time the engine had failed.

'We're about three hundred feet going down,' he said.

Robert leaned towards Janine and placed his arms around her in a protective embrace. Then Steven did the same for me. Even at the time my mind was clear enough to acknowledge that selfless heroic act by Robert and Steven to put the safety of another human being before their own. My last thought was to pray, 'Excuse me, God. If you can hear me, please don't let me die.'

The first tree hit with a high-pitched screech as it scraped the metal under the right-hand wing. Then another, then another, until the cabin was being lashed at by a frenzied rush of branches and leaves pounding and screeching. I could see them whipping past the window then, in the next confused violent seconds, my world seemed to be tumbling over and over, throwing my body around like a rag doll. The aircraft finally nosed down, tossing me forward against the restraint of the lap belt, knocking the wind out of me.

The Best I Can Be

Then it crashed onto the ground, pushing me down into my seat.

Silence.

Complete silence.

I opened my eyes taking a moment to focus. Dazed and disorientated, I looked down and saw there was something sitting on my lap. Oh, my God, it's a brain!

I started screaming, over and over again.

'Nigel, I'm dead. Nigel, I'm dead.'

I reached down and pushed it onto the floor, suddenly realising that my head was intact and it wasn't my brain.

Trying to gather my thoughts, I looked up in horror to see that my dear friend, Allan, was very, very dead. I couldn't see Peter but I knew there was no chance he could have survived. The door on Peter's side appeared to have been ripped off and the whole cabin was sprayed with blood – there was so much blood. I was in extreme pain, but it was masked by the scene around me. Janine was slumped over. I could see that she was breathing.

'Janine, Janine!' I called.

But there was no answer.

Robert was sitting upright. He was unconscious as well, but his breathing was laboured. I was bent across, leaning on Steven. He had slipped down in his seat. I looked up at his face to see his head was tilted back and his eyes were open, staring, completely lifeless.

I was breathing heavily, panting desperately for oxygen. I made a conscious effort to calm myself. I knew I was badly injured. My body was scrunched down and it felt that my head was too close to my lap. I was speckled with blood all over. I had a hold of the back of Janine's seat with my left hand trying to support my body, which felt as though it had been snapped in two. I had immense pain in my back as if the top half and bottom half of my body had been separated. I pushed myself up slightly with both arms in an attempt to right myself. As I lifted, I felt a rush of intense pain grab me, and I felt splintered bones grinding together in my lower back. I ran my hand down my spine and felt a lump of bone sticking out under my skin. My back was clearly badly broken.

I am in serious trouble and I am going to die, I thought. There are so many things I still haven't done in my life. Like having babies. I am only twenty-three and I'm truly going to die out here. I wanted to live so badly. I didn't care about anything but living another day.

Instinctively I continued assessing my condition. Patting the tops of my legs, I was relieved to find there was some feeling in them. But I couldn't feel my feet. I tried to look down below my knees, but I couldn't see anything. Janine's seat had slipped back on its track and was pushed hard up against my knees. Oh, God, why can't I feel my feet?

I wondered if they were still attached to my legs. It didn't feel like it. I tried to move my legs hoping to somehow get out of the wreckage, but I was pinned in. All I could do was sit holding up the top half of my body with my arms.

The midday sun beat down unforgivingly. There was not a breath of wind to relieve the stifling heat and thick smell of blood that was becoming suffocating. Outside I could see parts of shattered windows and jagged metal pieces. Instant panic overwhelmed me. What if we catch on fire? I can't get out. I tried to move my legs again, but they wouldn't budge. Oh, God, please don't let me burn.

There was a horrendous pain along my stomach where I had taken the impact with the seat belt. I looked down but I was bent over so far I couldn't see why it was hurting so much. It felt like the belt had cut right through me, slicing me in two. I tried to locate the buckle to undo it, hoping to relieve the pain. As I reached down I felt something sticky. Picking it up, I realised it was a piece of flesh. I didn't know if it had come out of my stomach. There was so much blood and gunk all over me, I couldn't tell, so I put it back where I'd found it. I was afraid that if I undid the seat belt, all my insides would literally fall out. So I left it in place.

Janine was still breathing but she hadn't moved. I tried calling out to her again but she wouldn't answer me. I couldn't reach out and touch her, although I tried. All I could see was her left shoulder rising and falling with each breath until finally she took a deep sigh and stopped breathing.

'No, no!' I called out. I couldn't help her. I couldn't move. I felt so helpless.

I was alone. Would anyone be able to find me out here? I didn't know. There were a lot of tall trees around and I knew how difficult it would be to see us through the canopy. About ten minutes had passed but it seemed like hours. I was gripped in agonising pain that was getting worse by the second. I was scared and alone. Robert was hanging in there, but it didn't look good for him. I wanted to help but he was too far away from me to even place a reassuring hand on him. I felt sick and went through waves where my vision went blurry. And I felt dizzy, wanting to vomit or faint. Is this it? I thought. Am I dying now? Each time it happened, I'd concentrate on my breathing and fight for consciousness.

I could hear someone groaning. I thought I was imagining it because I could see it wasn't Robert. It was coming from Steven who had started to stir. It shocked me at first because I'd thought he was dead. Then Steven became conscious and quickly went into an hysterical state.

'Get me out, get me out!'

He kept screaming and trying to sit up. I was still slumped over him, and each time he thrashed around I felt the pain of grinding bones in my back. Steven was obviously badly injured too and for both our sakes I had to calm him down.

'Steven, please stay really still. You don't want to hurt yourself anymore. You have to stay as still as you can. Help will be here soon. Everything will be okay.'

I tried to keep my voice soft and calm and it worked. He stopped moving about, even though he was scared and confused.

How much longer can we hold on? Please somebody find us soon, I kept thinking. The search for the first plane had begun yesterday and it still hadn't been found. We could be out here for days. I knew Steven and I couldn't survive for too long. We waited as the minutes ticked by, trying to remain as still as possible, although Steven was continuously grabbing at the ashtray, located near the armrest on his right. He seemed to be trying to pull at it like a door handle. He wouldn't stop. I could see his fingers starting to bleed from doing it, but he still wouldn't stop.

I thought I heard something faintly in the distance. I strained to listen. The sound became louder and louder. It was a helicopter. I couldn't believe it. Please, God, let them know we're here. Please let them see the aeroplane amongst all these trees.

The helicopter seemed to be flying straight towards us. I couldn't see where it was, but soon I heard it hovering somewhere overhead. I couldn't believe they'd found us. I knew there must have been an emergency locater beacon on board PLD for us to be found so quickly. All our rescuers needed to do was home in on the signal, which would bring them straight to us. I also knew there was probably nowhere to land, but at least we were found.

Only a minute or two later a man dressed in a green flying suit pushed his way through the dense foliage in front of the wreckage. I could see him coming closer. His face reflected his obvious repulsion at the scene before him. His expression changed to a look of disbelief as I screamed out to him, 'Please help us!'

'You're alive!' he answered, making his way quickly to the back of the aeroplane.

'There are three dead,' I told him. Our rescuer said his name was Steve. He couldn't reach us in the back of the cabin so he decided to smash the rear windscreen.

'Cover your heads,' he said. The screen shattered, giving some relief as fresh air began to flow through what remained of the plane.

Robert still hadn't moved and his breathing was weak. Soon after Steve arrived, Rob also lost the fight and died in front of us. Nobody said a word, but I prayed for God to take my friends to heaven. The four of them were gone. I wondered if God had the same fate planned for Steven and me. I knew we were very badly injured.

Another man arrived wearing the same green uniform. His name was also Steve and that made three. I asked the last man for some water, but he told me it'd be dangerous to put anything in my stomach because we didn't know what injuries I had sustained. He wiped my face with a damp cloth though, and helped me tie back my hair which was falling forward into my eyes.

'Hang in there,' he said. 'Doctors and paramedics are on their way.'

'Can somebody please contact my husband at Camden Airport and tell him I'm okay?'

'We'll take care of that, don't worry.'

Nigel had begun work on the Pitts. He wanted it to be ready for our trip north. The airport was still closed to anything but search aircraft so there was no training on today. A friend of ours, Adam Smith, was casually monitoring the radio in an aeroplane on the other side of the hangar and talking to Nigel from a distance. The chatter on the search and rescue frequency was spasmodic and could be faintly heard around the building.

'Mayday ... Mayday ... Mayday ... ' Nigel's attention was immediately focused on the broadcast.

'What's happening?' Nigel called to Adam who was standing closer to the radio.

'One of the search aircraft is in trouble, but it's not PLD.'

Nigel was relieved to hear it wasn't the aircraft I was in and he continued with his work while Adam sat by the radio. A few moments passed and another broadcast was made.

'Nigel, it is PLD, mate. They've had an engine failure over the valley,' Adam confirmed.

Nigel was panic stricken. They both raced to the control tower to try to find out what was happening. The mood was tense. The air traffic controllers had their workload stretched to the limit as their focus extended to a second aircraft in distress. Even though we knew the controllers personally, they couldn't let Nigel into the tower, despite his pleas. By this time most people on the airfield had heard about the second crash.

Nigel and Adam made their way back to the hangar to keep a listening watch on the radio and to ring my family. On the way, Nigel met up with Greg Watson who is Janine's father. He had heard the news, also. Dad was home on his own when Nigel made the difficult call. Mum was finishing her Christmas shopping and wouldn't be home for another hour.

'There has been an accident, Gordon,' Nigel said. 'Allana is in an aeroplane that has crashed in the Burragorang Valley. We don't know much more than that.' This is any parent's worst nightmare and Dad's reaction was understandable. He went into instant shock. Nigel said he would call back as soon as there was any news, but all Dad could do was stand in the hallway, stunned.

Mum came home soon after and found Dad still standing in the same spot.

'What's wrong?' she asked.

Dad told her what had happened, although the story was broken and slightly vague. She rang Nigel instantly to try to find out exactly what was going on. Nigel was sitting right next to the phone when she made the call. How terrible it must have been for him to have to tell my parents of the tragic events that were taking place.

'It doesn't look good, May. We have to prepare for the worst,' he told her. Mum rang my sister, Leanne, who drove straight up with John to be with Mum and Dad. Derek received a phone call straight after. He decided to drive to Camden Airport to be with Nigel. Every half an hour, Mum rang Nigel to see if there was any update.

My arms were getting tired from holding up the top half of my body. Every time I tried to relax, the broken bones in my back rubbed together causing intense pain. I asked Steve to help hold me up while I rested my arms. He reached into the cabin through the back window and put his arms around my chest. It was a great relief to have a rest, but it still caused a lot of pain in my back. Steven was getting agitated. I was worried I was hurting him because I was still slumped over, half leaning on his body. I suggested to Steve, our rescuer, that he try to sit me up to get me off Steven. Steve still had his arms around my chest and slowly began to lift.

'Stop! Stop!' I screamed out. I couldn't bear the pain. 'Just leave me like this, it hurts too much,' I said, trying to be brave. I wanted to be strong and I didn't want to cry. I just wanted the pain to stop.

It had been almost an hour since the crash. There

seemed to be more helicopters flying around and more people arriving on the scene, but there was no attempt to get anyone out of the wreckage until the Westpac Rescue Team arrived. They had trekked through the bush carrying all their support equipment and they looked extremely heat stressed once they arrived at the crash scene. A man dressed in a blue uniform, whose name was Hugh Russell, took control. He began giving orders to people who were still standing around and, within a short time, the two seats in front of me were cleared away. There was a hype of activity. Hugh climbed inside the cabin and settled in a crouched position right in front of me. He was so compassionate, and he showed great confidence in his ability to cope in this disastrous scene. I knew I was in good hands as Hugh assessed my condition, took my blood pressure, put a neck brace on me and put a drip in my arm. He worked quickly and without fuss.

'We're going to have to sit you up now,' Hugh explained.

I didn't want anyone to move me. The pain from trying before was too much to bear, but I knew it had to be done.

'I know we have to do this, but please don't start till I tell you I'm ready,' I asked.

I took a moment to gather my courage and gave Hugh the okay. There was another man behind me reaching through the back window, although I couldn't see who it was. Hugh released the seat belt. Then, with them both holding on to me, I was slowly lifted. I screamed out loud. The pain was indescribable. The process seemed to take forever and, despite being in excruciating pain, I couldn't do anything to escape it or stop them from sitting me up. As soon I was upright, the pain eased instantly. I let out a sigh, much to Hugh's relief and mine. I felt ashamed at all my screaming and wailing. I had tried to be brave, but we all have our pain thresholds and mine had been exceeded.

'We're going to slip a backboard down behind you and strap you to it, then we'll ease you outside,' Hugh said. When the board was slipped down it caught on my back where it felt as though a lump of bone was sticking out.

Pain gripped me again making me scream, 'No! Stop!'

Hugh let me calm down for a moment before he decided to slide me forwards in my seat so there was more room for the backboard. He supported me behind my knees and dragged my body towards him. The backboard was sent in again and I was strapped securely to it, which made me feel a lot more comfortable.

'Okay, you need to brace yourself again, Allana, while we straighten your leg.' I looked down. Hugh had raised my right leg up and my foot was facing the wrong way. As he slowly started to twist it around, I prepared for the pain, but there was none.

Hugh looked up at me and asked, 'Can you feel that?'

'No!' I replied, realising I was in a lot of trouble.

I couldn't feel my legs. I didn't know anything about spinal injuries, except for what I'd seen on television. I kept thinking about a movie I'd watched some years ago where a young boy broke his back and lay in hospital for months, sandwiched in a frame which was rotated throughout the day giving him sessions of staring at the ceiling then facing towards the floor. I pictured myself in this scene and wondered if this would be me tomorrow. Hugh put my leg in the brace and with a few more helpers started to ease me out of the aeroplane. It had been over two hours since the crash.

Once outside, I was amazed at how many people were around. It was like a battle ground. The crew from Careflight were working on Steven and using the 'jaws of life' to cut into the wreckage so he could be freed. Other emergency service workers were clearing away debris. There were police in uniform, TV camera crews and reporters. A policewoman introduced herself as Sergeant Helen Curtain. She asked for my name and address. After she had noted it down, I asked her if anyone had called Nigel. I knew he'd be going through hell, not knowing what was happening. Helen said she would make sure he was called.

'They've been found, Nigel!' The call came from one of the young instructors. Radio reports had confirmed it. The first report indicated there were people outside the wreckage waving to rescue helicopters. The survivors were being picked up and transported to a sports oval in Camden for transfer to Camden Hospital. Feeling a little relieved, Nigel rang my Mum instantly, then jumped in his car and drove to the oval where a police car waited for the helicopter to land. Nigel was standing next to the patrol car, explaining to the police officer that his wife was one of the six people in the aeroplane crash. Then over the police radio they heard a chilling report confirming that there were two people dead in the wreckage and the rest were still trapped. The first report had been incorrect.

Right: My first day at school, with my new, self-cut hairdo.
Below left: Fishing at Sussex Inlet, with Bill and 'the one that didn't get away'.
Below right: Outside the Washington Naval Yard Chapel, with Dad, Mum and my brother, Derek. I was eleven years old.

Left: Meeting my great-grandmother in Canada.

Below: Mum [centre] and Uncle Pete [in striped shirt] ready for their ballooning adventure.

Ballooning in Sydney in 1988.

Above: Nige [right], looking very much like Biggles, prepares the Black Tiger Moth to take my brother, Derek [seated], flying.
Below: Allan and Oscar.

Above: My fairytale wedding.
Right: The honeymoon sailing trip in the Whitsunday Islands wasn't such a fairytale.

Above: What remained of the Cessna 210.
Left: Memorial plaque erected at Camden airport in memory of those who died on 22 December 1990.

How this mix up occurred, we don't know. But poor Nigel had to return to the airport and again ring my parents. Minutes passed like hours as Nigel wandered around waiting for more news. Phoebe's daughter, Rachelle, stayed with Nige, trying to keep him calm. Another report reduced the odds again. There were now four confirmed dead. The only survivors were a man and a woman. However, they were still trapped in the wreckage and there was no report on their conditions.

Nigel knew now that there was a fifty-fifty chance I had survived. And if I had survived, I would surely be severely injured. Nigel and Greg Watson passed each other in the car park. Each knew one of their girls would not be coming home. It must have been terrible for both of them. Nigel rang my parents informing them of the news. It wasn't good and everyone had to prepare for the worst. Mum and Dad also knew that if I were alive my condition would be critical.

I had been placed on the ground in the shade of a tree. Hugh continued to work on me. He took off my remaining shoe and handed it to Helen. He was crouched at my feet saying, 'Wiggle your toes – Can you feel this? – What about this?'

I didn't know what was going on. Of course, I couldn't feel that. He wasn't touching me. I couldn't feel anything at all. Near me there was a group of people discussing how to transport Steven and me to the helicopters. A police 4WD was on the way, but it would be too risky to use a vehicle, they were saying. We had to be kept as still as possible because of our obvious spinal injuries. The only choice was to carry us.

Hugh checked me over again before I was picked up. There were three men down each side of me. They walked for a few minutes then delicately placed me back on the ground and rotated their positions. The oppressive heat made it hard going for them. Once we reached the helicopters, I was slid into the back and the stretcher was locked in place. Hugh took a seat next to me and Stewart, who was the other crew member, settled into his seat as well. I asked Hugh if he could get the pilot to call Camden tower on the radio and tell them to assure Nigel I was okay.

Rachelle was sitting with Nigel in his car. It was getting late in the afternoon and the stress of the day had taken its toll. The frustration and despair of not knowing my fate had left him feeling helpless and afraid. Then they saw a helicopter flying over the airport. It was the bright yellow Westpac Rescue Helicopter. Nigel had an overwhelming feeling of peace and he knew it was me who was being taken to hospital.

'She's going to be okay, Rachelle,' he said.

The flight to Prince Henry Hospital took about forty minutes. During this time I started getting a shooting pain down my right leg. It was getting worse and I was really frightened. I asked Hugh if he could hold my hand, which he did for the whole flight. It was the longest forty minutes of my life. The pilot turned to us and said, 'We are coming in to land.' The touchdown was so soft I didn't even realise we were on the ground until the door of the helicopter flew open. A team of doctors and nurses took me into the emergency room. Hugh was still with me. He told one of the nurses that I was worried about my husband. Could she phone him? The nurse asked me for the number. I knew Nigel was working in the hangar so I gave her his work number. She went immediately to make the call. It was 4.30 p.m.

The telephone at the hangar was answered by one of the Camden Aviation flight instructors who was a friend of ours, Greg McGovern. Greg was given the message that I had arrived at Prince Henry Hospital. Instantly he went looking for Nigel who was still wandering around the car park area with Rachelle and my brother, Derek. As soon as the message was delivered, Derek and Nigel drove straight to Prince Henry. The trip took about an hour. Despite my pleas during the day for someone to call Nigel and tell him I was alive, this couldn't be done until I reached the hospital because my rescuers didn't know the extent of my injuries. There was a real possibility I could have died at any time during the day.

Doctors and nurses were all around me. First, they cut my clothes off which exposed the gruesome haematoma across my abdomen. The swelling and multi-coloured bruising followed a line where the lap belt had restrained me on impact. I was in a lot of pain so one of the doctors gave me something that eased it instantly and made me feel even more groggy. The next few hours are a bit of a blur, but I remember being asked to wiggle my toes. There were doctors endlessly pin-pricking my legs. Some of it I could feel, but most I couldn't. I remember Mum coming in and, of course, Nigel. I have a vague recollection of being in a sort of tunnel for the purpose of taking X-rays.

Back in the emergency room, a doctor explained that I had to go into surgery. The impact I had taken on my stomach was so severe, he needed to perform an emergency laparotomy to make sure none of my major organs had been damaged. He also told me that the X-rays showed my back was clearly broken, but the priority was to make sure I had no internal bleeding or injuries before my back could be attended to. I was in a very heavily sedated state and it all seemed like a bad dream, but I still managed to sign the authority for surgery before being wheeled into theatre just before 6 p.m.

While I was in theatre, Mum, Dad and Nigel stayed in the waiting room with some of my friends. At 6 p.m. they sat, shocked, as they watched my rescue headlining on the national news.

'Wake up, wake up, Allana, wake up,' the voice seemed distant but intrusive enough to waken me. I was so drowsy, every part of my body was heavy and lethargic.

'Come on, Allana, wake up.'

I opened my eyes, a nurse was standing over me, checking the drip that ran into my arm.

'You're awake, how do you feel?' she asked.

I tried to talk but my mouth was too dry and my throat felt like someone had cleaned it out with a wire brush. All I could do was form the words, 'I'm okay.'

'I'll just be at the desk if you need anything.'

I looked across to see that the nurses' desk was on a

raised platform next to my bed. It was comforting to know. My stomach was very sore, not sharp pain, but a sort of burning pressure. I felt as though my body was wired up to every machine possible. There were tubes coming out of everywhere, even my nose. My neck was stiff and sore. I felt battered and bruised all over.

A sudden feeling of nausea overwhelmed me. I started gesturing towards the nurse.

'What's wrong?' she asked.

'I'm going to be sick!' I answered in panic. Not being able to roll over, I was afraid of choking. The nurse ran and collected a syringe and hooked it up to the tube that ran through my nose into my stomach. The nausea was relieved instantly, once my stomach was emptied. Exhausted by the ordeal, I drifted back to sleep.

Sometime during the night, I woke with a fright when one of the nurses accidentally banged a long blue pole against my bed. She was with a team of surgical dressers and the pole was part of a frame they were constructing.

'What's that for?' I asked.

'This is a Jordan frame, Allana. We're going to use it to lift you off the bed so you don't get pressure sores.'

'Lift me! You can't lift me! What about my back?' I exclaimed. I felt so fragile. Any movement at all caused excruciating pain in my back and the bones still ground together when I tried to move.

The nurse handed me a button that was connected to my drip regulator.

'If you want something more to ease the pain, just push the button and extra morphine will go straight in through your drip,' she said. 'Stop panicking, you'll be okay.'

Her words were reassuring, but I pushed the button straight away anyway because I knew it was going to hurt. Then I pushed it again just to be sure.

The steel poles of the frame went on either side of me, connecting at my head and at my feet, then long plastic slats had to be fed under my body and secured at either side. The sections at my legs were easy to do but I was perspiring so much, due to the drugs and sheer terror, that the plastic strap kept sticking to my skin, pulling it as the nurse tried to pass it under my back. I cried out in pain. I just wanted to be left alone. The nurse coated the next strap in talcum powder, which made the job much easier.

'We're ready to lift,' she ordered once all the straps were secured. There were six helpers, three down each side. 'Ready after three,' she said.

I pushed my button one more time and took a deep breath.

'One, two three, lift.'

'My back! my back!' I could feel bones moving around. 'Please let me down,' I begged.

'We have to give you a minute to get your blood circulating. You're all right. Stop panicking,' she said again.

Oh, please God, stop the pain. I didn't feel right. My body had been snapped in two. It was so fragile and here they were holding me up, suspended in the air. The frame looked weak as I realised I was gripping onto it so tightly on both sides that my knuckles had turned white. What if it breaks, or what if one of the straps comes loose?

'Please let me down, please let me down.'

The minute passed, despite my pathetic pleas. Once gently rested back on my bed, I was relieved it was all over, but exhausted by the experience. I drifted quickly back to sleep only to be woken two hours later to go through it all again. In fact this had to be done every two hours and each time was just as horrific.

Chapter 6

The Pain of Recovery

'I'm not happy with her lungs ... congestion ... she needs assistance with her breathing ...' As I slowly woke I could hear pieces of a conversation. There were two nurses at the end of my bed looking at my medical chart. I hadn't seen them before but I could sense they were concerned about something. They saw I was awake and came over beside me.

'How do you feel this morning?' asked one nurse.

'A little better. I don't feel sick like I did last night.'

'That's good news. We can go ahead and take this tube out of your nose.' She undid the tape that was holding it in place. 'This might feel a bit strange.'

She started pulling it out. I could feel it coming from right inside my stomach. It kept coming and coming. My nasal passage was stinging. I wondered how much more could be in there until finally the end came out, much to my relief.

'Are you okay?' asked the nurse.

'That felt awful,' I replied.

'I need to explain something to you. Your lungs are congested which means you aren't getting enough oxygen. We're going to use CPAP which is continuous positive airways pressure to help you breathe. We'll put a mask on you that fits tightly over your nose and mouth and blows air into your lungs. Sometimes it's a bit claustrophobic but you must relax and try not to breathe against the machine. Just let it breathe for you.'

The other nurse was wheeling the strange looking contraption over beside my bed. 'We'll leave it on you for ten minutes.' The nurse placed the mask over my face. The straps fed over my head and they were very tight, pulling at my hair. The machine started a slow breath of air feeding into my lungs. As they filled and expanded it was as if they were stuck, as if the walls of each lung were gunked together. As they inflated, I felt as if the walls of my lungs were being pulled apart like gooey peanut-butter sandwiches. It gave me a fright. I tried to breathe out, but the machine wouldn't let me. In panic, I grabbed at the straps and pulled the mask off.

'No, you have to leave it on.' The nurse wasn't far away. 'Let's try again. This time, relax.'

It was difficult trying not to breathe. I even tried to breathe in time with the machine but I kept getting out of sync. After five minutes I'd had enough and signalled to the nurse.

'Five minutes is a good start,' she said, taking the mask away. It had been on so tightly I could feel its outline left on my face. When Nigel walked in only minutes later, I must have looked like the cartoon character, Fred Flintstone, with the outline of shadowy whiskers on his face.

I was so relieved he was with me. It had been a really rough night.

'Hi, sweetheart, how are you feeling?' He pulled up a chair next to my bed and held my hand tight. Nigel was trying to be strong for me, but I could see it had been a rough night for him as well. 'Everyone is thinking of you and everyone sends their love. The phone hasn't stopped ringing and you wouldn't believe all the people who are here at the hospital wanting to make sure you're okay.' I listened to his words as the tears swelled in my eyes and ran down my cheeks. He wiped them away saying, 'Everything will be all right, we just have to get you well.'

'Nige, I have to tell you something.' I was almost sobbing and finding it hard to get the words out. 'Peter and Allan didn't make it.'

'I know, but we're going to be okay.' His voice was soothing and comforting, but I continued in my blubbering state.

'Nigel, Janine and Robert died too. Everybody was dying all around me. There were bits of everybody all over me and I couldn't move. I tried so hard but I couldn't help them. They were dying all around me, but I couldn't help them.'

I was distraught, but I had to tell Nigel what had happened. He sat listening to every word, stroking my face and holding my hand, comforting me as best he could. I felt relieved to talk to someone. It helped to off-load the burden of what I'd seen and what I'd been through. I hadn't been

The Pain of Recovery

offered any counselling. In fact, it'd be a week or so before I'd receive the token emotional support available through the hospital system. These days emotional healing is dealt with immediately and is considered an important part of recovery, but back in 1990 it was approached with less urgency or attention.

When I finished telling Nigel about what had happened, he could see I was exhausted.

'I want you to get some sleep. I'll be back soon,' he said. Only minutes after he left, I drifted off to sleep.

'Wake up! Wake up!' It didn't take much to rouse me, I was getting used to it. The nurse was standing next to me holding The Mask. 'Oh, no, not again.'

Nigel walked back into the room right at that moment. 'What's that for?' he asked.

'It's to help her breathing. She doesn't like it very much, but we have to leave it on for ten minutes.'

It was much easier this time but the initial unsticking of my lungs felt disgusting. With Nigel's help, I made it through the whole ten minutes, but I was glad to finally peel it off.

'Do I look funny?' I asked him as I tried to massage my face back into place.

'No, you are still as beautiful as ever. For all your poor little body went through, you haven't got a mark on your face. It's a miracle.'

I hadn't thought about the other injuries I might have sustained. So much emphasis had been placed on my back and on my abdomen, I had forgotten about the rest of me.

'Excuse me nurse, do you have a mirror?' She wheeled

over a large mirror that was attached to a frame, suspending it over my bed. The mirror was on a pivot so I could move it around. With this I could see my whole body and all around the room. I was so pale, it shocked me for a moment. But Nigel was right, there wasn't even a scratch on my face. My hair was a mess and still covered with dried blood although some attempt had been made to clean it up. I ran the mirror further down my body, pulling the sheets away, exposing a hideous multicoloured bruise down my left side. The imprint of the webbing from the seat belt had infused into my skin. The dressing from my operation covered most of my stomach. 'There must be a big cut under there, Nige.'

'Yep, it took thirty stitches to close you up,' he replied.

My legs lay at the end of my bed like slabs of dead meat. I couldn't feel anything at all below my knees and only bits and pieces at the tops of my legs. It was as if they were completely detached from my body. Through the mirror I could see all the way down to my toes, my right foot sitting up supported on each side with sandbags.

'Why isn't my leg in plaster?' I questioned Nigel. After all, my foot had been facing the other way, surely it must be broken.

'You didn't break a single bone in your leg. You tore all the ligaments in your ankle.'

Nigel pulled the sheets back for me to see. My foot was badly swollen, the bruising black and blue. Now I could see both my feet sticking out from the sheets. With all the ongoing tests on my legs, the pin-pricking and endless 'can you wiggle your toes', this was the first chance for me to see them for myself. The doctors kept saying they weren't moving, but surely they must be wrong. I could feel them moving. I wiggled my toes as hard as I could. In my head, they were moving perfectly. I could feel it happening. But as I watched – nothing. My feet didn't even twitch. I tried again, concentrating with all my might. Surely this time they'll move, but nothing happened.

'Nige, I don't understand any of this. Am I going to be in a wheelchair for the rest of my life? People keep giving me the impression I'm not going to be able to walk. Am I ever going to be able to run in the mountains again? I can't feel my legs. I'm so scared.'

'I talked to the doctors last night,' he said. 'There's a good chance your spinal chord is being obstructed by some of the bone fragments, and once it is cleared the feeling and movement will come back into your legs.'

'So there is hope?'

'There is always hope. Everything will be all right, you'll see.'

The surgical dressers came back into the room. 'It's that time again, Allana,' one of them said. They knew I hated being lifted on the Jordan frame and I knew they didn't like hurting me, but it simply had to be done.

'We are going to wash your hair after this,' the nurse explained. I was relieved. I knew my family was coming later in the afternoon and I didn't want them to see me in such a mess. Plastic sheets went down around the floor and after I was lifted, the dressers moved me up my bed hanging my head over the edge with the nurse supporting it. With a few more hands on deck and several buckets of water, the job was done. They even brushed it and put a ribbon in it for me.

I was so tired and groggy, the afternoon was spent drifting in and out of sleep. Mum, Dad, Derek and Leanne came to visit and doctors were constantly checking on me, continuously testing the feeling and movement in my legs hoping for any change. Nigel hovered around protectively, watching my feet intensely every time this was done. At one time, my big toe flickered.

'Did you see that!' Nigel exclaimed. 'It's not much, but it's something.'

'Well, it is a positive sign,' the doctor agreed. 'Your condition is stable enough, Allana. We are going to schedule you for surgery on your back tomorrow.'

High doses of drugs were continuously pumped through my body sheltering me from the pain, but they also allowed me to sleep, escaping the reality of my situation that was all too confronting. During the night, drifting in and out of my continuously interrupted sleep, I cried for Peter and Allan. I would miss them so much. I remembered how excited we'd been about flying up to Hamilton Island. I prayed for their families and for Janine and Robert's families too. I wondered how Steven was getting on.

What's going to happen to me? What if Nigel is wrong and everything is not all right? What if I can't walk again, what will I do? I pictured Nigel and I strolling across the dark grey tarmac at Camden Airport only yesterday. Will that be the last time we'll walk together? I tried to remember everything about those few moments, and how I took for granted walking one step after another, oblivious to the fact

The Pain of Recovery

that they could be my last. I couldn't believe what I'd done to my body. It was young and beautiful. Perfection, Nigel would say. I was so confident with the way I looked. I loved to be naked with Nigel. I loved the way it felt when he used to run his hand down the full length of my body, but now there were parts of me I wouldn't be able to feel if he did that. Would he be able to love me with my body so scarred and broken? We had only just started our life together. Our wedding was less than two years ago. It wasn't fair. How could this be happening to us? These thoughts haunted me. Fear was my constant companion.

I was alone and afraid. How I longed for Nigel's reassuring touch. I closed my eyes and prayed so hard.

'Excuse me, God, if you can hear me, please let this be a dream. Please make this awful nightmare stop. Please let me wake up tomorrow in my own bed ...' As I continued, a warm and comforting hand ran down my body. I opened my eyes, knowing it must be Nigel, but there was nobody there. I could see the nurse checking on another patient across from me, but there was no one else in the room. It didn't frighten me really, although I was confused. I don't know if it was the drugs that were playing tricks on me, but I like to think that it was God's hand that touched me that night.

The morning was busily spent preparing me for surgery. Many doctors and nurses were in and out checking me for this and testing me for that. Nigel came in amidst all the activity. It was going to be a big day for us. Our whole future would be determined by the outcome of this surgery, and we knew it. We held together, giving each other strength as the neurosurgeon, Dr John Matheson, explained the procedure to us.

'There is a chance that the fragments of broken bone in your back are obstructing the spinal chord, and we hope when we clear them you might get feeling and movement back into your legs. Nevertheless, we have to perform a spinal fusion. Two vertebrae in your lower back have been broken and we need to put them together. We will probably use a few screws to secure the bones.'

As he went on, the fear in me grew. I felt like a character in a bad movie. But it was me, it was happening to me. I just wanted everything to stop. I didn't want to hear about broken bones and wheelchairs any more. I didn't want to know how the movie ended. I just wanted it to stop.

It was time to go. Nigel kissed my forehead. 'Everything will be all right.' The nurses wheeled me through a maze of corridors into the operating room where a doctor put a needle in my arm. My ears began ringing and I could smell a strong stench like ammonia. The room was spinning as the anaesthetic took hold. The light faded, I simply couldn't keep my eyes open any longer.

Beep – beep – beep. I woke to the rhythmic sound coming from a machine beside me. The room was bright and it took a few attempts for my eyes to adjust. The light above me was reflecting off the white walls of the ward. I was in a place that was unfamiliar. My eyelids were heavy and I had to struggle to stay awake and make sense of where I was. My body felt cold and numb apart from an agonising pain in my back. It felt like I was lying on a big lump of rock. It was pushing into my spine.

The Pain of Recovery

There was someone at the end of my bed. I tried to focus but my body just wanted to sleep. 'Can you wiggle your toes?' I could hear a man's voice. I gave a pitiful attempt to move my feet as my body won the battle for sleep.

'We didn't think you'd ever wake up.' I looked up to see the familiar face of the surgical dresser who had helped lift me on the Jordan frame. He was wheeling me back into the intensive care ward. I was pleased to be back in a place I knew. Dr Matheson came to visit me, again going through the ritual pin-pricking and toe wiggling while I lay in a state of semi-conscious awareness. My body felt drained and I continued to sleep most of the day.

It was late in the afternoon when I finally woke feeling reasonably alert. Nigel was beside me, he had been sitting there for hours. The pain still in my back made me agitated and uncomfortable but at least I wasn't alone. Just having Nigel with me was a comfort. His smiling face and encouraging words were hiding something though. I could see behind the facade that he was disturbed.

'Have you spoken to Dr Matheson?' I asked.

'Yes, I spoke to him a few hours ago.'

'What did he say?'

'It's too early to tell. There is a lot of swelling in your back. He'll come and check on you in a few days, then we'll know more.'

'But I still can't feel my legs or move my feet. The operation was supposed to fix them. What else did he say?'

'You've had major surgery on your back. He had to put two screws into your spine. You need to give it time to heal.'

That seemed reasonable to me. I could wait a couple of days for the feeling and movement in my legs to come back. Then everything would be fine. I would just have to wait a few more days.

'Nige, my back is so sore. It feels like someone is pushing their fist into it, or like I'm lying on something round and hard.'

The surgical dressers arrived for my routine two-hourly lift.

'Oh, no, please not the frame. I'm way too sore,' I begged. Surely they weren't going to try to push the straps under the lump in my back.

'No, it's all right, Allana, your spine has been fused together. From now on, we'll be log rolling you.'

I was relieved. I didn't quite know what he'd meant but it had to be better than the Jordan frame. With two men supporting my body and the nurse holding my head, they rolled me onto my side.

Nigel was standing behind me. 'No wonder it feels like you're lying on a big lump, Lan. You are lying on a big lump. There's a lot of swelling and you have about ten stitches down your back,' he explained. It felt good to ease the pain, even though it was only for a minute.

Mum and Dad came to visit me that evening along with two of Nigel's brothers. Nigel is the eldest of five boys. They didn't stay too long but I was really pleased they'd come to see me. Apparently as they were leaving, one of the boys fell into an epileptic-type fit and had to be treated in the hallway outside the intensive care ward. This drama occurred without my knowledge. Nigel didn't tell me until some weeks later. He didn't want to upset me. 'You had enough to worry about,' he said.

Despite my ongoing routine of log rolling, checking my temperature, topping up my drip and so on, I rested well at night.

'Merry Christmas!' The nurse was pulling the curtain around my bed. 'Merry Christmas, wake up.' I couldn't believe it was Christmas Day. I didn't feel very merry. The past few days had been so confusing, one day merging into another, I had forgotten all about Christmas. 'I am going to give you a sponge bath and then we'll be moving you to Ward One.' I was quite glad, my condition must be improving if I'm finally leaving intensive care. It can't be long now before my legs are working again.

A nurse named Elizabeth came to escort me to the ward. She was very chatty and had a broad English accent. As I was wheeled into the back of the ambulance for the short trip to my new home, I caught the scent of the crisp sea breeze and felt the warm sun on my face. It was wonderful to escape the clinical smells of the hospital and breathe some real air. As we made our way through Prince Henry Hospital's grounds to Ward One, the surroundings were well known to me. I remembered the buildings and that distinct salty air from a long time ago in my childhood. We passed a three-storey building. It was the Children's Ward where I had been treated for my kidney condition, and I remembered how you could look straight out to the ocean from the Children's Ward. It was a beautiful view, and I wondered what the view would be like from Ward One.

Elizabeth took me in through the automatic doors. I was passing beds on either side. There were patients in almost all of them, some with empty wheelchairs parked beside. We went through another doorway all the way to the end of the room.

'Bed one, this is you.' Elizabeth settled me in. 'You are right next to the nurses' desk so if you need anything I'm not far away.' There was a similar mirror to the one in intensive care that enabled me to look around. There were six beds in total and only narrow windows high up on the wall that filtered in a little bit of sun. I wouldn't be seeing the ocean from here.

'I heard I was getting a new neighbour.' The voice was coming from my left. I manoeuvred my mirror over to the bed next to me and saw a young guy reflected in his mirror.

'I'm Carlos,' he said.

'I'm Allana. What's wrong with your head?' I asked.

Carlos had a metal apparatus coming from the temple area on each side of his head. It went around to a point above and was attached to sandbags that hung off the end of his bed. 'I broke my neck and this brace is drilled into my skull to keep my head still.' It sounded horrendous. We chattered for ages and it turned out that Carlos had been at a party and was pushed into a swimming pool. He'd hit the bottom and broken his neck. Carlos had been admitted to the hospital the same night as me. It was nice to have a young person to talk to for a change, although the painkilling drugs that were still being pumped continuously through me made me eventually fall back to sleep.

It was early in the afternoon and Nigel had arrived with

The Pain of Recovery

a small television. We set it up behind my bed and I was able to watch it through the mirror. Elizabeth came over, pulling the curtains around me.

'You can stay,' she said to Nigel. 'I'm just going to take the drain out of Allana's stomach.' I didn't even know I had a drain in my stomach, but once the dressing was removed it revealed where the surgeon had cut right down the middle of my tummy. The cut was about twenty centimetres long, weaving around my belly button. There weren't stitches but metal staples and, at the end, was the drain. Elizabeth whipped it out so quickly I didn't even feel it.

My whole family came to visit that day. They brought me Christmas presents that I enjoyed opening and I tried to join in the festive celebrations. Leanne gave me a beautiful new bathrobe. I gave her a hug to thank her and, as she stood talking with me, I ran my fingers through my hair. To both our distress, huge clumps of hair came out in my hand. I got such a shock. But I didn't want to make a fuss. I'd heard that trauma can cause this sort of reaction, but I didn't want to get upset on Christmas Day. In the afternoon, a few friends came to visit, including Adam Smith who was the young instructor with Nigel when the first mayday call was heard on the day of my accident. He had ridden his bike from home and he spent several hours with me. It meant so much to me to know he cared and wanted to be with me, especially on this special day. It was a very strange Christmas Day, but one I know I'll never forget.

Over the next few days, I continued to pull out clumps of hair but the head nurse assured me this was common after a trauma and that the problem would pass. I became accustomed to the monotonous hospital routine. Most of it was bearable. However, some procedures that were required to take care of the most basic of bodily functions were outright humiliating. These times were so difficult that they always left me feeling invaded and ashamed. I would keep reminding myself that the quicker my legs got back to normal, the sooner I could go home and I'd have my life back.

It was the day after Boxing Day. Dr Matheson was coming to see me some time during the morning. I couldn't wait although I was a bit apprehensive. There was still no change in my legs, but it was only a matter of time before they improved because I knew the operation must have gone well. I just wanted to know when I could go home.

Nigel sat quietly holding my hand as Dr Matheson again ran a pin down my legs, pricking me strategically. Some I could feel, but there was generally no change. 'Wiggle your toes,' he asked. I could see through the mirror that nothing happened when I tried. Dr Matheson had a young female doctor with him. They conferred with each other just out of earshot, then Dr Matheson turned to me.

Standing at the end of my bed, he said, 'When we operated on you, we found the injury was worse than we expected. The base of your spinal chord and all the nerve endings that run off it, called the caudo cauna, were torn out of the spinal column and found floating around in the muscle. We've put everything back in place and secured your broken vertebrae with screws, but we don't expect you'll be able to walk.'

What was he saying, it didn't make sense! That wasn't what he was supposed to say.

'No, you must be wrong,' I replied. I felt like I was in a time warp. I felt sick. This couldn't be happening. 'What if I work really hard and exercise every day?' I asked.

'Allana, you have to accept that you are not going to walk. You will be in a wheelchair.'

'I just want to go home,' I said, looking across to Nigel whose face was no longer strong and reassuring, but very pale. I'd seen that look before. 'You knew, didn't you?' I asked.

'I couldn't bring myself to tell you,' he replied.

An overwhelming sense of anger enveloped me. 'They don't know me, Nigel. How can they just write me off like that. I'll show them I'm not going to give up that easily. I don't want to hear any more talk about wheelchairs. I will not be in a wheelchair.' Nigel just listened as I went off. I made him promise not to talk about the doctor's diagnosis ever again, and promise not to tell my parents.

Days passed. Mum kept asking about Dr Matheson, wondering if we'd seen him. Nigel and I managed to deceive her and change the subject every time she asked the question, until one afternoon she arranged with the nurse on duty to have a meeting with him. Dr Matheson was busy but the female doctor who assisted him came into the ward. I was frantic. I didn't want Mum to hear those horrible words. Derek, Leanne and Dad were there as well, making their way outside the ward with the doctor. Some time passed and Nigel sat with me. He was silent. I dreaded to think what was being said out there.

The doctor sat down with my family and described what had been discovered during surgery and how screws had been used to secure my broken vertebrae. She continued on to explain that the paralysis and loss of feeling in my legs was permanent.

'We don't expect your daughter will be able to walk again,' she said.

Poor Mum was devastated. She sat crying. The four of them tried to comfort each other. At last Derek said, 'I don't care if I have to carry her on my back for the rest of my life, Mum, she is still with us and that's all that matters. She is going to get through this.'

Finally, Mum came walking towards my bed, and the others weren't far behind. It was obvious she had been crying and was still very distressed. 'I knew it would destroy you, May,' Nigel said.

'Will you all stop it,' I shouted. 'You're all being so morbid. Mum, don't look at me like that. Everything is going to be fine. These people don't know me. I am going to walk.'

Anger was my first line of defence. It was my only way of coping. My body simply didn't feel unable to walk and I fully expected that after eight weeks in bed, as the doctor had prescribed, I was going to get up and walk out. Why was everybody telling me otherwise?

Several doctors and counsellors came to visit me during this time. One particular social worker called on me often, continuously trying to prepare me for life as a paraplegic. 'You'll have to accept your paralysis, Allana,' he'd say. Often, when this subject of wheelchairs and paraplegia came up, I'd give my social worker an earful. Sometimes I was downright rude and aggressive, telling him to 'piss off and leave me alone!'

'You're in denial. The sooner you accept the way things are, the quicker you can get on with your life,' he'd say.

'Get on with my life. What is my life without walking? I have to walk,' I'd say. This new condition of 'denial' became a separate issue that my carers felt they needed to deal with.

One day Dr Stella Engel, a spinal injury specialist, came to visit me. She spoke about personal issues, assuring me I could still have children. However, there would be obvious difficulties, like getting into and out of my wheelchair with a big tummy. The conversation was going well until that point. 'What wheelchair?' I said. 'I won't be using a wheelchair, I'm going to walk.'

'On special occasions with supports on your legs, with crutches and someone to help support you, there may be a chance you can be on your feet for short periods. But mostly your life will be spent in a wheelchair,' she said.

There came a point when I got sick of arguing and simply said, 'Whatever!' This noncommittal uninterested response I'm sure frustrated the staff even more, but in my own mind I was saying, 'I'll show you, I will walk. I won't rely on a wheelchair.'

This upsetting time was made worse because my continuous supply of pain-killing drugs was stopped, making me rely on three hourly injections of pethidine. For the first two hours I'd be comfortable and able to sleep, but the last hour had me stricken with excruciating pain in my back. It felt like there was a clamp around the lower part of my spine and, as the minutes ticked by, the clamp kept tightening. Burning pain radiated outwards, causing my whole body to tighten up with stress. Sometimes I'd realise I had both hands firmly gripped onto the metal tubing on the bed head. Tensing up my body like this made the pain worse so I'd consciously have to relax all my muscles, put my hands by my side and breathe deeply, trying to focus on happy soothing thoughts. By loosening my muscles, the pain would momentarily increase then slowly settle down. I'd close my eyes and work through my agony. Sometimes I thought the pain would kill me.

There was a clock on the wall just to my right above the nurses' desk. I tried so hard to keep my attention away from it, but the pain was too intense, and the time left until I could get relief was all I was concerned about. When I felt ten or fifteen minutes had passed, and it was getting closer to my injection of pethidine, I'd open my eyes and look up at the bland white face and straight black hands, and one minute would have gone by. This would make me panic. I didn't know how I could bear another minute more. My obsession with the clock made the passing of time more agonising. When there were only ten minutes to go, I'd get the nurse on duty to prepare the syringe and have it sitting next to my bed ready so I didn't have to wait a second longer. It was exhausting dealing with this lingering agony. Day after day, night after night, it continued.

It was more than a week after the accident when Nigel arrived one morning at 8 a.m. just as he had every day. The nurse came over to us. 'I'm going to take your drip out,

Allana, and you can start drinking and eating lightly,' she said. All I wanted was a cup of tea and although I had to drink it out of a straw, it was the best cuppa I've ever had. The nurse also took alternate staples out of my stomach. Each one had to be attached to a gadget that released it like a claw. One by one they came out and hurt like hell leaving my stomach red and very tender.

'I got a Christmas card in the mail yesterday,' Nigel said, holding an envelope.

'That's nice. Who's it from?' I inquired.

'It's from Allan. He must have sent it the day before the accident. With all the confusion, I only cleared the post box yesterday.' Nigel handed me the envelope. It was an official air force greeting card appropriately with two aeroplanes on the front. Allan had written, 'Nigel and Allana, Pretty nifty card, huh! Thanks for your support and friendship in 1990. All the best in '91.'

I looked at the words and imagined Allan sitting down to write it. 'Nigel and Allana.' In all the time I'd known Allan, he'd never said my name. It was always Ma'am. His air force discipline, I guess. I held the card in my hands, opening it, closing it. I looked at every part, running my hands over the paper, knowing it was in Allan's hands only days earlier. I missed him so much. Poor Al, I couldn't get the picture of what remained of him after the plane crash out of my mind. It haunted me at night time. When the room was quiet, the picture was clearest, despite my battle to escape from the memory. I knew I'd have to carry the burden of what I saw for the rest of my life.

I thought about some of the fun times Nigel and I had

had with Allan, and they were usually flying times. Allan and I had flown to Griffith together one year in a small two-seat aeroplane called a Citabria. We had stopped off at Bathurst because of poor weather where Allan did the worst landing, hitting the runway hard which made us bounce back into the air. We had bounced three or four times before settling on the ground. He was so embarrassed, and it was made worse by Nigel, who was flying another aeroplane near us and saw the horrible landing. His shrieks of laughter came over the radio. 'How many landings was that, Al?' Nigel had asked. I pictured Allan, Peter, Nigel and I flying up to Hamilton Island. We were supposed to be there right now. It made me so sad to know we were never going to make it.

I remember the first time I had met Allan. I had been finishing up a balloon flight breakfast at Phoebe's. There was a buzz around the airport that a real F-18 top-gun pilot was on the airfield doing some test flying on the new composite aeroplane, the Ultrabat, which was the first prototype of the plane Nigel and I later worked on in America. We'd heard Allan and his friends were coming up to the house for brunch. I conjured up images of a Tom Cruise look-alike striding in through the garden, strong and manly, suave and worldly wise. When Allan arrived, he was nothing like my picture at all. Medium height, blond hair, very slightly built, he didn't look old enough to be flying anything, let alone F-18 fighter planes. If he reminded me of anyone, it was 'Goose', who was 'Maverick's' co-pilot in the *Top Gun* movie. Allan became a great friend to Nigel and I over the years. 'We'll never forget your friendship either, Allan,' I said handing the card back to Nigel.

Nigel left early that evening to go back to the airport and do some work. During the days, I had a constant stream of visitors and was never lonely but at night time when things were quiet and there was nothing to distract me from the constant pain – and even worse, the demons in my head that kept reminding me of my uncertain future – I felt very alone. That night I couldn't sleep and neither could Carlos. We lay chatting to each other for ages. The visitors had gone home and it was getting very late.

Several nurses pushed a new patient into our ward and settled him in across from Carlos. He was a young boy named George. He was only fourteen years old and he was accompanied by his whole family, uncles, aunts, cousins, the lot. The nurse on duty was Liz. She was a new face on the ward and very competent. Poor Liz tried to explain the rules of only two visitors at a time, regardless of the fact that it was after visiting hours. But they all wanted to stay with George and I didn't blame them. He was very sick. George had been diving into the Georges River. He had done the right thing and checked the depth first but, when he passed through the water, he went headfirst into a log that had floated downstream.

As a result, George had broken his neck and had actually drowned. Fortunately someone was able to drag him out of the water and revive him. But George's lungs had become infected and still contained some of the river water. This was to complicate the treatment of his spinal injuries. After some time, George's family left and Liz spent most of the night trying to help George clear his chest simply so he could breathe. It was a long night for all of us.

Across from my bed was a man in his late twenties or early thirties. He had an electric wheelchair next to his bed. I had called out 'hullo' to him a few times the day before but with no response.

'Who's that?' I asked Carlos.

'Oh, that's Romar, but I don't think he speaks any English.'

'What happened to him?'

'Romar is a bag snatcher. He grabbed a lady's bag but was chased by police into a building. When he was cornered, he jumped out of a window aiming for a tree. He missed and landed on his head breaking his neck.'

'A perfect example that crime doesn't pay,' I answered.

It was hard to believe this was my ninth day in hospital. Tomorrow was the start of a brand new year. There was still no improvement in my legs, and every day I'd think, surely I'll wake up tomorrow and they'll be back to normal. After breakfast, two physiotherapists came to begin passive movements and manipulation of my legs. They introduced themselves as Liz and Andrew. Here was a third Elizabeth – I seem to attract names in threes. Liz and Andrew worked with me for about twenty minutes. It felt fantastic to relieve my cramped up joints and get the circulation going again.

'We'll be doing this twice a day now, Allana,' they explained.

During the morning, the final staples were taken out of my stomach and the dressing was left off. 'It's very sore,' I told the nurse. 'It might be a little tender for a few days but it's looking okay,' she assured me.

I had plenty of visitors that day which surprised me

because it was New Year's Eve. Nigel stayed with me till he was kicked out well after visiting hours ended. Grunya, our regular night nurse, came into the ward at the start of her shift armed with streamers, balloons, party hats and champagne. She was always very bubbly and she made sure we saw the New Year in with a bit of fun.

We were a bit weary the next morning but were still woken at our regimented time of 5.30 to be sponge-bathed and fed. The routine never changed. It was like being stuck in the movie, *Ground Hog Day*, where a man wakes up every day and nothing changes. All the people around him do the same thing. The weather's the same. Everything's the same ... every day.

Chapter 7

New Year – New Strength

I pointed my mirror to my feet. The first day of the New Year. Surely my feet would move today, I thought. I looked down and squeezed my toes as hard as I could, but still nothing. They'll move soon, I assured myself.

Liz and Andrew came again for my exercises. They were worried that my right ankle was still very swollen. They decided to put it in a cast to give the ligaments a chance to heal. As it turned out, it would have been better had I broken my leg.

Nigel arrived at lunchtime looking slightly worse for wear after celebrating New Year's Eve with some of our friends. 'Can you look at my tummy,' I asked him. 'It's sore and very red.'

'I'm not happy with the way that looks,' he said as he went to find a nurse. She agreed it was very red but assured us it was nothing to worry about. The next day I showed the nurse again. The pain and redness weren't easing.

'Stop being so paranoid,' she said. I felt sorry for the nurses in Ward One. They were short staffed and were doing their best to attend to all their patients, some of whom were very ill.

After lunch, Nigel and I were watching the television together. 'I can feel something running down my stomach,' I said to Nigel. He pulled back the sheet. I could see through the mirror that part of the wound was bursting open and copious amounts of brown-red gunk were pouring out.

Nigel screamed for the nurse. She ran over to me and saw the mess then disappeared, presumably to get some help. Nigel grabbed a pile of clean towels trying to contain the mess. The stench was horrendous as blood and pus kept pouring out of me. I didn't know what was happening. I thought all my insides were coming out and as I watched I saw two new areas bursting open. Within minutes a team of doctors and nurses were crowded around my bed. Even a surgeon had been called urgently from theatre. He pulled away the towel, pushing my stomach down on either side of the wound, causing another overflow.

'We're going to have to open this up. It's badly infected,' he said. Nothing could have prepared me for the next few minutes. There were four people holding me down as the surgeon took a scalpel in his hand. There was no time to waste, no time for a local anaesthetic or any pain-killing drugs. This emergency had to be dealt with immediately. So, ignoring my whimpering terror because I knew full well what was going to happen, the surgeon cut into my skin, slicing open the holes and making them stretch to where I could see the muscle wall of my stomach.

I felt the knife touch my skin then, as he moved it along, it burned. I cried out for him to stop hurting me, but he continued until the three areas where my wound had broken down were wide gaping bloody incisions. I thought of the movies I'd seen of the days before anaesthetics when patients were forced to endure torturous procedures without pain relief. But at least, I thought, they got a bullet to bite down on!

I don't know how I dealt with the pain, but the surgeon moved quickly and the ordeal lasted only seconds. Somehow I coped. I hated being weak, but I was crying in fear of what was happening to me and of not knowing what would happen next.

'Please, someone tell me what's happening,' I begged. A young doctor I hadn't met before placed her hand on my shoulder. 'You're all right,' she said. 'You have a postoperative infection that we have to irrigate, then we'll pack it and allow the wound to heal from the inside out.' It didn't sound all right to me, but at least I was being informed.

After cleaning out the ugly cavern left down my middle, a nurse soaked half-metre lengths of gauze in a saline solution and proceeded to pack them into the void. Several lengths were packed into every corner through the open incisions now exposed. Apart from the pain and repulsion for what I was being subjected to, I remember thinking, 'What a mess.' And I imagined the hideous scar that would be left on my once young and beautiful body.

Nigel was with me for the whole day and other visitors filtering through the ward included my friends, George

Markey and his partner, Robbie, who brought me fresh fruit almost every day.

Twice a day the packing had to be removed and fresh gauze replaced. This horrendously painful procedure became part of my daily routine. Wake at 5.30 for a sponge bath, breakfast on dried-out baked beans or a chewy piece of toast, then physio. After physio, my dressings were done. Then lunch at midday, dinner at 4.30, and more dressings in the evening. Carlos and I would be starving at 8 p.m. As time went on and thanks to the wonders of modern technology in the form of my mobile phone, we would sometimes ring for pizza to be home delivered to the ward. The local Pizza Hut was quite used to receiving orders from Ward One. We'd give the nurse on duty enough money to pay for the pizza. When the delivery boy arrived he'd hand her the box, say hullo to the patients, then leave. It was a regular occurrence.

I'd been thinking about the day of the accident constantly and how the man in the blue suit, whose name I'd forgotten, had looked after me so well. I hadn't thanked him for saving my life and this was worrying me.

One day when Mum came into the ward we were talking about the accident. She said that in all the confusion after the plane crash, and with all the phone calls coming in from my family and friends in Sydney when she got home from the hospital, she hadn't rung my uncle and aunty in South Australia. She'd planned to call them the next morning, but my Uncle Richard and Aunty Bev had bought the Sunday paper before Mum had a chance to ring. It had me on the front cover being carried from the helicopter into intensive care. This was how they discovered I'd been injured.

'They sent the paper down to me,' Mum said. 'I've got it in the car if you want to have a look.' Before she ran off to the car, I told her how I wanted to find the man who had looked after me on the day of the accident. I asked her to go to the Westpac Rescue base to find out if he was there. We agreed she would do this after lunch. Mum returned with the folded-up page from the newspaper. I opened it up and there he was carrying my stretcher, the man in the blue suit.

'Mum, that's the man I've been telling you about. You've got to find him and ask him to come and see me.'

The helicopter base was located in the hospital grounds not far from my ward. She showed the secretary on duty the article, pointing out the man who had saved me. 'That's Hugh Russell,' the secretary said. 'He isn't rostered on today, but I'll give him the message your daughter would like to see him.'

A couple of days later Hugh paid me a visit. I was so pleased to see him. We had the chance to talk about the accident and I thanked him for being my hero that day.

On Mum's next visit to see me in hospital she handed me a letter she'd received during the week. It sported an official Department of Defence, United States of America symbol and was from the Department of the Navy, Washington, D.C. The letter read:

New Year – New Strength

Dear Mr and Mrs Thomson,

Just prior to last Sunday's Protestant worship service at the Washington Navy Yard Chapel, Alice Bulkeley informed us of the injury to your daughter. We delayed the opening of the worship hour to tell the congregation of Allana's accident and injury. I showed the congregation the newspaper articles you sent to Alice. We then bowed in prayer for you and your daughter. It was, and shall continue to be, our prayer that God's strength and healing will be with each one of you.

Alice showed us a copy of an old picture of Allana standing in the front of our WNY Chapel. The picture must have been taken about ten years ago. Realising that you had visited our chapel gave us a special bond.

Although you do not know me or most of the congregation, I do want you to be aware of our prayers for all of you. Prayer has a way of transcending miles. For that reason, it is our collective prayer that those of us at the Chapel, who are so far away from you in miles but so close in our hearts, will be a source of comfort and encouragement. God bless you.

Captain W.L. Perry, Chaplain.

I had received so many lovely letters and cards from people in Australia and around the world but this one held special significance. It reminded me of the time I had visited my family in North America. I'd always known them to be courageous people who'd shown strength in times of tremendous hardship. I remembered travelling to America and Canada when I was eleven to meet my relatives, who up until that time were only characters in the extraordinary stories I'd been told by Mum and Gran ever since I was about seven.

I'd met my great grandmother (Grannie) in Toronto, Canada. She'd been 88 years old and she'd appeared to me to have survived unscathed, despite the harrowing events of her life. She'd lived with my Great Aunt Leilah, who was also a woman of tenacity. And it was on this trip that I had visited the naval barracks in Washington, D.C. with my Aunt Alice and Uncle John. They'd taken us to the chapel where their son John Jnr. played the organ. He'd proudly showed us around the little church and we'd all stood at the front steps and had our photo taken. Uncle John was a three-star admiral and truly an amazing man, a hero to his family and his country. His very presence had left me in awe.

Now, at this most challenging time in my life, I needed heroes. I thought about the strength of spirit that had been shown by so many of my family in situations that often seemed hopeless, and many times, life threatening. I hoped this strength was a family trait and could help me through the many difficult times I knew lay ahead of me.

My family's story has been a truly remarkable feat of survival. My mother was born in Kowloon, Hong Kong, the daughter of Edith and Arthur Hamson. The Asian influence

New Year – New Strength

in my family tree shows Edith's grandmother was Japanese and her grandfather was German. Arthur's grandfather was Chinese and his grandmother was English. It certainly makes me a Heinz variety. But it helps to explain why, as a child, my mother lived in Kowloon Tong, on mainland China.

They had a large home in which Mum's Aunt Leilah, who was thirteen, and grandmother (Grannie) also resided. They were all British subjects.

On 7 December, 1941, the Japanese planes began attacking Hong Kong. During the next two weeks of confusion, Kowloon Tong was evacuated. My grandparents fled, taking with them Aunt Leilah and my mother, May, who was five, and her brother, Richard, three, in an attempt to escape incarceration by the Japanese.

Along the road, their car was stopped by a Japanese officer at a checkpoint. They were all bundled out of the car. My grandfather was forced to move to the other side of the road while Grandmother Edith was directed to return home with the children. In the meantime, my grandfather was escorted with nine other men to a spot on the Tai Po Road and ordered to sit in the gutter. They had their hands tied behind their backs and were subjected to blows across their heads with the butt of an officer's rifle before being moved to a nearby location and held as prisoners.

With the car confiscated, Edith and the children began the long walk to return to Kowloon Tong, only to be attacked by three Chinese bandits who took away the bag she was carrying. That left them with nothing but the clothes on their backs.

A month later, Arthur was reunited with his family at

the Kowloon Hotel, which was then being used to hold the internees. Grannie was also with them. Three weeks later, they were all moved to the Stanley Prisoner of War Camp and there they remained for three years and eight months.

Edith's sister, Alice, had married a US naval cadet named John Bulkeley a few years before the war broke out and they had left Kowloon Tong and were living in America. To best describe the horror of my family's life in the Stanley POW Camp, I wish to quote from a letter written by my grandmother to her sister, Alice Bulkeley. This letter is dated 3 September, 1945. The war was over and the family had just been released.

> Dear Alice,
>
> At last we are free – free to breathe again. The world has progressed while we have been asleep. You can imagine what we feel like being under British Rule again. We have all suffered in one way or another. We all know what hunger is. Hunger pains were common complaints. The children used to wake up crying with hunger pains in their tummy. My heart used to bleed to see them suffer and unable to help them. Some people suffered terribly, by the hands of the Japanese. They slap your face for the least excuse. There have been some severe beatings of internees. We even had some executions.
>
> At Stanley Camp we only had one meal a day, rice and watery soup, no bread, no tea, no sugar, no light, no soap

and many of us no bed to sleep in. We slept on the floor of a draughty hall for six months before we had a room and beds of some description. The first six months of our internment was really terrible. The children suffered terribly. Many times we went short to give them more. We just drank water to fill up the empty spaces. I have worked hard on the garden to raise extra food and have done very well, otherwise we would be in a sorry plight. To tell you what we have eaten when we were very hungry – potato leaves, banana skins, inside of Papia trees etc. Many internees suffered from beri-beri, sores that won't heal, lost memory, temporary blindness and forgetfulness. I had to sell my wedding ring to buy extra food and it was an awful wrench and I felt very sad in doing it, but health comes first before sentiment. Another thing we suffered was no shoes. The children had worn no shoes for 3 years. During winter it was very pitiful to see their chapped feet. Clothing was a problem, we came into the camp with just the clothes on our backs, nothing else. We have lost all our personal belongings.

First year in camp May was very ill. She had Shega dysentery. It came on all of a sudden and during the night she had four convulsions. Dr Philip Jones, who is our good friend in the camp, saved her life that night by a special injection which he happened to have with him. We had to wait an hour to see the effects of that injection – whether she would live. That hour I shall never forget, it was the longest I have ever waited. All that hour Arthur was on his knees. Her temperature was 107 degrees and she was unconscious for three days. Richard caught it the next day and even our doctor was ill with it. We had a very anxious time. May was up and well in 10 days and everybody said it was miraculous.

As for bombing, we did not escape that either. On Jan 16th of this year a plane accidentally dropped a bomb on bungalow 'C' and 14 people were killed. It was very sad and it shook the camp up pretty badly. On July 25th Bungalow 'A' was hit and we suffered. No one could identify the plane that came over. Arthur and I just went down to the library which was in the St Stephens block. Without any warning this plane suddenly appeared and swooped very low over our bungalow and dropped 11 bombs. Seven out of the eleven dropped around the bungalow and two came through the building. The bomb dropped into a bath full of water and burst into our room, breaking the dividing wall and flung all the bricks and glass and debris onto Mother, Leilah, May and Richard who had the misfortune to be there. May and Leilah were rather badly hurt, bruises and cuts all over the body. Both have a bad gash on their arm which I am afraid will leave a scar. May had a piece of brick taken out of her arm. Richard was flung out on to the verandah and escaped without injury, Mother was badly bruised. Believe it or not, one bomb out of 11 burst and it had to be the one in our room. These bombs were Amonis bombs and the action of water on these bombs explodes them. This one had to fall into a bath full of water. Ripley would love this.

New Year – New Strength

It was an awful shock to us. I rushed up to the bungalow and the first person I saw was a man carrying Richard who was looking terrible covered all over with grey dust and half conscious, the man who carried Richard said May was all right, not daring to tell me she was hurt. I went to the clinic with Richard then. May was brought in to us covered in blood. I nearly fainted from shock. Poor May, she was a dreadful sight. While the doctors were attending the cases, the Japanese came along and told us all to leave the building because a bomb dropped into a room two doors away from the clinic and they were afraid it might explode any minute. What a mad scramble there was, we all rushed to the next block, it was here I saw Leilah stretched out like a corpse, unconscious. Both Leilah and May went straight to the hospital. It is all over and done with now and best forgotten. It left May in a state of nerves. I hope she will steady down later.

Now to our immediate future: we must still remain in camp at Hong Kong as the city of Hong Kong is in a terrible state. There are very few livable houses, I and the children will go to Australia as soon as plans are made. I thought of coming to you but doctors advise against going to a cold country as our health can't stand it, so it looks like Australia is the place. Mother has other plans for herself and Leilah.

I remember as a young child asking Mum, 'What's that big scar on your arm?' This was the first time she had told me

The Best I Can Be

the story. I was then about the same age as she would have been when the bomb exploded, and it helped me understand her appreciation of life. Over the following years, I'd heard so many incredible tales of hardship that my family were forced to endure. Yet they had survived to live happy fulfilling lives. I wish that for myself too.

The war stories Mum told me also included one about how Alice's husband, John Bulkeley, had become an officer in the US Navy and was in charge of the new patrol torpedo (PT) boat program. Uncle John was sent into Filipino waters, under the command of General Douglas MacArthur. On 7 December, 1941, Japan attacked Pearl Harbor. The Japanese war had begun. Then the Japanese attacked the Philippine islands. The American military there was hit hard.

It wasn't until late February, 1942, that President Roosevelt ordered General MacArthur out of the Philippines for Australia. The Japanese knew there would be an attempt to get MacArthur out, but they expected this to be done by plane or submarine. MacArthur chose to leave using the PT boat squadron, under the command of the leader he called 'Buck' – my Uncle John.

As the sun went down on 11 March, Uncle John led his squadron up to Corregidor dock and collected MacArthur and his family. Other VIPS followed. With three more PT boats following, Uncle John successfully moved General MacArthur out of the region, undetected by the Japanese. Coincidentally, 11 March was also to be my birthday many years later.

There have been many books written about MacArthur's departure from the Philippines. John Wayne even played 'Buck' in the film, *They Were Expendable*, telling of the events around this time. Uncle John died on 6 April, 1996. He held the honour of being America's most decorated war hero, being awarded every medal the United States has to offer, including some two or three times. He was greatness in every sense of the word.

Early in 1998, Alice and Leilah travelled to Australia to see my grandmother and the three sisters were together again. I made sure to spend as much time as I could with them listening to their stories about the war times. It would make a great book!

My great-grandmother had passed away, aged 96. Aunt Leilah told me she would wake up each morning, surprised to be alive. She was very frail in the end and she was ready to go. 'This dying business is a great bother,' she would say.

Lying in hospital, I could only admire the legacy of the three generations of women who had shown such strength in surviving all those years. And I hoped I could show the same grace in adversity. I prayed their strength would be in me, too, for my war had only just begun.

A month passed, we were into February, and my legs were strengthening. But there was no neurological improvement. There was still no movement in my feet and no feeling had returned. However, my hopes weren't dashed. Once I can get out of this bed and try to stand, they'll get better for sure, I told myself.

Almost seven weeks I'd been lying here. It was Friday morning at the stupid hour of 5.30 a.m., the nurse had left me to finish my sponge bath and the curtains were pulled around my bed giving me a moment of welcomed privacy. I pulled the sheets away from my frail body. It didn't look like me at all. I had lost so much weight, the skin around my shoulders outlined the bone joints. I looked like a Biafran. Surely this emaciated figure couldn't be me. I had been lying on my back for so long my breasts had migrated under my armpits, exposing my ribs that stepped down my chest. The multicoloured bruising, dark and angry, still ran down my left side. My stomach was sunken and covered with a dressing that would have to be changed again after breakfast. My hip bones stood up prominently at the top of my weak and wasted legs. Look at what's happened to me! Tears flowed onto my pillow. I wiped my face and covered myself up, horrified and afraid. What's going to become of me!

Nigel arrived at 8 a.m. as usual. He could see that I was distressed. 'What's the matter, sweetheart, you're not yourself today?' he asked.

'I'm so scared, my body is just wasting away.' I asked him to draw the curtains so I could show him. We pulled the sheet down. Nigel had seen my naked body almost every day since the accident, so it was no shock.

'Look at my breasts, Nige, they've moved. I'm never going to be able to put my arms down beside me because my boobs will be in the way.'

He laughed. It did sound a bit funny. 'Once you sit up they'll fall back into place,' he assured me. 'We do need to put some meat on those bones though.' Nigel had prepared a 'health shake' as he called them. He'd brought me one almost every day for the past month. It was basically a milk shake laced with a multitude of vitamins and minerals designed to help me get well and put on weight. 'Your Mum should be here soon,' he reminded me as he opened the curtains. I hadn't forgotten. It had been four days since she'd been in to see me.

'Hi there, darling,' Mum said as she put her bag down beside my bed. It was good to see her. We chattered and she updated me on the happenings at her work and home and of the get well messages that were still coming in. 'I spoke to Gran this morning,' she said. 'The preparations for Lynda's wedding are going well. Everyone is really excited. The family send their love and will all miss you terribly on the day.'

I had completely forgotten about my cousin's wedding. Lynda was three months younger than me and although she lived five hours away from Sydney at Wagga Wagga, we had grown up together and we were like sisters. Her wedding was to be on the second of March. Lynda and Phillip had met at high school and had been going out for years. He already felt like part of our family, so when they had announced their engagement last year we were very excited. The wedding was another opportunity for our close-knit family to be together. I couldn't not be there. I did some quick thinking. I was due to be up and out of bed in a week. That would give me two weeks in physio before the big weekend.

'What do you mean I'm not going. Of course I'm going to the wedding,' I said to Mum.

'Well, it's a nice thought. But, Allana, you won't

possibly be well enough to travel all that way in three weeks' time.'

'Yes, I will. I'm going, Mum. Tell Lynda and Phillip I'll be there.'

Mum learned long ago not to argue with me, so she opted to just humour me for now. 'We'll see,' she said.

Nigel and Mum stayed with me for the day until Professor Jones, my spinal specialist, did his 4 p.m. rounds, just as he did every Friday. The professor checked me over, testing my legs and looking at my chart.

'We'll be getting you up in a week, Allana. I've scheduled one of our orthotists to come on Monday to fit you for a body brace.'

I had already met three of the orthotists. They'd been wandering in and out of the ward working with various patients. They made all the leg and back supports for the patients with spinal injuries. Professor Jones explained that I'd have to wear my new brace to support my back when I sat up in my wheelchair.

'Oh, that's good, because I'll be going to Wagga Wagga for a wedding in three weeks,' I announced, feeling confident and assured that it would be approved.

Professor Jones looked at Mum and said, 'It will be way too soon for you to travel that far, Allana.' Mum agreed with him.

'Well, I'm sorry, but I'm going!'

'We will just have to wait and see,' he said.

On Monday, I was measured up and a mould was taken of my torso so the orthotists could make a turtle brace. The brace, which I'd have to wear for six months, was in two parts with a front and back that attached at the sides and extended from my hips to the top of my chest. It was waterproof, made of plastic and padded with foam, so I could wear it at all times to support my back, even showering. Only when I was lying flat on my back could I take it off. I was excited at the prospect of finally sitting up, after almost eight weeks. The final fitting was completed on a Thursday. Professor Jones would be around in the morning to check it and give the approval for me to get up.

Mum and Nigel arrived early for the big day. Professor Jones turned up at 10 a.m. with the orthotist. They put the brace on me. It felt tight, making it hard for me to breathe, but I really didn't care. This was the first step I'd take to being able to walk again.

'We have to sit you up very slowly, Allana, you've been lying down for so long your heart isn't used to pumping the blood uphill. If we get you up too quickly, you'll faint,' Professor Jones explained. I was prepared and eager. I laughed at my joy and excitement at finally being able to sit up in bed. I'd been waiting for this simple pleasure for almost two months. How amazing it would be to see the world from a sitting position.

First, a nurse lifted up the back of my bed. I felt pretty good, and after a while it was lifted up further. The room looked different seeing it from my new upright position. Mum had brought my cosmetics from home. She pulled the curtain around me. I looked at myself in the mirror and I lifted up my hospital gown, pleased to see my breasts back in their rightful place. My hair was filthy. It had only been washed once since I'd been in intensive care. I ran a comb through it, but clumps of hair were still coming out in my hand. My face was very pale and thin. I took a few minutes to put on my make-up. That made me feel a lot better and look a lot healthier.

After lunch, Professor Jones checked on me again saying that I could be lifted into a wheelchair if I felt all right. Before he left, I reminded him I was going to Wagga Wagga and it was only two weeks away.

'I don't think we can let you go, Allana' he said. I didn't want to get upset, and I assured myself that somehow I was going to that wedding.

Two of the surgical dressers and a nurse came to sit me in a wheelchair. They picked me up, supporting me beneath my knees and around my chest, then eased me into the seat. I was fine for a while, then I suddenly felt strange. My ears were ringing and the room around me was spinning.

'I'm going to faint!' I called out. One of them quickly tipped the wheelchair back letting the blood rush to my head. I was lifted back into bed. It had been a big day, but it was the start of my recovery. I just couldn't wait to try to walk.

Chapter 8

One Step at a Time

Instead of my usual sponge bath the next morning, I was placed on a commode chair and taken for a shower. The room was large, stark and clinical with a few shower hoses coming out of the wall. One nurse helped to wash me while another stood behind, continuously having to tip me back when I felt faint. The whole process was exhausting not to mention embarrassing, but at least I could wash my hair and my body felt clean for the first time since the plane crash.

By mid morning, I was sitting slightly upright in bed thinking about Lynda's wedding and imagining all my family celebrating without me. I wanted to be there for Phillip and Lynda. Somehow I would have to convince Professor Jones to let me go.

A young doctor came over to me armed with a kidney dish full of needles and swabs. 'Hi, I'm Dr Joanna Colhagen. I have to give you an arterial blood test,' she said.

'I hate those things,' I answered. This would be my

third since being in hospital. The needle is injected into your wrist all the way into the artery where the blood is taken from. It's an extremely painful process.

'Don't worry, I'm going to give you a local anaesthetic so you won't feel a thing,' she said.

'You must be new. I haven't seen you on the ward before?'

'Well, you'll get used to my face because I'm the new registrar for this ward. I'll be checking on you every day.'

I was quite pleased because Joanna seemed very nice. She finished my blood test and it didn't hurt me at all.

'You wouldn't happen to be Lynda Browning's cousin would you?' Joanna asked.

I was confused by the question, wondering how she knew of my cousin. I answered, 'Yes, I am. Did you know she's getting married in two weeks?'

'Yes, I know,' Joanna said. 'I know because I'm going to be one of her bridesmaids. Lynda and I went to school together. She told me her cousin was a patient here.'

I couldn't believe what I was hearing. 'You're kidding,' I exclaimed. I couldn't get my words out quick enough to explain how I needed to go to Wagga Wagga for the wedding, but Professor Jones wasn't going to let me. 'I've begged and pleaded with him but he still won't let me go. But if you're going to be there, surely he couldn't refuse,' I said.

I asked Joanna if she'd speak to him for me and explain that she was going too and would be able to help me if I had any medical problems. A few days later Professor Jones came to see me. Joanna had spoken to him. He was amazed at the coincidence, but he agreed to let me go to the wedding.

In the meantime, my first day for rehabilitation was scheduled. Nigel brought a tracksuit from home for me to wear. After showering, a nurse helped me get dressed. It was very difficult squirming around on the bed, rolling from side to side trying to pull everything on. I felt weird being clothed again after such a long time. Two surgical dressers helped me into a wheelchair that had been allocated to me to use until one could be made to measure. Then a nurse fitted a pair of Artificial Foot Orthoses (AFOs) onto my lower legs and ankles. These braces were designed to hold my feet at ninety degrees so I wouldn't trip over them when I tried to walk. They fitted neatly into my brand new Reeboks that had been bought for me by a group of my friends.

Craig, the physiotherapist, helped me into the back of a truck with several other patients in wheelchairs to be driven down to the other end of the hospital grounds. It was very degrading and I felt we were being herded like cattle when they moved us out of the truck and into the gymnasium.

Early in the session I practised rolling my body over while lying on a bed. My legs were heavy and flopped around out of my control. I also learned how to get from the wheelchair onto a bed using a slide board. My legs were so weak that I had to lift them with my hands. I wasn't prepared for these minuscule tasks to be so difficult. Maria, the physiotherapist assigned to look after me, wheeled me over to the parallel bars where I was to try to stand for the first time. This was the moment I'd been waiting for, the moment of truth.

Nigel was with me and he stood behind the wheelchair ready in case I fell. I grabbed hold of the bars and with every bit of determination hauled myself up. My legs were shaking and I felt the pain in my back as the weight of my body pushed down on my spine. I had to take most of my weight with my arms but at least I was up. The ground looked a long way down and my legs felt strange. It was like I was standing on nothing or standing on stilts because I couldn't feel anything at all beneath my knees. I couldn't feel my feet on the ground and I had to look down to see what they were doing. The whole sensation frightened me. There was a mirror in front of me where I could see my pathetic figure standing precariously with Maria holding me tightly. My body was so thin I could barely recognise myself. My knees continued to tremble. I couldn't hold myself up any longer and I fell back into the wheelchair without taking one step.

I was dejected and angry. I thought I would walk today. I really did believe it'd be easy to stand and walk. I knew I'd be weak, but I'd prepared myself for the fact that it would be a bit hard. I had intended to prove my carers wrong by taking a few steps. I'd imagined how I was going to make them eat their words. Now that I had tried and failed, the reality of the battle I had ahead of me hit home. 'You won't be able to walk again,' had been relentlessly drummed into me over the past two months. I had tried to remain positive even though those words had distressed me. I wouldn't allow myself to believe them. But all of a sudden I knew I may never be able to walk again or, if I could, I wondered to what capacity. My journey to recovery was going to be long and hard. I felt the urge to give up. I just wanted to lock myself away and hide from the world.

Craig pushed me along towards the truck that was waiting to take us back to the ward. I couldn't bear the added humiliation of taking my place like one of the herd in the back.

'No, Craig. I'll push myself up the hill,' I said. I had to work off all the anger I had inside and I started the long push to Ward One. It was a sticky hot summer's day. There was not even the familiar sea breeze to give me relief as I pushed on. My arms were tired and my back ached, but I continued. A third of the way I stopped to rest, perspiration dripping off me. Craig was walking with me. 'You're exhausted. That was a great effort. Now let me push you the rest of the way,' he said.

'NO!'

I persisted with my challenge counting ten pushes, then resting for a moment. Only a third of the way to go. I was stuffed, puffing out the words to Craig, 'I can't go any further.'

'You did well. You can be proud of your effort. You've had eight weeks of bed rest. It'll only take you a week or so to make it all the way to the top of the hill,' he said.

'Well, just wait a minute. No, I'm going to do it.' I had thought that I was going to walk today and I didn't. But one day I would. It was an enormous mountain to climb and it was going to be harder than I thought. But if my reward at the top was to one day be able to just walk, then I decided I was ready to climb. This was only one little hill and it was my first hill. I would never give up.

I took a deep breath and with my newly found motivation continued on. The last little bit seemed to never end until, at last, the slope began to level out. I was making progress by inches, grunting through the strain as I tried to draw the last little bit of strength from my body.

'You did it.' Craig was just as impressed as I was. I peered back, acknowledging my triumph. Although I hadn't walked today, this had still been my first step.

After lunch, Nigel took me for my first outing away from the hospital. We went to a shopping centre not far away so I could buy a new tracksuit. This was my chance to experience the outside world from my new perspective. I wasn't thrilled to be using the wheelchair, but I was excited about getting away from the hospital even if it was just for a little while. Freedom at last, I thought, as we passed the security station at the main entrance to Prince Henry Hospital and drove onto the open road. I must admit it was a bit scary leaving the doctors and nurses, and I hoped I wouldn't have a medical problem while I was away.

Nigel walked beside me as I pushed my wheelchair past people and shop windows looking up at faces whose stares lingered, making me feel nervous and self conscious. I hated being stared at. The expression on the faces seemed to say, 'Look at that poor young girl in a wheelchair.' I didn't want to be different. I despised myself this way and I felt like a carnival freak show. I had been so keen to leave the hospital. I'd thought an afternoon of shopping would be fun. But now all I wanted to do was go back to the spinal unit where I would be safe. Nigel never left my side. Without his comforting hand in mine, I felt isolated and alone. He could see my distress, but there was nothing he could do but stay by my side. I fixed my eyes on the ground and continued, trying to keep my anxiety under control. But I still felt their eyes caving in on me until my umbilical chord of safety was demanding I go back to the hospital that I'd started to call home. Poor Nige didn't entirely understand what the problem was.

'I've just got to get out of here,' I said after only half an hour.

Professor Jones came to see me later that day and I reminded him about the wedding that was only a week away. He suggested Nigel take me home that night for the weekend to see how I coped being away from the hospital.

Going home! It had been so long. I remembered walking out of the door that last day when we were rushing to get to Camden. I hadn't had time to run with Ben through our mountain track. Would I ever again? I had so longed for this day. It felt like I had been in hospital for a lifetime. To sit in the sun and listen to the birds singing at home was something I had missed so much. But I was still very apprehensive, especially after my panic attack in the shopping centre.

The nurse prepared my medications and medical supplies to take home – the bags of bottles, syringes, swabs and so on seemed to take up half the boot of the car. I still had wounds that needed to be dressed daily and other apparatus to help with my bodily functions that required monitoring. It was late in the afternoon when we drove out of the hospital gate and made our way to the mountains. The trip took over an hour. I couldn't believe Nigel had driven this distance twice a day to be with me.

We made it home and drove into our driveway. The familiar sounds and smells were comforting. Although I had missed my home, I felt strange to be back after so long. Nigel stood back and let me push my wheelchair around the house. He had borrowed some money from a friend and employed a builder to help make our home a bit more wheelchair friendly, so there were a few changes. Ben was very apprehensive when he saw me, then he gently nuzzled his soft and furry face into my arms. He had remembered me, but I think he knew I was hurt and fragile.

We went to Mum and Dad's for dinner later where Mum, who is a nurse, checked me over to make sure I was okay. We were all a bit nervous. When we got home, I settled into my own bed and took my body brace off. It was so warm and cosy. The room was dark and quiet, unlike the continuous hospital noises I was used to. The stillness made me feel nervous but I snuggled up to Nigel. The warmth of his body against my skin made me feel safe and I slept peacefully until the morning sun filtered into the room and my birds were singing to me outside the window.

We hadn't planned anything particular for the day, only to relax at home. Nigel brought me a cup of tea in bed and ran a bath for me. And so began our morning routine. First, I had to put my brace back on while lying flat on the bed. Then Nigel carried me into the bath where I washed myself, still with the brace on. When I was finished, he picked me up out of the bath and put me back onto the bed where he had laid out towels. I took my brace off and wiped it over with a cloth then dried myself and put my clothes on. The brace went on over a singlet top. Then I finished getting dressed. Somehow this process took hours. Nigel worked with me methodically, but I could see the strain in his face at times and knew he hated seeing me so incapacitated. It wasn't until lunch time that I was ready to face the day. The builders had arrived at the house and there was a hive of activity outside although, because of all the rubble around, I was restricted to watching them through the window next to our front door. We spent some time with Mum and Dad late in the afternoon and the next day. I think it helped Nigel to have their support.

I cried a lot that weekend. It was so humiliating and frustrating having to rely on someone else for everything. But I tried to stay positive, knowing things could only get better. Nigel was great. There were times he had to help me above and beyond the call of duty. We were both relieved at the end of the weekend to have survived without any complications.

Nigel took me back to the hospital on Sunday evening. I was a reluctant patient and I tried every trick to con him into letting me stay home. But I knew I had a lot of hard work to do with my physios and it wouldn't be too long before I could go home for good. I really wanted to work hard this week because the next weekend I'd be with my family at Lynda's wedding.

I was already in the gym early Monday morning when Nigel arrived. Maria was lining me up on the parallel bars ready to stand again. Craig had the video camera set up to record the moment. 'I'm so glad you're here, Nige. I'm going to take a step today and I didn't want you to miss it.' Again I hauled myself up, gripping onto the cold metal bars. A rush of pain attacked my lower back and I grimaced until it passed. Maria was supporting me, holding onto my brace. Nigel was again behind me, holding onto the wheelchair.

'Okay, I want you to take a step forward with your right foot,' said Maria. My concentration was intense. I tried to lift my right leg but it didn't move. It felt like it was stuck to the floor. I tried again, leaning my body weight onto my left leg and heaving the other forward, throwing from my hip. My foot jumped forward and landed on the floor with my toes pointing dramatically to the right. That's weird, I thought. It wasn't very graceful, but it was a step. Maria crouched down and tried to direct my next step, but my left foot also darted out of control, landing with its toes pointing outward. The next step did the same. I was tired and sore but I had taken three shaky steps. Maria and Craig told me that my feet tended to point outwards because the muscles in my legs were so unbalanced. There would be techniques I could work on further down the track to try to correct it, they told me.

My motivation was high and that day I worked on the exercises Maria had set me with great vigour. They were designed to strengthen my legs and my arms. I'd see all my family on Saturday. I wanted to show them how I could stand.

Exhaustion allowed me to sleep soundly that night and I was keen to get back to work the next morning, even arriving at the gym before Maria. The morning session went well and I managed a few more steps. But I was feeling a bit lethargic and by lunch time I was looking very pale.

Back in the ward for lunch, the nurse on duty became

concerned and took my temperature which was 38.5 degrees. 'You have a fever, Allana. It's best you stay in bed for the afternoon,' she said. I was disappointed but I felt so ill. All I wanted to do was sleep, which is what I did. I woke up late in the afternoon, drowned in perspiration and feeling very cold. Joanna came to see me and ordered my temperature and blood pressure be taken every half hour. The nurses piled me high with blankets, but I couldn't keep warm.

During the night I woke again, sweating profusely, but this time I pushed all the blankets off me. I felt like I was burning up. This ridiculous hot and cold cycle continued throughout the next day and my temperature soared to 39.5 degrees. It wasn't fair. I had lost a whole day at the gym. It was now Thursday and Lynda's wedding was on Saturday, I'd have to leave tomorrow for Wagga Wagga or I'd miss out. Joanna came to see me again in the morning. 'If your temperature doesn't go down by this afternoon, I'm going to have to put you on a drip. If we do that, you're not going to be able to come to Wagga,' she explained. It simply wasn't fair. I'd come so close and now I was probably going to have to miss the wedding. I'd thought Joanna was a gift from God, an answer to my prayers. I didn't understand why this was happening to me. Was I being punished for something? I didn't know. My temperature had been high for two days now and by mid morning my body had started to object. Every part of me began shaking violently. My muscles ached and felt cramped. Even a few cards that were hanging on my bedhead fell onto the floor as the whole bed trembled.

'What's happening to me?' I asked the nurse.

'It's a reaction to the fever. It's a condition called the rigours.' She summoned Joanna again.

'I'm going to start an IV, Allana.'

'No! You said I had till the afternoon.'

'We need to get fluids and antibiotics into you or you could get very sick. Your temperature is still 39.5 degrees and we have to bring it down.'

'Just another few hours. Please!' I begged and pleaded because I knew once the drip was in that would be it. I couldn't go to Wagga. Joanna gave me a reprieve until 2 p.m.

I prayed hard. But this time I was really pissed off, wondering why my goal to make it to Lynda's wedding had come so close and now it was being taken away from me. I felt cheated.

'You won't believe this, Allana, but your temperature has dropped slightly,' said the nurse. 'We'll check it again in half an hour.' My next half-hourly obs proved it had gone down a little bit more and, when Joanna came back in the afternoon, although it was still high, the pattern over the past few hours had showed it steadily decreasing. We were amazed. By the next morning it was almost back to normal.

Mum, Dad and Nigel came to the hospital to pick me up at 11 a.m. for our drive to Wagga Wagga which would take five hours. We drove in separate cars but stayed together, stopping for a break every hour or so. Nigel had brought several pillows from home so I could pack them around me to be as comfortable as possible in the car. I had the front seat laid back as far as it could go but my back still became sore from sitting for so long. I was very tired. It had been a big week but, despite that, I enjoyed being out in the country and away from the hospital.

I was relieved to make it to our motel room where I rested on the bed for a while before Nigel drove me to Aunty Heather and Uncle Merv's house where there was to be a family reunion with more aunts, uncles and cousins. I felt nervous about them seeing me in a wheelchair. I couldn't have coped with an emotional scene. Lynda and Phillip's wedding was a happy occasion and I didn't want to put a dampener on it. I should have predicted the hugs and kisses, laughing and hilarity. There were no morbid comments or grim and gloomy looks from any of them. Being with my extended family was just as it had always been, outrageous fun. I was Allana, wheelchair or not, and they made me feel no different.

I made sure to start getting ready early the next morning so we wouldn't be late, but I still managed to get into a fluster trying to get dressed. I was able to disguise my plastic body brace cleverly under a black top and it felt great to be dressed up with my hair and make-up done. When we arrived, Lynda had arranged for her ushers to take Nigel and me into the church through a side door. There were quite a few steps at the front that would have required me to be lifted. I was pleased to escape that humiliation. We took our position in a row of seats elevated behind the altar away from the rest of the congregation, as access to the lower level was difficult. Leanne, John and Derek joined us. The bridal march began to play and everyone stood except me, which didn't matter. From my perfect vantage point I could see right down the aisle, where Lynda, as pretty as a princess, was walking towards me. I couldn't believe I had made it.

This time was an important part of my recovery. It was essential for me to be with my family. We're so close – they are my strength. My emotions were fragile though and when the song, *Can I Have this Dance For the Rest of my Life*, started to play we all remembered that this was the bridal waltz Nigel and I had danced to almost exactly two years earlier. It was too much for poor Leanne who raced out of the room in tears. I'll never forget my wedding day and how it felt to be a bride. I'll cherish that moment forever. To make it to Lynda and Phillip's wedding was an important challenge to me and I had done it. Dr Jo, in her bridesmaid's dress, checked on me a few times. But all went well. I didn't get sick and my temperature remained stable.

Monday morning I was back working in the gym. It was necessary for me to strengthen my upper body, which would carry most of my body weight until my legs were strong enough. Maria prepared a fitness program designed to strengthen my arms as well as my legs. I was very motivated. When she set me fifty repetitions to do on the apparatus, I'd do one hundred. I just wanted to get on with it and get out of hospital.

After lunch, one of my occupational therapists took me for a driving lesson using hand controls. My legs and feet didn't have to do a thing. The car was a station wagon, which was a larger vehicle than I was used to. It had a sign on it saying something like, Disabled Driving Instruction. I didn't like that label very much, but I ignored it. The steering wheel had a rotating handle, like a ball, attached to it so I could steer with one hand. The throttle was a lever that you pushed in and out just like the throttle in an aeroplane. This should be easy, I thought. To make the car go forwards, you pulled back on the lever and to stop, you pushed it in. Everything was back to front.

My two instructors were deep in conversation about some hospital matter as I shakily manoeuvred around the quiet suburban back streets near Prince Henry Hospital. They just let me go, not giving much advice. I decided they were allowing me time to gain some confidence. Once or twice I went to stop, but accidentally accelerated and vice versa. I was nervous and driving very slowly but I was enjoying the freedom to just go wherever I wanted.

I noticed a car speeding up behind me. It would come up close then pull back, then race ahead again sitting on my bumper bar. It contained a group of four or five young guys just mucking around. I put my indicator on and moved onto the side of the road so they could go around me.

As they came tearing past one yelled out, 'Get off the road, you f . . . ing freak!'

His words cut me like a spear through my heart. I knew they must have been referring to the disabled sign on the car. Disabled was one thing, but they had called me a freak! I was mortified, I couldn't believe anyone could be so cruel. Instantly those words had made me feel like a worthless piece of broken nothing. Suddenly my whole being felt that I was of no value, no importance to life. Freak! Why had they chosen that word? Ugly, grotesque, deformed – that's how 'freak' made me feel.

My two passengers hadn't stopped talking and they appeared not to have noticed what had just happened. But as I watched the car disappear, the boys were laughing and jeering, turning around and looking at me. I fought back tears and wondered if one day any of them would regret their heartless act, probably not.

I had been trying so hard that day. But these cruel people with those few words had dropped me like a rock into the depths of despair. My whole being was numb. I didn't want to think, I didn't want to feel. I just wanted to be who I was before. I didn't want to need hand controls to drive, or callipers on my legs, or a wheelchair. When would this nightmare end!

When we drove back into the grounds of Prince Henry Hospital, I was asked to schedule my next driving lesson.

'No, thanks. I'll drive when I can use my legs,' I said.

'But, Allana, you don't have the function in your legs to use them to drive a car.'

'Well, I won't drive at all then.'

I was angry and I left my therapists standing dumbfounded. It wasn't their fault, but I never wanted to be labelled freak, disabled, crippled or anything but normal ever again. I was sick of being told what I would and would not be able to do. Being constantly told, you can't, you won't, you will not be able to, is very disheartening.

'Allana, you'll have to accept life in a wheelchair!'

'Allana, you won't be able to walk!'

No! No! No! No more! These negative comments had taken their toll. Boundaries and restrictions are things that only you can place on yourself. I knew that I didn't want to fall into the trap of making excuses for myself because of my paralysis. These thoughts made me remember a story I had heard at a motivational seminar once about how to train a flea. As we all know, fleas are renowned for their ability to jump hundreds of times their own height. If you take a flea and put it in a jar with plastic wrap over the top, the flea will jump up and hit the clear cover. Then the flea learns to jump only to a height just short of the see-through lid. If you remove the plastic wrap, the flea will continue to jump at its restricted height even though it's no longer inhibited. The flea has created its own limit. I didn't want that to happen to me.

It was time to take control over my future. My poor body had been badly broken and disfigured. Over the past ten weeks I had been subjected to endless tests and procedures that were painful, intrusive and degrading. I had been prodded and poked in every place imaginable. My legs and arms were bruised beyond belief from ongoing needles. I'd had so many X-rays, I was sure if I swallowed a coin I'd light up like a pinball machine. Enough was enough!

One of my doctors came to see me that afternoon. 'We've booked you in for nerve conduction studies on your legs tomorrow,' he told me.

'What does this entail?' I asked.

'We inject electric probes at the top and bottom of your legs and send electric shocks between both probes.'

'I don't think so!' I said.

'But you have to have this test.'

'Why? What is the test going to do?'

'It's going to enable us to gauge the messages getting to

your legs. In six months we'll do the test again and see if there's any improvement.'

'Is this going to make me walk?'

'Of course not.'

'Well, I don't want the test.'

I didn't want to go through any more pain and I didn't want people touching me any more. The doctor went ahead and booked the procedure for the next day. I didn't turn up and he was very angry. But I'd had enough.

The hospital routine focused on my rehabilitation. George, the young guy who had broken his neck in the Georges River, made his daily trips to the gym with me and was making great progress. He was also determined to walk. Carlos was very lucky and had gone home weeks earlier, thankfully with no lasting paralysis despite the injury to his neck.

Nigel was back at work but still came to see me every second day, and on weekends I got to go home. I looked forward to it all week, but I usually cried during our trip back to the hospital on Sunday afternoons. One night, Nigel dropped me off at 7 p.m. I had only just wheeled myself into the ward when one of the nurses started screaming, 'ARREST! ARREST!' Medical staff came running from everywhere. One of the patients was suffering a heart attack. They couldn't revive him. About fifteen minutes later, the patient next to me had an epileptic fit. It was very distressing. I sat outside for hours, crying.

I finally settled myself into bed but it was almost midnight. A new patient had arrived while I was at home. He was directly opposite me. His eyes were fixed on me. They looked terrified and confused. 'I know who you are – I know what you're up to,' he started to yell. It gave me such a fright and it woke the whole ward. It turned out he was a head patient but the brain injury ward was full so they had him brought to the spinal unit. He'd kept everyone awake all weekend. How I longed for the peace of my own bed at home. That night the man thought he was flying a spaceship around the planet, Zoltar, and then later he was being chased by a group of men trying to kill him. It was a long night.

My walking was steadily progressing and Professor Jones was very pleased with the way I was advancing. He told me I could go home in seven weeks, but by now I really had come to the end of my patience. I told Professor Jones and Maria that I'd be signing myself out of the hospital in a week. I had a life that I needed to put back together, a family, a marriage and a home that needed tending to. Being away from Nigel for so many months was taking its toll on our relationship and I felt him drifting away from me. It was time to go home and somehow work out the new life Nigel and I would be having together. My decision wasn't received favourably and they both tried to change my mind. But they soon realised it was in vain.

I was measured for a wheelchair. It would be ready within the week in time for me to go home. Craig was helping take down the dimensions.

'What colour?' he asked.

'Fluorescent pink, blue, green and yellow. Let's make it as bright and lairy as possible.'

I didn't want to look sorrowful sitting in my wheelchair. It was depressing enough to know I'd have to use it for a while.

'You have to give it a name like Fred or Harry,' Craig added.

'I'm not planning to get that attached to it, Craig.'

My last week went quickly and by the time I left Prince Henry Hospital, I had begun to learn to walk with Canadian crutches, which have hand grips so you can hold up your body. The supports around the wrist assist your balance. With someone supporting me on either side, I was able to take ten steps. Craig had also worked intensely with me, teaching me the wheelchair skills that would enable me to negotiate obstacles like steps and gutters. But I must admit I wasn't very good at it. To go down over a gutter or step, I had to balance my wheelchair on its back wheel then move it forward, keeping it balanced precariously as I went over the edge. Then I'd let the front wheels down. This whole process was very scary and I had far from gained the confidence to use these skills in the outside world. But I knew somehow I'd tackle these obstacles in my own way. Arrangements were made to continue my rehabilitation as a day patient at Governor Phillip Special Hospital only ten minutes away from home at Penrith.

It was on 22 March, exactly three months after the accident, that Nigel helped me put away the beautiful cards and letters I had received off the pin board behind my bed. We packed my clothes and loaded everything into the car. It had been a harrowing experience. I had been through so much in the hospital but, with the help of the nurses, physios, rehabilitation specialists and doctors, I had made it through. These people had spent so much time with me, they were like family. Maria, my physio, was especially sad to see me go. She'd wanted to watch me walk out of the ward.

'We send so many people home in wheelchairs. I wanted it to be different for you,' she said. I understood that my ability to walk, even a little, was Maria's achievement as well. I promised her one day I'd give up the chair for good. As the staff wished me farewell and we drove through the main gate, I knew I still had much ahead of me to conquer.

Chapter 9

The Long Road Ahead

The Governor Phillip was almost like a nursing home, I thought, when Mum took me there for my introduction and assessment. The gym was small with very basic equipment. However there was a brand new hydrotherapy pool that I couldn't wait to try. Nigel was back at work full time. He'd leave home at 7 a.m. and rarely arrive home before 6 p.m. so my family rallied around to help get me to the physiotherapy sessions. Between them I was picked up in the mornings, usually by my brother-in-law, John. He'd take me to the hospital and then in the afternoon, Mum would pick me up on her way home from work. This was a Monday to Friday routine. At lunch time I'd go into the activity room where all the old people gathered to do craft activities and have lunch. For some reason, the men sat on one side and the ladies on the other. I'd sit eating my lunch, listening to petty quibbling and childish gossip. I'd had enough of this after a few days and I put my lunch on my lap and pushed outside onto the front verandah.

'Hi blossom.' It was a warm and friendly male voice. 'I'm Barry,' he said. Barry was also paraplegic and was sitting with two other men in wheelchairs. They introduced themselves. Wayne was quadriplegic and lived at the hospital. He was only young, about twenty-four. The other man was Ray who had had both his legs amputated above his knees.

'We've seen you coming and going over the last week,' Barry said. The four of us talked all through lunch time sharing our stories. We struck up a great friendship and continued to meet for lunch each day.

My morning physiotherapy sessions were spent in the gym, strengthening my legs and practising my walking. Barry often came to watch. He was also trying to gain strength in his legs to be able to stand. Three afternoons a week I went into the hydrotherapy pool. My freedom in the water amazed me because I was able to take my body brace off. The buoyancy helped to support my back and enabled me to stand and walk around in the water pain free. Barry came in on one of my sessions. We were swimming laps together. The physios kept an extra cautious eye on Barry because only a month earlier he had been concentrating so hard on swimming his laps, that he'd forgotten about the wall at the end and he'd swum straight into it, knocking himself out cold. Luckily the staff saw him do it and dragged him out of the water before he drowned.

My Monday to Friday routine continued and, on weekends, I relaxed at home. Nigel had decided to compete in the Australian Aerobatic Championships. We had discussed selling the Pitts Special we had owned with Allan, but Nigel had developed an obsessive desire to learn aerobatics and compete in the little aeroplane. His practice took up most of his spare time outside of work and, just under a month after I came home from Prince Henry Hospital, he flew to Griffith for the competition. I wasn't confident about staying at home by myself although I was reasonably independent by now, so I went to Mum and Dad's for the week he was away.

I wasn't feeling very well one day so I chose to cancel my physiotherapy session and rest instead. Mum and Dad were at work and I was enjoying having a quiet day to myself. I wheeled into the lounge room and noticed two videotapes sitting on top of the television. One had a hand-written label saying, 'Allana's air crash'. The other had a printed label saying, 'Memorial Service'. I turned the television on and took the first tape, placing it in the video machine. The tape began with a few recorded commercials then the beginning of the National Nine News of 22 December, 1990.

'Four killed during the search for a missing plane!' began the headlines. I watched horrified as the scene, which had devastated my life, was played. My rescuer, Steve, was shown talking to me through the back window of the wreck that had been clearly smashed in. I was reliving the pain of that moment, not only physically but also emotionally. I could see myself being carried away on a stretcher, my body covered with a silver survival blanket. Hugh had placed a damp cloth across my forehead. Why did this happen to me? – why! why! I closed my eyes and took myself back to the moment I had stepped into VH-PLD. I had climbed aboard in such a hurry because Allan was keen to get going. I remembered how every little step felt. They had been my last. I remembered how my feet had felt sitting in the leather slip-on moccasins I'd bought a week earlier. They were a little bit tight and a small blister had developed on one of my toes making it a bit sore. An hour more, and I'd never be able to feel a blister on my feet again.

I was shaken by the footage I saw. I dared myself to continue and I placed the next tape in the machine. It began with the smiling faces of Peter, Allan, Janine and Robert. The four photographs showed each of them in their enjoyment of life. I couldn't watch any more. I turned the TV off and sat in my wheelchair, sobbing. How unfair life is. I wished they were all here with me. Why did they have to die? What am I going to do? What sort of future do I have? I looked up through my tears and saw my little bluebird sitting on the mantelpiece. It was the one Gran had given me after Grandad died. I picked it up and held it to my chest, trying to draw the comfort it had always given me. But there was nothing. Will I find happiness? Is there any hope? My childhood innocence was shattered. I'd seen things that had scarred my emotions and I had experienced severe trauma that had already begun to harden me.

I caught sight of my reflection in the television. I looked so pitiful sitting in my wheelchair. What's going to happen to me? If I was somehow going to get myself up and walking again, it would be completely up to me. I knew that all too well. I prayed that I was a strong enough person to make it through!

★

Nigel competed in the Sportsman category and at the Nationals and he kept in touch over the competition days. I could tell he was having heaps of fun. The past four months had been murder for him and he was enjoying being away for the first time from the pressures and the reality of our difficult adjustments to life. Mum, Dad and I were thrilled to receive his call on Sunday evening to tell us he had taken first place. No one could have been prouder, but I would love to have been there with him when he won. The celebrations at Griffith that night were somewhat out of control from what I heard and, although I was happy for Nigel's success, I couldn't help but feel a little bit left out. Mum and Dad came over to our house for dinner to celebrate Nigel's win on the night he came home, but he seemed depressed and preoccupied.

'What's wrong with you?' I finally asked.

'I didn't want to come home to you and this nightmare. Our future is so uncertain,' he said.

I put my head down. I couldn't bear to look at Mum and Dad.

'Well, at least you're honest,' I said. My injuries were a life sentence but if I could walk away from them, I certainly would. I never wanted to be a burden on Nigel and never wanted to see myself as his invalid wife, but that's how he made me feel. I have never felt more unattractive than at that moment. I felt like half a woman, like a freak. It would have been so easy for Nigel to stay away, and part of me wished he had. I really didn't know why he'd come home.

Nigel and I had a heartfelt discussion about our future

that night. I understood his week away had given him an escape from the realities of our lives.

He kept asking me, 'Do you think you're getting any feeling back in your legs? Do you feel your legs are getting stronger? Do you really think you'll be able to walk?'

I knew I couldn't promise Nigel miracles and my future frightened me too. All I could say to him was, 'I don't know what's going to happen to me. But I promise you with all my heart that I'll be the best I can be, with whatever I have left.'

I committed myself to making my life as normal as possible. I wanted everyday life to be the way it had been before the accident too, and that included taking over the mundane household tasks I used to do. One day Nigel was in the back garden pruning some trees. I watched him for a while from the new verandah that led off our bedroom. I had managed to strip the sheets and doona off the bed earlier in the day and wash them, then put them in the dryer. The bathroom could do with a once over, I thought, so I wheeled my way into the laundry and got out the cleaning items I'd need. It was awkward working from the wheelchair but after a lot of grunting and straining, I cleaned the bath and the toilet and even mopped the floor.

The dryer had finished its cycle. I dragged the linen out and placed it on my lap, pushing my wheelchair into the bedroom. Replacing the bottom sheet and pillowcases on the bed was the easy task. Putting the doona cover on was going to be tricky, but I wanted to give it a go. I grabbed the two ends of the doona, one in each hand, and fed them in through the opened seam all the way to their respective corners. The fabric had enveloped me, wheelchair and all. Most of the doona and its cover were on my lap and on the floor in front of me. It was getting tangled up so I wheeled myself back a little to free it. But I wheeled over the back end of the doona cover and it got stuck. I wheeled forward to release it, then wheeled over the front section of the cover's opening. The harder I tried to escape, the more entrapped I became, until both ends of the doona's opening were well and truly jammed under my wheels, with me and the chair inside. There I was, stuck in a doona cover. How humiliating. Nigel's going to get a lot of mileage out of this one, I thought.

'Nigel, help!' I kept calling out, giggling at how stupid I was going to look.

He walked into the room. 'What are you doing?'

I could hear his voice from beneath my ghostly disguise of the white cotton shroud. I couldn't see him. 'I'm stuck,' I said.

'What were you trying to do?' he asked.

'I was trying to put the cover on the doona.'

Nigel roared with laughter and decided to sit on the bed next to me for a few minutes, discussing something trivial and inappropriate. He wanted to savour my embarrassing predicament for a few moments more before helping me out. We were both laughing so much, but we managed to finish making the bed together.

From my seated position, I managed to cook our meals every night, and dust and polish items within reach. I tried to sweep and vacuum, though it wasn't very successful. But I was having a go and that's what mattered to me. Mum came over once a week to help with the household chores that I couldn't manage.

I was cleaning out the bottom of my wardrobe one weekend, sitting on the floor amongst all my beautiful high-heeled shoes that I used to wear to work every day. I had dragged them out, cleaned the floor and was putting them back in. Deep down I knew I'd never be able to wear any of them again. It was so difficult letting go of the past. One part of me still believed I'd wake up some day and be back to normal. But another part of me said it was time to cleanse myself with a symbolic gesture to accept the things I would never be able to do again. I really needed to say goodbye to the way I had been, physically, before the accident. I collected all the shoes except for the ones I wore on our wedding day. I started putting them into a garbage bag. Nigel walked into the room in the middle of this, horrified at what I was doing.

'No, don't touch them,' he said. 'Leave them right where they were.' He took a shoe out of my hand and put it back in the cupboard along with the rest from the bag. I was dumbfounded. I felt like an impostor. It was as if they weren't my shoes to touch. Nigel was still holding on to the beautiful, fit and active woman I had been before the accident. He wasn't ready to come to terms with letting that person go. He needed time to adjust and I needed to understand that.

After three months at Governor Phillip, I was reassessed and graded a non priority patient, which meant that physiotherapy was reduced to three days a week and there would be no more work in the pool. Generally, I was still confined to the wheelchair but I was gaining strength and confident enough to take ten to twenty steps without the support of anyone by my side, although I was using my Canadian crutches and had calipers supporting my feet. I was pleased with my progress, but I didn't want to waste two week days without exercising.

I'd heard about a gymnasium in Penrith that was owned and run by Ron Oxley, the former conditioner/trainer for the Penrith Panthers rugby league team. Nigel drove me to meet with Ron one Saturday morning. He turned out to be the nicest man. He took me under his wing and agreed to work with me. Ron helped me focus on the strength in my upper body because my arms had to carry most of my weight around when I walked. Paralysis resulting from a spinal injury is normally permanent. In my case it was. To strengthen my legs, to a point where they were supporting my body when I walked, would take an enormous amount of time and effort – if they were able to improve them. So, in the meantime, my back, stomach and arms got a lot of attention. I also needed strength in my arms to help my balance, which was still non existent. This was because my feet and ankles didn't work. I had asked one of the physios at Governor Phillip one day why amputees who had false legs with fixed wooden feet had more balance than me. The reason was because they compensated with other muscles in their upper legs and especially the gluteal muscle. My gluteal muscle had been affected by paralysis as well.

I felt comfortable at Ron's gym. There were no mirrors on the walls and his other clients were down-to-earth people, there to work out seriously. There were never any prancing show ponies as I called those gym addicts who strut around showing off their beautiful bodies, or steroid heads flexing their muscles.

At this time Nigel had to take a business trip to Germany. Now that I was a little bit more mobile and independent I chose to stay at home by myself. On the night Nigel left, I was making myself a cup of tea. I could do this standing now. By leaning on the cupboards for support, I could stand and use my knees to balance on the cupboard door in front of the sink and that would leave my hands free to cook or wash the dishes. I looked across and noticed my car keys sitting on the kitchen bench. Nigel had left my car in the driveway. Having to rely on other people to take me around was becoming very frustrating. I hadn't tried to drive using my feet so I thought this was as good a time as any to give it a go.

The distance from the front door to the car took me about twenty steps, but there was a lot of rubble around from the workmen who were still helping us with renovations. I knew I'd be unsteady, especially on the uneven ground. I pushed my wheelchair up to the front door, then gingerly stood up, gripping intensely onto the handles of my crutches. Then I carefully negotiated my way to the car. Once settled in the driver's seat, I turned on the cabin light so I could see my feet. I practised pushing the pedals. I couldn't feel what my feet were doing, but there had to be a way I could make this work. I placed my foot on the brake, looking down to confirm it was in position. Then I sat up, analysing how every part of me felt with my foot in that spot. I did the same with the clutch. It felt a little bit different and so did the accelerator. I'd been sitting for almost an hour practising accelerating, braking and changing gears.

It was 11 p.m. and the streets were quiet so I turned the key and started the engine. It required considerable effort to push my leg down onto the clutch, but I got it all the way in and I put the car into reverse. My coordination between accelerator and clutch took a few attempts, stalling the car each time. Perseverance paid off. I reversed all the way up to the top of the driveway. It was so exciting. I'm going to be able to master this, I thought. I rolled the car back down and planned to try again the next night.

I waited until late and went through the same ritual. But this time when I reached the top of the driveway, I put my car into first gear and drove up the road. I made it all the way around the block even though my feet got tangled up. I kangaroo hopped most of the way and even stalled twice, but I was confident I'd get better. I kept practising every night and was improving. I told Mum and Dad who were very encouraging. On Sunday, Mum took me to a shopping centre so I could drive around the car park. A few times I couldn't find the brake with my foot and had to quickly use the hand brake. Mum was as cool as a cucumber, praising me for my determination.

Nigel was due back in four days and I wanted to surprise him. But when he rang me from Germany, I couldn't contain myself and proceeded to tell him how I could drive.

'I'm so proud of you, darling,' he said.

Over the following two weeks, my confidence grew and

I was finally able to drive myself around. This gave me back my freedom and independence.

Some weeks before I'd left Prince Henry Hospital, a young guy named Lee was admitted as a patient. He'd been in a car accident and broken his neck as a result. Lee was from Penrith, which wasn't far from where I lived. I'd heard there was to be a fundraising night for Lee at a local club and Barry and I planned to go. Nigel was still in Germany so Barry agreed to pick me up from Mum and Dad's place. His car was equipped with a contraption used to hoist his wheelchair onto the roof. But it wasn't working so before Barry left home, his adult son had put his chair in the boot. Once I was settled in the passenger's seat, Dad put my wheelchair in the boot as well.

'How are you going to get these out once you get to the club?' Dad asked. 'Do you want to take your walking sticks with you so you can walk around to the boot?'

'No, there'll be plenty of people around to help, don't worry,' I assured him.

Barry was driving with hand controls, which still looked awkward to me. Driving into the car park at the club, there were a few other cars arriving. But by the time we'd found a vacant spot, all the people were inside. We waited for a few minutes until another car drove in, but he parked away on the other side of the parking lot. Neither of us could walk to the back of the car to get the wheelchairs out so we simply had to wait for someone to come along and help. About ten minutes went by. We were laughing at our silly situation as each car that drove in parked too far away for us to call out for help.

'This is so funny, Barry, I'm going to write a book one day and I'll have to put this in it,' I said.

Not long after, a car pulled up next to us. I had my window down and casually asked the driver, a man, who was with a few friends, if they could help us by getting our wheelchairs out of the boot.

'Certainly,' he said, looking a bit confused. Once we were settled in our chairs, the group of men wandered into the club. Barry and I met them at the front desk where they were signing in. The driver asked, 'How did you get them into the car in the first place?' We decided to keep that a secret.

It was a fun night. Even Wayne from Governor Phillip Hospital was there. But the biggest surprise came halfway through the function when Lee arrived with one of the nurses from Prince Henry. His mum, Gail, was so proud of him. I met Gail some years later in a coffee shop by accident. She told me Lee was living in Queensland with his girlfriend, who was a nurse. I was pleased to hear he was so happy.

My physiotherapy at Governor Phillip Hospital came to an end a few months later, but Barry and I kept in touch. In fact Nigel and I went to Barry's wedding a few years ago. He married a gorgeous lady, Pauline, who was an occupational therapist at Governor Phillip. They had both been working hard on Barry's rehabilitation and they celebrated by dancing the bridal waltz together with Barry standing. It was a beautiful moment.

It had been six months since my accident. I took my report from the physios at Governor Phillip to Professor

Jones during one of my regular check-ups. He was pleased with my progress and gave me the all clear, at last, to remove the body brace I was still wearing each day.

Even though I was using my wheelchair, I showed Professor Jones how I could walk. It was very gawky looking but that didn't matter.

'So what are you doing with yourself during the days?' the Professor asked.

'I go to the gym,' I said.

'And what about the future?'

'I'll keep going to the gym.'

'But what are your goals, what do you hope to achieve?'

'One day I'll walk without crutches, and one day I'll throw this chair away for good.'

'I think that's a bit ambitious. Soon you'll have to accept the way things are,' he said.

Professor Jones and I always had a bit of a stand off when we talked about my walking.

'We'll see,' I said.

My wheelchair skills hadn't really improved since leaving Prince Henry Hospital. I didn't want to become too comfortable in the chair for fear of giving in and deciding it was easier to accept life without walking. Once I saw a young guy jumping his wheelchair down a small flight of stairs outside a shopping centre. He made it look so easy. Even negotiating a gutter frightened me. I had developed my own method to get around town, which always commanded a second look from passers-by. When I came to a gutter, I'd make sure there was a light pole or something solid for me to hold on to. I'd wheel up to it, then stand up grasping onto my support. I'd pick the wheelchair up with my free hand, lifting it over the obstacle. Then I'd sit down and wheel away. I know people were thinking, if she can stand, surely she can walk.

At the gym, Ron Oxley monitored my progress every day. I was getting stronger. Then I heard about a personal trainer who worked for the Commonwealth Rehabilitation Service. His name was Roman and he was said to be an excellent motivator, experienced with spinal injury patients. I made arrangements to meet with Roman for an evaluation one day in Sydney at the centre where he worked. Nigel and I were ushered into a small gymnasium filled with unusual equipment. Roman was a slightly built man who was very fit. He spoke with a very broad Russian or Ukraine accent.

'Come in, come in, welcome, welcome,' he said, waving us towards him. I was in my brightly coloured wheelchair and expected my assessment to take about half an hour. Roman took hold of my hands and helped me to my feet. He began to step backwards, walking me all around the room, analysing my walking gait until he helped me back into the wheelchair. Roman paced backwards and forwards. His determined strut revealed he was deep in thought.

'I want you to get onto the floor,' Roman directed. I was baffled by this request and looked towards Nigel for support. He looked as puzzled as I was.

'Why do you want me to get on the floor?' I asked.

'Don't ask, just do!' came the demand.

Once on the floor, Roman had me crawling along the ground forwards and backwards. He had me throwing heavy medicine balls to him and doing other obscure tasks.

Each time I questioned why I was doing these odd things, Roman would say, 'Don't ask, just do!' At the end of our session, which took almost two hours, I was exhausted. Roman was eager to work with me further and we agreed to meet once a week at the Parramatta office of the C.R.S. Nigel and I left feeling confident we had found someone who would make the difference with my walking. Roman was tough. He would make me work hard and I knew, with Roman's help, one day I would reach my goal to walk without sticks.

My exercise program continued every day at the gym in Penrith where I concentrated on my general fitness and overall body strength. I looked forward to my weekly sessions at Parramatta, which I was now able to drive myself to. Each time Roman would have a new task for me to master, sometimes preparing an obstacle course for me to walk around or teaching me to get off the floor using a chair for support. I even learned how to walk up and down steps. Sometimes I'd be sent home with odd equipment and bizarre instructions. I learned never to ask why. I just did as I was told. One day, Roman strapped specially made weights around both my ankles and told me to walk with them. My legs were so heavy that all I could manage was a shuffle. I was required to take the weights home and do three sessions a day, five minutes each with them. At the end of the week, I could just lift my feet off the ground and take a few steps with the weights.

Another time, he sent me home with a stool on wheels and told me not to use my wheelchair in the house. I was to push the stool around the floor, using my legs. Roman kept me motivated and his assistant, a young physiotherapist named Wendy, also became an important part of our team. The three of us got on like a house on fire and we worked very hard making great progress.

I kept pushing myself to improve and my walking was going well. Every day I'd set new challenges. The registration was due on my car so I drove down to the R.T.A. office, parking in the disabled spot which was closest to the front entrance. My wheelchair was in the back of my car. As usual, I walked around on my crutches, popped the boot and started to drag it out. But then I hesitated, looking at the distance between me and the door, thinking I bet I could walk all the way inside and back again. A surge of enthusiasm engulfed me as I slammed the boot in a determined manner, deciding to give it a go. Then I took a deep breath, concentrating on one step at a time. Remember your balance, you can do it. I was walking for the first time alone, outside the security of the gym, or on the arm of someone to support me if I stumbled. Inside, the room was full of people. I took a ticket with a number placing me in a queue to be served. Almost every eye was on me. I felt suddenly anxious and self conscious. My heart was pounding hard but I hoped nobody noticed how nervous I was. A kind man stood up from his chair and helped me into the seat.

'Thank you so much,' I said.

My hands were glowing red and sore from gripping tightly onto the handles of my Canadian crutches. It was a relief to rest. I've made it this far, I thought. It wasn't long before my number was called out. I gingerly walked to the counter where a lady took my paperwork and entered into polite conversation about the weather. I had a strong hold on the solid bench, feeling stable and safe. I looked around as the lady continued to punch data into the computer in front of her. People were still staring at me. I smiled slightly and turned back around, momentarily losing my grip. I grabbed for the counter but felt my hands slip away. As if in slow motion, my body fell back. A woman behind me screamed as I landed flat on my ass. People crowded around me straight away and the lady behind the counter stood up, peering down at me sitting on the floor.

'Are you all right?' she said. I nodded to her, but it had given me a bad fright. I quickly assessed my condition and realised I hadn't hurt myself. Roman had taught me how to get up off the floor using a chair or a piece of furniture for support. But as I looked around, there was nothing to use as a prop. A sea of faces kept asking, 'Are you all right? Are you all right?' How could I tell them I was okay, but I just couldn't get myself up onto my feet. Oh, God, please get me out of this horrible scene with some dignity.

At that moment a man pushed his way between the two people next to me. He was a male nurse from Governor Phillip Hospital.

'What are you doing down there, Allana?' he said, making light of my humiliating situation. With no fuss, he picked me up, balancing me back against the counter. He put my crutches back in my hands, dusted me off and walked out the door.

My face must have been so pale. I was still shaking and fought back the urge to cry. The paperwork was ready. I thanked the lady and walked back to my car ever so carefully. I knew that to give up my wheelchair for good, I'd have to make myself leave it behind more and more. I had to accept I was going to fall many times. It doesn't matter that I fell over. I had achieved something new today and that was all that mattered, I told myself.

On my next visit to see Roman, I told him what had happened and we spent the whole day's session learning how to get off the floor using nothing but my crutches.

Nigel helped to motivate me and set goals as well. One day, we parked at the shopping centre ready to buy our groceries as we did every week.

'Don't use your wheelchair today, Lan. We're in no hurry. I want you to walk with me,' he said. It would be the furthest I'd had to walk since the accident. But I was ready to try so off we went. I was exhausted even by the time we reached the turnstiles. I pushed on regardless, all the way through the vegie section, making sure not to slip on the occasional squashed grape or wet section of floor. I reached the end of the aisle, totally disinterested in the selection of food that was mounting in the bottom of our trolley. I peered down the next aisle that seemed longer than the last. The muscles in my arms and shoulders screamed out for a break and a burning pain in my back made each step increasingly difficult. There was a display at the top of the drink aisle where cartons of soft drink cans were stacked.

'I can't go any further. I need to rest,' I said to Nigel as I propped myself up, sitting on the corner of a box. Nigel whizzed around selecting the essentials we needed for the week. When he was done, we slowly walked back to the car, both pleased that although I'd only made it down two aisles, I had never walked this far.

The next week we did the same and I made it through four aisles. This became a medium by which I could measure my progress and, during the days between our trips to the grocery store, I'd work really hard with Roman and Ron, keen to improve every time. It took a few months of hard work until the day I walked down every single aisle. This was a goal Nigel and I had set. We were both so excited when I did it that we went out for dinner that night to celebrate, toasting our glasses to the conquest of Woolies.

My confidence grew as I made progress quickly. Mum and I now did regular trips shopping for clothes at the mall. We'd usually park in the disabled parking spots. I'd become used to the idea of using these. They were always close to the entrance which meant I could leave my wheelchair behind because I didn't have to walk too far to go inside. However, people often abused me when I pulled in, despite the fact that I had the required notice in my windscreen. I've tried to analyse this behaviour. It seems people think if you're young and drive a nice car, there couldn't possibly be anything wrong with you. Mum always took great offence when this happened and would fly to my defence. One lady made such a scene one day that a crowd gathered as she stood screaming at me like a rabid dog. I let her continue yelling at me for a while, not saying a word, then casually reached for my crutches and eased myself out of the car door. She quickly realised I had good reason to use the parking spot, especially when she looked across and saw my disabled sticker in the window. She choked on the token apology before slinking away beneath the glare of the onlookers.

Once inside the shops, I could leisurely browse, enjoying the freedom of complete accessibility around the racks that was sometimes impossible to do in my wheelchair. I made sure to take advantage of a quick rest though, whenever there was a bench or chair to sit on. This kept me from tiring too quickly and allowed us to shop longer.

Mum took me to buy some new shoes one day. I was limited to flat and practical. We picked out a smart pair of leather ankle boots and asked the sales lady for my size. I was a bit embarrassed having to expose the plastic supports on my lower legs, but I continued on, quickly sliding into the new shoes, trying to ignore the sideways glances from other customers in the shop. Before I stood up, I pushed down with my thumb around my toes to make sure they were all sitting straight. The danger, when you can't feel your feet, is having a toe crunched up or bent. After leaving it like this all day, it can cause all sorts of damage. I found that out the hard way. Once upright, I realised the heel was slightly higher than I was used to. Maybe only by millimetres, but it was enough to disrupt my balance.

'How do they feel?' asked the young sales girl. I looked at Mum, who was also waiting for an answer. 'Well, I don't really know how they feel.' The sales girl was confused, so I continued on to explain I had no feeling in my legs and feet. She was very nice and immediately crouched down, feeling for my toes, assuring me they were a perfect fit. They looked quite smart. I decided to buy them and wear them straight away. I walked out of the shop, pleased with my new purchase. Yet people continued to stare. I caught sight of my reflection in a shop window, initially trying to see how my new boots looked. But, as I walked along watching my movements and seeing myself awkward and ungainly, I realised how pathetic I appeared to people. No wonder they stared. I turned away, not wanting to see any more.

These shopping days provided great exercise for me. But we were restricted to staying on one level, unless there was a lift close by. The escalators were plentiful but they terrified me. I was getting around okay but my balance was still shaky. The thought of trying to get on and off a moving platform was inconceivable, although I wanted to try.

I contacted the manager of Westfield Shoppingtown at Parramatta and explained my problem. He was eager to help me in any way. I arranged to be at the centre with Roman and Wendy early one morning before the shops opened. The manager met us and let us in, turning on a set of escalators near the door. Roman spent a few minutes getting on and off himself, trying to work out how I could do it without falling over. He sat me on a nearby chair and practised with my crutches.

'Okay, this is how,' he said, walking through the procedure for me.

I stood ready with Wendy supporting me while Roman waited at the bottom of the moving stairs.

'Whenever you're ready,' he called. I was braced, lifting my foot several times, trying to time myself with the flow of steps. They were mesmerising. The longer I stood watching them, the faster they seemed to be travelling.

'Whenever you're ready,' Roman called again. I moved quickly forward, stumbling onto a step.

'I did it, Roman. Look, I did it! Oh shit, Roman, how am I going to get off!'

I was carried steadily down where I could see Roman's stance preparing to save me. He looked like a baseball catcher. 'I'm scared, Roman.' I had visions of us both falling flat on the floor.

'You'll be right. I'll catch you.'

I could see where the steps disappeared into the floor and I lunged onto that spot, staggering slightly as Roman held me upright. The three of us screamed with delight. Roman was always so enthusiastic.

'Quick, get the video camera, Wendy,' he called. I prepared to go again. I was still very wobbly and it was very frightening, but my confidence grew quickly and after a while I was almost doing it by myself. Each time I stepped off, we celebrated, making such a racket that a security guard came by to see what all the fuss was about. We tried to explain it to him. I even showed him how I could get on and off the escalator by myself. Again, the three of us shrieked with delight. I'm sure he walked away thinking we were all mad. The manager returned after an hour to let us out the doors. I showed him how sure-footed I'd become during the time and I thanked him for being so kind to us.

One morning, Roman surprised me with a brand new set of walking sticks that he had ordered some weeks earlier. This was a big step for me. The Canadian crutches I was using had supported me high above my wrists, assisting my balance and stability. Now we began working with one stick and one crutch. I felt extremely vulnerable. The walking stick swayed from side to side each time I put pressure down on it. Roman realised that my wrists would need to be strengthened to enable me to keep them under control. He sent me home with suitable exercises to work on during the week. The next week, I practised with both walking sticks. It was as difficult adapting to my new canes as it had been learning how to use the Canadian crutches. Often I stumbled off balance and fell onto the floor. But I was an expert at falling over now and I didn't make too much fuss when it happened. I just got up and tried again.

It only took a month before I threw the Canadian crutches away for good. I was very proud of my efforts. I had worked hard to strengthen what muscles I had left functioning in my legs. My walking still looked a bit odd, but anything was better than being stuck in a wheelchair. I still had no feeling below my knees and only a patchy feeling in the tops of my legs.

To get around on my feet still felt as though I was walking on nothing or walking on stilts. I couldn't feel when my feet hit the ground with each step so I tended to stamp my feet down. To hear my foot hit the ground was the only way I knew I'd taken a step. Still, I was adapting to my new body and discovering new techniques to make my walking stronger every day.

It was coming up to Christmas, one year since the accident. I waited for that day, hoping that on the anniversary I would wake up in the morning and find that my body was back to normal. It didn't happen. On my birthday in March, it would happen, I told myself.

Nigel and I were talking in the hangar one day. I was balancing against a bench and my walking sticks were resting against it as well. Nigel wanted to show me something on an aeroplane he was working on. For some unknown reason, I forgot that I couldn't walk and I stepped forward towards the plane, stumbling into Nigel's arms. It happened purely by accident, but I had taken three steps before I fell. We both got a fright initially. Then we realised what had happened.

'Do that again,' Nigel said. I balanced myself back on the bench and stepped forward, still only making three steps before falling. Nigel caught me again. We were elated. 'I'm going to be able to do it. I'm going to walk without these sticks,' I said.

Roman knew this was my goal, but he hadn't pushed me until I told him what had happened in the hangar. At the end of our next session, Roman and Wendy placed chairs and tables strategically around the room. Each item was separated a distance of two or three steps. I walked through the course without my sticks, staggering and falling onto each support. At home I did the same and tried my best to get around the house on my own. After several months, I could walk a considerable distance – twenty or thirty steps – without my sticks, although I had to continue wearing supports on my ankles. I was practising in the hangar one day when one of our friends, Paul Grey, came to visit us.

'Hi, Clive,' he said.

'Clive? Who's Clive?' I asked.

'You are. You look like Clive the orang-utan in *Any*

Which Way But Loose.' I hadn't noticed, but when I was walking I would wave my arms in the air to give me balance and, combined with my clumsy waddle, I really did look like an orang-utan walking. Every time I went to take a step that day, I would fall over laughing at myself. My technique obviously needed attention.

Eventually I was able to walk without swinging my arms around. But my accentuated waddle remained. After walking like this for a while, I would have to spend an hour lying flat because the pain in my back, knees and hips was unbearable. I had worked hard every day to reach my goal and now I could walk without sticks. I wasn't relying on the wheelchair. But I had to accept that if I continued putting pressure on my spine and my joints by walking around unaided, it wouldn't take long before I did damage to myself. X-rays showed that I had already begun to develop osteoporosis in my ankles. I decided it was better to protect my body and maintain it at its potential best, rather than flog it to prove a point. I decided to continue using my walking sticks to get around. I didn't see this as failure. I wasn't compromising on my promise to Nigel to be the best I could be. I had challenged myself and I had won. I had done my best!

Chapter 10

Fighting for Me

January, 1992, and Nigel was training in earnest again for the National Aerobatic Competition. I was watching him fly the little red bi-plane around, drawing intricate patterns in the sky. When he taxied in and shut down he asked me if I wanted to go for a fly. He had our friend's aeroplane, a Chipmunk, ready to go on the tarmac. I hadn't flown in a light plane since the accident and had put this day off again and again. But now seemed like the perfect time to get back into the air. Nigel helped me into the front seat, strapping me in securely, then he climbed into the pilot's seat behind. I was very anxious which made me feel nauseous, but Nigel was understanding and he continued to reassure me that I was safe and nothing was going to go wrong with the plane. I trusted him as he gently flew me around the valley. By the time he turned us around to return to the airfield, I wasn't afraid at all. The grass runway was up ahead. We were approaching from the north. Everything was looking good.

I could see the river coming up and I was scanning the valley, enjoying the view, when I looked straight down to see we were low over the trees at the perimeter of the airport. My mind flashed back – I could hear the high-pitched screech of trees, scraping beneath the wing, and the cabin being lashed at by leaves and branches. The frenzied, confusing moments were real again. I was back there. I could vaguely hear Nigel speaking to me over the intercom, but at that moment my mind was in another place. At first I couldn't speak.

'Are you okay?' Nigel kept repeating until I finally replied.

'The trees, the trees.'

When we were on the ground, Nigel helped me out of the aeroplane. I was pale and still shaking. He held me tight.

'You're okay. I won't let anything bad happen to you,' he said.

My first flight had been extremely traumatic. I wondered if I'd ever overcome my fear of flying. It had been such a big part of my life. I'd loved to fly once. I wanted that passion back so badly.

Nigel was doing some work on a high performance aerobatic aeroplane called an Extra 300. He had just put the propeller back on and cowled up the engine. 'I'm going to take her for a test fly, Lan,' he said.

'Can I come too?'

Nigel was surprised. He hadn't tried to encourage me to fly since the last episode.

'Of course you can,' he said.

We flew all the way to Mittagong, the round trip

taking us almost an hour to complete. The whole time I was in the air, my eyes were fixed on the propeller, convinced that Nigel hadn't secured it back on properly, despite him repeatedly answering my questions with, 'Yes, Allana, I tightened every single nut and bolt. The prop is not going to fly off.'

I wasn't panicked or hysterical but I prayed during that flight – God, please get me back onto the ground safely. I promise I'll never ever fly again if you get me down in one piece.

I persevered, however, playing pillion whenever Nigel had a spare seat in the aeroplane. I fought my inner battle each time, but some flights were worse than others. One day we were flying back from Bendigo. The aeroplane we were in had two fuel tanks and the fuel supply to the engine had to be alternated between them. When Nigel swapped over, the engine coughed and spluttered. Nigel warned me each time so I was prepared for it, but once he forgot to tell me he was changing tanks. The engine ran roughly and momentarily stopped. This time, I became hysterical. I was so frantic, thinking we were going to crash, that I started to hyperventilate. I was gasping for air and tears poured down my face.

Nigel was in a separate cockpit behind mine and he couldn't even reach out to touch me. I know he was frightened. We were six thousand feet up in the air and he couldn't do anything to help. By this time the engine was running smoothly again and Nigel started yelling at me through the intercom, 'Allana, calm down. I'm sorry, darling, I forgot to tell you I was swapping tanks. Just calm down.' We landed at a nearby airfield where I managed to compose myself before the final leg home.

Sometimes, when I was flying, I wondered why I was pushing myself. It would be so much easier to stay on the ground. But something inside kept driving me. I was doing what I had to do, but I didn't know why.

It was late March, 1992. My birthday had come and gone, and again I was surprised to wake up on the big day to find that my legs weren't any better. Waiting for a miracle can be a tedious job and it was starting to get me down. Nigel had been practising hard for the National Aerobatic Championships that were only a week away. His obsession was all consuming. I wondered what was motivating him. He spent almost seven days a week at the airport and he was often distant and preoccupied when he got home at night. This was worrying me.

My car was loaded up with Nigel's support equipment and I drove to the competition at Griffith on Thursday morning. This was a very distressing time for me. I had been falling into a deep depression since my birthday. I wanted my nightmare to end. I wanted to be able to walk and run like everyone else. Why did this have to happen to me? I had put so much effort into getting physically well and proving myself to Nigel that I don't think I gave myself time to heal emotionally.

The competition lasted four days. Being there reminded me of the time we'd spent at Griffith with Peter and Allan only two years earlier. I could still picture Allan polishing the shiny silver propeller on Oscar. He was so proud of his little aeroplane that year. I pictured Peter poking around the planes with his blue Cessna cap on. I was keeping a diary at the time and I made an entry in capital letters on the Saturday afternoon, 'GOD, WHY DIDN'T YOU JUST LET ME DIE!'

I couldn't bear to be around people. The effort involved in just engaging in small talk with people was way too much to bear. This overwhelming grief that I was feeling seemed to be escalating so quickly, and I was unable to control it. My thoughts and emotions were dark. I had so much anger inside me. That Saturday night all I wanted to do was run away and hide. Instead I got into my car and drove to the airport.

It was late at night. The field was deserted and there was light rain falling. I sat on the cold grass outside the aeroclub and sobbed for hours. This was my time to grieve. It was more than a year after the accident and all my emotions were pouring out. I was grieving for the four people who I'd watched die. I missed Peter and Allan so much. But I was also grieving for myself. I didn't know who I was any more. The lives of my friends hadn't changed, but I felt like I was living on a completely different planet to everyone, even Nigel. It was almost like I was living in a glass cage, where I could move around the people I used to know and the places I used to go, but I wasn't a part of my surroundings. I desperately wanted to break out and join the 'real' world again. But I was trapped and I didn't know how to escape the despair that had become my barrier.

My depression sank lower and lower over the months following. Most days I'd sit in front of the television absorbed in daytime soap dramas or talkback shows where I'd get wrapped up in other people's misery. One day I was standing in the kitchen washing up some dishes when it finally hit me – this was it! I wasn't going to get better, I was going to be paralysed for the rest of my life. The day that I was waiting for, the day I would wake up and find my body was back to normal, wasn't going to come. I stood frozen for a few moments, still with my hands resting in the warm water and soaked in suds. Then I went to pieces, falling to the floor huddled in the foetal position. I was in a corner of my kitchen crying out convulsively. I was frightened of myself. I was suicidal and I even took a sharp knife out of the drawer and held it to my wrist, only to be disgusted with myself because I couldn't bring myself to do it.

Time became irrelevant. I don't know how long I sat there, but some time during the afternoon I managed to phone a psychiatrist, Dr Hugh Jolly, whom I had seen earlier in the year for legal reasons. His secretary sensed the urgency of the situation and put me straight through. Dr Jolly calmed me down and rang my local GP, who in turn made arrangements for me to see a local psychiatrist, Dr Shail Chatervardi, urgently.

Months went by and I continued to seek help from my doctor. But I was absorbed in my own self-pity. I even had trouble leaving the house. Some days my biggest challenge was to simply get out of bed. Nigel was away one weekend and he became concerned for my safety after phoning me during the day. I'd been talking about ending my life. Nigel rang Mum who found me sitting on the floor in my lounge room halfway through a bottle of scotch beside an ashtray piled high with cigarette butts. I was a mess. I was self-destructing. My life was a labyrinth of fatalistic thoughts. I was drowning in my own sorrow and enjoying it. I didn't care how I looked. I didn't care about my health. I was interested in nothing. I was pathetic.

I thought nobody understood me. Life for everyone else in the world was unchanged. But look what was happening to poor me. I continued in my spiral dive, hiding my pain away from the rest of the world. Whenever I had to be around people other than Nigel or my parents though, I made sure I did my hair and put my make-up on and I was smiling and charming. This was my 'clown face' as Nigel called it.

Sometimes he saw me hiding away from people, gripped in an emotional turmoil, only to gather my strength a few minutes later and return fresh and bubbly as ever. They would never have known. I realised nobody could help me. I had to find my own way out of this maze, but I didn't know how.

Nigel became even more preoccupied with work and took on a greater role in the Aerobatic Club. Life for him went on regardless. He was going to committee meetings and functions a few times a week. He went alone to practise at weekends and he also went alone to the New South Wales Aerobatic Competition. I wasn't only losing myself. I was losing him as well. Our relationship was strained, which was made even worse by our deteriorating financial problems. I was trying desperately to fund a legal case for compensation for my injuries and I was forced to take ongoing loans from the bank to do it. Borrowing large sums of money was too much for me to cope with, and it just compounded my emotional problems. Mum and Dad even had to help out financially at times. This was extremely distressing for me.

I felt I was in a hopeless situation. Physical problems, depression, relationship problems, finance problems. My luck had to turn eventually. And out of the blue, it did. Right at this time, when I needed help most, I was contacted by Comcare, an organisation that looks after workers' compensation for Commonwealth employees. They offered to assist me financially. Although I wasn't being paid to be part of the search and rescue team on the day of the accident, I was still considered a Commonwealth employee and therefore I was eligible to make a claim. Without too much fuss, a lump sum payment based on pain and suffering and loss of wages, was approved. I knew I'd have to be careful with it. My plan was to use it to allow me to continue fighting my main case for compensation against two American companies which, the lawyers had warned me, could go on for several years. My prayers were answered.

Things were strange with Nigel at this time. He was acting very peculiarly. He was going through stages of overwhelming affection towards me, then other times shying away. This made me feel very insecure. Our relationship problems escalated. He was working late and still regularly driving an hour into Sydney to attend endless meetings.

Eventually I became aware that Nigel was having affair. This news sent me plummeting further into depression. Within three weeks, I'd lost almost a stone in weight and I was having trouble eating and sleeping. My health was suffering terribly.

The Best I Can Be

I was in a miserable state. I couldn't believe what Nigel had done. I didn't know who this man I had married was any more. Our relationship had always been based on honesty and trust, but he'd shattered that. I wallowed in my anger for days. When I began to calm down I realised despite what had happened I loved Nigel and I didn't want to lose him. We sat down and talked it out, realising we both wanted to save our marriage.

Nigel's affair had shocked me into action and, ironically, it broke me out of the depression that had plagued me for so long. I knew I had to pick myself up, dust myself off and join the real world again or I'd lose everything. I wanted to be happy. I knew I had to make major changes in my life to do so.

I stopped playing sad songs on the stereo. I turned Rikki Lake and Phil Donohue off and I started thinking happy thoughts. If I was feeling down, I would take myself shopping and buy a little treat to remind myself that I was a good and special person. When I felt sorry for myself, I tried to look at the good points in my life. I still had a pretty face. My body was a bit battered and bruised, but it was intact. I was alive, and that in itself was a miracle. I had been spared for a reason and I'd been given a second chance at life, so I decided to live it.

March, 1993: I couldn't believe Easter was coming around again. I always knew because that's when we began preparing for the National Aerobatic Championships. Nigel had just taken possession of his brand new aerobatic aeroplane, Russian Sukhoi he'd decided to buy. It had arrived from

Moscow a month before the competition began.

There was quite a crowd of us who travelled to Luskintyre in the Hunter Valley for a ten-day training camp in practice for the Nationals that would be held straight after. Luskintyre is a privately owned airfield, where a group of enthusiasts had bought shares in the property to keep the old flying days alive. Sometimes known as the home of Tiger Moth, it is tucked away amongst the wineries.

I had taken a chair inside the hangar trying to stay out of the stifling heat as the sun beat down unrelentingly, and an army of flies attacked in endless raids. I took off my shoes and calipers to try to cool down my body, relaxing while watching as one after another pilot and machine went through their choreographed routines in the sky.

A very distinguished gentleman came and took a seat next to me. He was casually dressed in shorts and a sports shirt. I recognised him as Kevin Weldon, one of the owners of Luskintyre whom I'd met briefly some years earlier at a fly-in. I didn't expect he'd remember me so I politely introduced myself. After the initial small talk Kevin asked, 'What did you do to your legs?' I explained how I'd broken my back in a plane crash and that it was the resulting paralysis that had caused me to wear the equipment lying on the floor. Kevin was interested to hear more and he soon realised he'd heard about my crash. I felt comfortable with Kevin. We must have been talking for over an hour when Nigel returned from his practice flight.

'Hi, Nigel!' Kevin said. These two had known each other for years, since the early days when Nige was flying the Ryan around to air shows. But they hadn't been in touch since way before Nigel and I met, so Kevin hadn't realised I was Nigel's wife.

Kevin stayed at Luskintyre for the weekend and several other enthusiastic Tiger Moth pilots flew in to watch the aerobatics. There was a young girl, maybe a little older than me, doing circuits in one of the yellow bi-planes.

'Who's that?' I asked Kevin.

'That's Lace Maxwell. She's learning to fly. She's also a wing-walker.'

'You mean she gets up on the wing while the aeroplane is flying around?'

'Yes, isn't it amazing? Would you like to meet her?'

At the end of the day, everybody gathered for the constitutional beer in the coolness of the evening. That was when I met Lace Maxwell for the first time. We hit it off straight away. She was bright and friendly, but one of the first things I noticed about Lace was her incredible compassion. She asked me about my injuries and about my accident. The questions seemed to come naturally to her and I found myself talking comfortably about deep-seated emotions that she could understand. It wasn't until later the next day that Kevin told me she worked for Canteen, an organisation set up to support teenage victims of cancer. I knew then that personal tragedy was no stranger to her.

I was sitting on the grass in the shade of a tree watching Nigel fly through his aerobatic sequence. He was finding it difficult to master his new aeroplane. It was so different to anything else he'd flown and I thought it was very brave of him to be flying it in the national competition with such little time to practise.

Lace came over and sat with me. 'Tell me about your wing-walking,' I asked.

Her face lit up as she told me how she'd met a pilot named Bob Copaz and together they'd made plans to put a frame on the top of a Tiger Moth to do wing-walking displays at air shows and other public events. She told me how she would climb onto the top wing and brace herself against the frame, then Bob would take off flying around the sky.

'What's it like up there?' I asked.

'It's just like being a bird. The sky and the clouds are so close, you can almost touch them,' she said.

'I would love to do that one day!'

'We're having a Canteen camp here in a few months. The kids get to go for joy flights and we put on an air show at the end. You should come up and watch.'

Nigel didn't place at the Nationals that year, but I was very proud of his effort in the new plane. Allan had spoken many times to us about one day owning a Sukhoi. 'It's the ultimate machine,' he used to say. We had made this dream a reality, for Allan as well as for ourselves. He would have been proud of you too, Nige.

A few months later, Lace called me at home and asked if we were still coming up for the air show. It fell on the weekend of Dad's sixtieth birthday and the family had planned to celebrate at a dinner on Saturday night. I assured her we'd come up for the day. Nigel and I borrowed a friend's aeroplane, an Extra 300, which was also a top-of-the-line aerobatic aircraft, except that it had two seats, unlike the Sukhoi that had only one. As we flew towards Luskintyre, we could see all the kids out on the grass. Nigel flew over the top and pulled up into a vertical roll and then he dived straight down towards the earth before joining the circuit and landing. He is a showman through and through.

Lace was standing beside the wing before we had time to shut down. She was excited to see us and she greeted us both with the biggest hug. Some of the kids were up flying. There were four Tigers up constantly so they would all have a turn. The flights were donated by the Luskintigers, an enthusiastic group of pilots who often gave their time to help Canteen. There were about twenty kids at the camp in varying degrees of health. Many were suffering the obvious effects of chemotherapy.

I will never forget meeting Brett for the first time. He'd rushed over to the aeroplane and was such a gusher, saying how fantastic our arrival had been and how fantastic the aeroplane was. He just loved everything.

'Come on, I'll take you for a fly,' Nigel said. Brett was over the moon with excitement, but Lace slipped into her protective mother role and made Nigel assure her that it'd be a gentle flight with no aerobatics because of Brett's health problems.

'We'll be right!' They bounded off and were strapped into the aeroplane. Lace and I walked back to the group sitting around on the grass. They all welcomed me with hugs and kisses. I don't know if it was because of my obvious disability, but these new friends adopted me instantly.

Nigel and Brett taxied down the grass strip and flew off way into the distance. The Extra has a distinct sound and I could hear its pitch varying so I knew Nigel was up to something. So did Lace as we strained to see where they were.

'There!' I pointed to a large billowy group of clouds. Every now and then you could see the boys pop out between valleys and turn and fly back in. I remembered my first time playing in the clouds and how magical the experience was. I wondered if Brett's soul was singing too.

One of the aeroplanes taxied past us to fill up with fuel. It was the one with the wing-walking apparatus on top.

'That's it?' I said to Lace.

The frame stood right on the very top of the wing and was just over a metre high.

'I can't wait to see you do it!'

'Well, you won't because you are going to do the wing-walk today,' she said.

I laughed. 'Very funny!'

'No, I'm serious, it has all been taken care of.'

The pilot came over to us at that moment.

'Hi, you must be Allana, I'm Bob Copaz. I hear you're going to be my wing-walker today.'

It was true, they weren't kidding. I turned to Lace with a shocked look on my face.

'You did say you would love to try it one day, so here's your chance,' she said.

A mass of thoughts rushed through my head. I don't think I was serious when I said that. I could get hurt. It is still difficult for me overcoming the fear of flying without standing on top of an aeroplane in the open air.

Some of the kids sitting with us had heard the conversation and began overflowing with enthusiasm.

'Allana's going to do the wing-walk, Allana's going to do the wing-walk,' they kept calling to me.

Nigel and Brett had landed by this stage and, hearing the commotion, they strode over towards us. Nigel stood over me, silhouetted by the sun. 'You're not serious are you?'

'I think I am.'

'Your parents are going to kill me!'

The air show was planned for later in the afternoon but it would still give us time to fly back to Camden and make it to Dad's party. The hours ticked by, giving me time to contemplate my fate. The idea of doing the wing-walk was terrifying. I really wanted to do it, but my fear had a tight grip on me, making me wonder what could go wrong. I looked at the sea of little faces, some of which were so pale and sick. Two little girls were engrossed in conversation discussing how they both wanted to be wing-walkers one day. My hugs and kisses from the kids continued. They were all a-buzz waiting for the air show that would begin with my flight.

Allana before the accident had been fearless. She would have been jumping out of her skin to climb on top of that aeroplane. I wished *that* Allana could be here now.

I have to do this, I thought. I can't let these children down. But most importantly, I can't let myself down. The inner battle continued as I realised this was the start of the fight back to becoming the person I had once been. And it was a fight I was determined to win. If I was to stop doing things I wanted to do because of the fear of getting hurt, I might as well dig my grave right now because that's not what living is about.

Nigel came up to me while I was sitting alone in the sun.

'You don't have to do this you know.'

'Yes I do,' I said.

Bob and I ran through all the safety issues. He showed me the hand signals he and Lace used to communicate during the flight. He told me that if there was a problem with the aeroplane, I was to crouch down below the height of the frame. It would protect me if we had to make an emergency landing or, heaven forbid, flip over. Lace helped me into the harness that had to be attached to the frame in case I slipped or fell. The harness was adapted parachute equipment that I had to step into. Straps supported me around my crutch and continued up over my shoulders.

With the help of an army of strong men, I was lifted into place high up on the wing. It was a long way down to all the faces peering up at me, and we were still on the ground.

Nigel called out from the crowd, 'You are crazy, Allana Arnot!'

'I know it,' I called back.

Bob had settled himself into the pilot's seat and started the engine. Nigel couldn't watch. He walked into the hangar with our good friend Phil Unicomb.

What on earth was I doing up here? My heart was pounding as we taxied to the end of the strip. I could see our shadow outlined on the ground. I waved my arms and watched my shadow waving back. Bob pushed the throttle forward. A surge of power threw me back hard against the metal tubing.

I could feel the rough ground reverberating through the old machine beneath me as we continued to accelerate and float into the smoothness of the fresh country air.

'YES! YES! YIPPEE! YAHOO!'

I couldn't contain my exuberance and I continued to scream out in a defiant celebration.

'I'M DOING IT. I CAN'T BELIEVE I'M DOING IT!'

Adrenaline pumped quickly through every part of my body. It was a familiar old feeling and one I hadn't felt for a long time.

The valley was picture perfect and the sky was as blue as I'd ever known it. I stretched my arms out like a bird and felt the wind rushing past. I closed my eyes and tilted my head back, then opened them up again. All I could see were white patchy clouds painted against the endless sky. I was unaware of the wings beneath me.

'Look, Mum, look, Dad, I'm flying, I'm really flying.'

I started laughing hysterically. I felt on top of the world. It was just as Lace had said. I was up so high, on top of the wing towards the very front of the aeroplane, so that the propeller was just in front and below me. It was spinning around so quickly, I couldn't see it. If I looked straight ahead, my peripheral vision couldn't see the bright yellow Tiger Moth at all. I was a bird and I was flying alone. The sensation was pure ecstasy and the experience was completely spiritual. I was climbing higher and higher towards the heavens, now about five hundred feet up in the open air.

I looked around and saw another Tiger Moth formatting on us. A friend, Allan Coulthard, was in the passenger seat taking photographs. I waved to him.

'Look at me, Allan!' I screamed. I knew he couldn't hear me but I felt so triumphant that I wanted to share it with everybody.

Bob turned the aircraft around and descended, flying us low down the strip where all my new friends were waving madly. I could see Nigel standing in the doorway to the hangar with his arms crossed. I waved to them all feverishly, then gripped both hands back onto the cold frame as Bob climbed up a few hundred feet and began another slow turn to run down the strip in the opposite direction.

The outline of the biplane, shadowed against the grass runway, looked weird with my body poking up on the wing. As I watched it, the Tiger Moth, represented on the ground flying beside us, suddenly began to leave a trail. My heart jumped and I looked behind me to see smoke billowing from the back of the aircraft. I looked down where I could see Bob's face and gave him the thumbs-up sign, which he returned. The smoke was all part of the show and Bob had forgotten to warn me about it. I realised that's what it was when Bob confirmed operations were normal.

We had been in the air for fifteen minutes before we joined the circuit and came in to land, rumbling to a stop just near the crowd of spectators. Everybody cheered. Nigel was walking back from the hangar, shaking his head in disbelief as much as relief that I was safely back on the ground. Lace and Bob embraced me when I crawled down off the aeroplane. I thanked them so much for making my dream come true. I had conquered my fear and the old me was on the way back. I celebrated with the group for a while and watched more of the air show, but it was getting late and we had to get back for Dad's birthday party.

Nigel and I arrived at Camden at last light. I was still intoxicated by the adrenaline and I had had a permanent toothy grin plastered across my face for so much of the way back that it had made my cheeks ache. We arrived at the restaurant a little late but nobody had ordered their meals yet. Mum noticed my exuberant expression as I wished Dad happy birthday.

'What's with the grin?' she asked.

'Guess what I did today.'

'Oh no, we haven't heard that question for a long time.'

I had Dad's attention also as Nigel decided to slink away a few steps.

'I was a wing-walker at an air show today!'

'You what!' she cried out. Isn't it funny how some things change but some things stay the same. How did I know she was going to say that! 'Do you mean a wing-walker who stands out on the wing of an aeroplane?'

'Sort of, I was standing on the top wing of a Tiger Moth while it flew around the sky.'

Mum and Dad were not impressed. They had become very protective of me since the accident and who could blame them. They didn't really like it when I went flying these days. They had been through so much as a result of my accident. And I knew it. But this was who I was. Dad would have been happy to see me take up floristry or pottery or anything to keep me on the ground. But I yearned for adventure, and they understood that.

Chapter 11

Tragedy Again

We kept in touch with our friend Kevin Weldon during the rest of the year, although he was busy learning how to fly his new helicopter, an AS350 Squirrel. And Lace and I became great friends. I saw her at Luskintyre and sometimes while she was completing her flying lessons. And one weekend we went to Queensland with friends on an impromptu trip, where a group of us ended up sitting on the beach at Coolangatta at night talking and telling stories way into the early hours.

Kevin rang me out of the blue in January, 1994.

'I'm going to fly my helicopter right around Australia. Do you and Nigel want to come on the leg from Cape York to Darwin?' he asked. What an opportunity!

'Of course. We'd love to.'

Kevin gave me his schedule. We'd have to be at Horn Island, at Cape York Peninsula, the topmost tip of Australia, a week after Nigel competed at the National Aerobatic

Championships at Griffith over Easter. It was perfect!

I had only flown in a helicopter twice, first when I was taken from the crash site, and later in a Jetranger owned by Pat Soars of Australian Native Landscapes. Pat had kindly taken me for a fly when he visited Camden Airport one day. It was an amazing feeling. The helicopter was so versatile and responsive. Pat let me fly it by myself and since then, helicopters had held a fascination for me. It had made me think about learning to fly one myself one day.

I tracked on a map of Australia where we would be flying on our trip. It was coastal from the tip of Australia through the gulf country and up and over to Darwin, taking two weeks to complete the journey. Some of the areas would be remote, but I was open-minded about our safari through the Top End. On our way to the airport to catch the flight to Horn Island, Lace rang to remind me that the air show weekend at Luskintyre for Canteen would be on again in twelve days.

'Are you still coming?' she asked. I hadn't forgotten but I hadn't realised it was so close. I explained to Lace that we were going to be away for two weeks, but we'd be there if we could make it back in time.

'There's someone here who wants to talk to you,' Lace said.

'Hullo, lovely lady!' It was Brett. 'You are coming to the flying weekend, aren't you?' I assured Brett that we'd do our best to be there.

Horn Island was hot and humid. Kevin's friend, Paul Newlands, had flown the helicopter over from the mainland to pick us up and take us to Pajinka Wilderness Lodge, located on the very tip of Australia on the point of the peninsula. The resort was tucked away beneath a canopy of trees. It wasn't until we were directly overhead that you could see the little cabins. The flight didn't take much more than five minutes, but we had to wear our life jackets because it was mainly over water. Paul landed on the helipad which was a flat area at the top of a cliff near Pajinka. Although the landing site was covered lightly with grass, much of the surrounding area was nothing but barren rock leading all the way into the calm waters. Looking out towards the north were other small rocky islands leading to an infinite blanket of sparkling blue. Andrew, the manager of the lodge, was waiting for us with a 4WD to take us to the pool area where Kevin was sipping a refreshing fruit cocktail with friends who'd flown up from Coolangatta with him. It was great to catch up with Kevin. He'd been so busy with his flying that we hadn't seen him for months and months.

Andrew showed us to our cabin which was located at the end of a narrow path, flanked by thick, overhanging tropical vegetation. The open-style cabin was basic but clean and comfortable with breezy windows covered with fly screens and louvres. I noticed two little skink lizards on a wall. They were obviously going to share our room.

Before long, we were relaxing in the crystal blue pool. Paul was there too. I hadn't met him before today. He explained he was a crewman for Westpac Rescue Helicopters at Prince Henry Hospital and he knew all about my story. That night we had a feast of seafood.

'Is there anything you particularly want to see during this trip, Allana?' Kevin asked.

'Not really. But I would like to buy a traditional Aboriginal bark painting.'

Andrew piped up and told us to try to find a man called Dick Yambal. He was a well known artist from Ramingining, he said, which was located right in the heart of Arnhem Land. Apparently he didn't paint a lot any more, but Andrew assured us he was the best artist in the Top End. He gave us the phone number for the Community Council in Ramingining. Arnhem Land, the Aboriginal land east of Darwin, starts at the top western end of the Gulf of Carpentaria. For us to land at any site in this region, we had to gain permission from the relevant Community Council for that area. It's like landing in someone's backyard without asking. You don't!

The next day Kevin took Nigel and I flying to Somerset on the coast a few miles south-east of Pajinka. The landing spot was very tight and I was amazed how easily Kevin popped the chopper down snugly amongst the trees. Nigel and I were a bit anxious at first watching Kevin guide us, hopeful not to hit any of the many surrounding bushes. There were towering palm trees as well and some were simply long trunks with no foliage at the top. This was our first taste of how functional helicopters can be.

'Someone's flown a helicopter in here before us and chopped off some off the palm trees trying to get in,' I said to Kevin.

He laughed and replied, 'It's quite possible.'

After lunch Paul flew us to Thursday and Friday Islands, a few minutes north-west by air and he let me have a fly along the way.

Early the next morning, Kevin, Nigel and I left the group, who would be flying home commercially, and we headed for Weipa. On the western side of Cape York Peninsula, south of Pajinka, it is a one and a half hour flight.

I was sitting in the back seat of the helicopter and even there the visibility was perfect. We saw huge sharks, crocodiles, manta rays and schools of fish. I'd only ever viewed these in public aquariums. To see them in their natural habitat, in their vast ocean home, was quite spectacular.

On the beach north of Weipa, Nigel spotted the wreckage of two aircraft. Kevin hooked the helicopter around and landed on the sand for a closer look. They turned out to be World War II Thunderbolts that had been forced down en route to Papua New Guinea in 1944. It was a very sad sight. As you could imagine, after fifty years there wasn't much left of them. The wings and the cylinders of their radial engines were identifiable. But trees and palms had grown amongst the skeletal remains. There are said to be many World War II aircraft wrecks in the top of Australia. Because of the remoteness of the region, new sites are still being discovered. Many have been left untouched. I don't know if it's a sign of respect or that the job of retrieving the wrecks from these remote areas would be just too difficult.

The hotel we stayed at in Weipa had its own helipad. Kevin took care of securing the helicopter for the night while Nigel and I checked in.

'What's your car registration number?' the lady at the desk asked.

'We don't have a car. But the helicopter is parked out on the pad and its registration is VH-KVN,' Nigel said.

The receptionist thought he was kidding. She'd only been working there for a short time. She didn't know the hotel had a helipad. We felt very spoilt to be arriving by helicopter.

Each day we flew up to three hours which kept us well ahead of schedule. Kevin let Nigel and I fly some of the way, but he took over when we came in to land – apart from one time when Nigel showed off his flying skills and landed the chopper like a pro. He's a natural pilot who, I'm sure, could fly anything if he had to.

When we saw a pretty spot, we'd land on the beach, boil the billy and have lunch. One day, we landed in the football oval in a place called Karumba at the base of the Gulf of Carpentaria. We walked across the road to a seafood cafe and had a feast of fresh prawns. The helicopter gave us the freedom to go anywhere and do what we liked.

I was really enjoying the small amount of flying I was doing.

'I am going to learn to fly a helicopter one day. I'll fly myself all the way around Australia,' I told Kevin.

Whenever we were able to get to a telephone, we tried calling Ramingining Community Council but we still hadn't been able to contact anyone. The phone simply rang out. We needed to gain permission before we landed. This was a very sensitive issue and we respected that. But I was determined to find Dick Yambal.

We decided to fly to Ramingining anyway and see if the artist was there. On final approach to a cleared area near the town, we were surprised to see that the whole place looked deserted. But, by the time we were on the ground, little kids began poking their heads from behind trees and up through the long grass. There were dozens of them. They stood back, inquisitive but cautious, until two elders drove up in a FWD.

'I hope the natives are friendly,' I said to Kevin. 'You go out first.'

Nigel and I watched, tentatively waiting for a sign that we were welcome.

Kevin turned around and waved us over.

'This is Yambal,' Kevin said. I couldn't believe we'd come all this way to find a man who had become something of a myth, someone who I'd begun to think didn't exist. Even if he did, I'd almost accepted the fact that we wouldn't find him in this vast land. And here was Yambal in the flesh, meeting us at the helicopter.

He took to me straight away, showing great concern and wondering why I was walking with sticks.

Yambal had come up to me and given me a hug. 'You okay? What you do to your legs?' he asked.

'I hurt my back in an accident and I'm paralysed in my legs,' I replied.

'But you get better?' he asked.

'No, I don't think so,' I replied.

Yambal's distress at my disability was flattering. He hovered around me protectively, and he held my arm as we walked along towards the helicopter.

'I can't believe I've found you. I've been trying to contact you for a week,' I told him.

'I knew you were coming. You've come because of my paintings. I heard it on the wind,' he said.

Kevin and I looked at each other with curious expressions. I still don't know what Yambal meant by that. Had someone called him on the phone and told him we were coming? Or was it something deeper, something involving the traditional sixth sense of the Australian Aborigine. None of us questioned the comment, but I like to think that his mysterious knowledge of my visit was telepathic.

Mrs Yambal and the dozens of local kids followed us to the helicopter.

'Could you fly us around our land, Kev? We haven't been out to see our banana plantation since the Wet ended,' Yambal explained.

Kevin was only too happy to oblige. He helped Yambal into the front seat and his wife sat in the back while Nigel and I stayed behind. We were used to Kevin taking people for short joy flights that usually lasted ten or fifteen minutes. After they had been gone for half an hour, we started to become concerned.

The children were very curious of everything about us. We entertained them by drawing funny pictures in the sand. It was a successful form of communication because their pidgin English was impossible for us to understand.

We kept an eye on the time, and after an hour and still no Kevin, we were convinced something was seriously wrong. Since we hadn't been able to contact Ramingining by telephone over the past week, we assumed there probably wasn't a telephone that worked in the town.

'We should walk into the town and see if there is a phone, or at least a two-way radio to try to contact Kevin, or to raise an alarm if the helicopter doesn't return within the next hour,' Nigel suggested.

We continued discussing our options, hoping and praying Kevin and his passengers would return soon.

We didn't have to wait too much longer before they came scooting over our heads and landed on the ground in front of us.

'What took you so long? We were worried. Where did you go?' we asked Kevin.

'Sorry about that. I knew you'd be concerned. We'd only flown a couple of kilometres from here into a swamp area where a flock of geese flew into the air,' Kevin explained. 'Yambal became very excited and he asked me to land so he and his wife could collect geese eggs which are quite a delicacy. When I explained I couldn't land on the marshy ground, Yambal went to open the helicopter door saying, "I'll jump out from here then." Mrs Yambal prepared to do the same thing. They gave me such a fright. I told them both to stay inside while I landed on dry land on the outskirts of the swamp.

'They went walkabout for kilometres and kilometres across a dense marshy plain. They walked so far that I lost sight of them. All I could do was sit and wait for them to come back.

'I knew you'd both be getting worried, but there was nothing I could do.'

Yambal and his wife, safely home, seemed unaware of our concern for their delay. They were being swamped by the children who had spotted the eggs. Their eyes lit up as if the full plastic bag Mrs Yambal carried contained bright shiny Easter eggs, or was bulging with lollies.

Although Yambal didn't have any paintings to show me during our visit to Ramingining, he agreed to paint me a special bark painting and also make me a didgeridoo. He honoured his promise. Over the following months, he'd call me on the phone to give me an update on his progress.

'I went into the bush today and found a perfect tree. I cut the bark and it's drying in the sun,' he first told me.

'The bark is ready and I've made the brushes,' he said next.

Yambal told me the first paints he had made were red from the earth. I felt pretty special to know Yambal was putting so much care and so much of himself into his piece of art, and I was living its creation step by step.

When finally it arrived later in the year, I was flabbergasted. We'd had the chance to view many Aboriginal bark paintings during our adventures in the Top End. But when I saw Yambal's painting, I realised he truly was the master. The pictures on the painting were of a didgeridoo and water birds. Yambal painted for Kevin as well, telling a story of gathering geese eggs, which seemed very appropriate.

It took us ten days to reach Darwin and the experience opened up a new world for me. Kevin's enthusiasm for life was infectious and his generosity in allowing us to join his adventure had given me the motivation to continue reaching for my own dreams.

Kevin included Nigel and me in other unusual trips, including sailing an old boat around Holland in 1993. That time, we met Kevin at a Tiger Moth fly-in at Woburn Abbey in England. The small air show had lasted three days, then

Kevin arranged for us to fly to Amsterdam where the boat was waiting for us. We spent four days discovering the waterways and negotiating through locks and narrow canals.

We had a husband and wife team who crewed the old two-masted ship, the *Avanti*, although the nine guests on board had been encouraged to help. Many times we'd dock in a little cobblestoned village to wander and look around the shops.

To disembark meant walking across a narrow plank which made for some anxious moments. When it came to my turn, Kevin would stand to one side, encouraging me.

'You can do it, Allana,' he'd say. In all situations, Kevin would allow me to cultivate my own potential. He would include me, but he wouldn't make allowances for my disability. To Kevin, I was just like everybody else. He helped me realise that life was to be lived, and there were no limitations to what I could do. His friendship means the world to me and I love him dearly for it.

It was late Friday night when Nigel and I flew into Sydney from Darwin. We were exhausted, but we were determined to make it to Luskintyre for the Canteen air show starting on Saturday. We couldn't get a two-seater aeroplane to fly, so Nigel took the Sukhoi and I drove up with Deidre, one of my closest friends. We arrived late in the afternoon to the warmest welcome from Lace and Brett. There were new faces in the group of teenagers, and others I remembered from last year.

On Sunday morning, the Tiger Moths were up flying again. The day was perfect and the backdrop of the Hunter

Valley wineries made the atmosphere warm and friendly. It impressed me how the young people from Canteen gave support to each other. The bond between them and the dignified manner in which they coped with their illness was extraordinary. The teenagers were encouraged to write down their feelings and express their emotions. Many had become budding poets, especially Brett. With his dry sense of humour, he was able to make light of the hospital routines and ongoing medical problems in witty little rhymes. I had seen him, earlier in the year, featuring on a special ABC-TV program, hosted by Andrew Denton. The cameras had caught Brett in full flight, standing around a camp fire delivering one of his favourite poems.

The families of these teenage kids with cancer were also encouraged to join in the Luskintyre weekends. After lunch, we gathered in the large living area of the guest house. First, the director of Canteen thanked the Luskintigers for making the weekend possible, and she presented them with a plaque that today is still proudly displayed on the wall. A young girl at the camp had lost her brother to cancer during the year. She had written a poem in his memory and she shared it with us. Lace was standing with her as support while she read the words, and everybody in the room shed a tear or two. As she continued, her emotions began to choke her so Lace stepped in, placing a comforting hand on her shoulder, and they read the last part of the poem together.

I remember leaving Luskintyre that day.

'Are you going to do the wing-walk?' some of the kids had asked as we filed outside for the remainder of the air show.

Me wing-walking.

Flying Kevin's helicopter to Friday Island.

Mrs Yambal and her geese eggs.

Ramingining. Yambal is standing next to me. He's the one wearing the hat.

Above: Learning to hover. Steve Dines shows me how it's done while I follow on the controls.
Below: The day ELF arrived. I couldn't wait to fly her.

Above left: The island of seals, just out of Albany.
Above right: Harry, with Jane in the side cart, leading their four-helicopter escort.
Below: The shearing shed that Harry took us to for a true outback breakfast.

Right: There were many beautiful waterfalls in the Kimberleys.
Below: Discovering the Arafura Swamp and its magical contrasting colours.

Above: Spectacular cliffs as we fly towards the Twelve Apostles.
Below: Taking a break for lunch after a morning's fishing; Jamie, Greg, Grant, Jim and me.

Above: Camping out just north of Derby.
Below: It took six weeks and four days but I made it around the whole country and back into Prince Henry hospital.

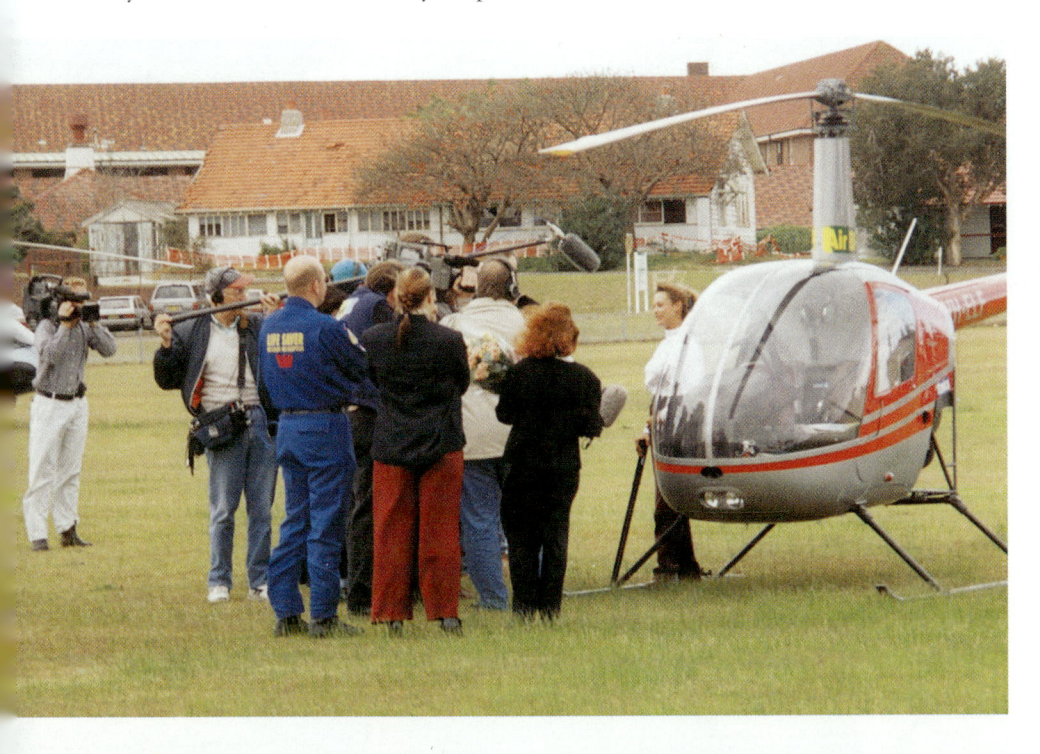

Above: Me and my rainbow.
Below: At my parent's place, writing this book.

'Not this year,' I said. Lace was standing nearby. 'Deidre and I have to get back to Sydney,' I told her. She thanked me for coming and we planned to get together again soon. She hugged me before running off to get ready for the wing-walk. Nigel had already left for the thirty-minute flight back to Camden. As Deidre and I drove out of the driveway, Phil Unicomb was doing his Dame Nellie Melba crazy-flying routine.

Lace waved goodbye and we headed down the dusty road. After thirty minutes, we had made it to the freeway and were discussing how strong Lace was and how incredibly emotional the day had been.

My mobile phone was ringing. When I answered it, there was a distraught voice on the other end, blurting out words that didn't make any sense. It was Phil Unicomb's girlfriend, Rebecca. She was saying something about an accident, something about Lace.

'Calm down, Bec. Tell me what's happened.'

'There has been an accident. The Tiger Moth has crashed, and I think they're dead.' Rebecca was hysterical and I didn't know if I was hearing the words correctly. 'I've go to go,' she said.

'What's happened?' Deirdre asked.

'There's been some sort of accident. I think it might be Lace.'

We were still on the freeway and I didn't have any of the phone numbers for Luskintyre with me. So I rang Nigel who had just landed at Camden. I told him about the fragmented message I had received. He said he'd try to find out what was going on and ring me back.

The next ten minutes seemed like hours. Deirdre and I were assuring each other that I must have misheard the message. It couldn't be Lace.

The sound of the phone cut through the air like a knife. Not knowing was somehow comforting. I answered it and, as soon as I heard the tone in Nigel's voice, I knew the news wasn't going to be good.

'Tell me what's going on, Nige.'

'Lace has been killed,' he told me. 'The aeroplane crashed while she was doing the wing-walk display. Bob has been taken to hospital, but he has been burnt from head to toe.'

I couldn't feel. I couldn't cry. I couldn't believe it was true. Lace was an angel on earth. She flew with her golden wings and brought nothing but good to the world. She couldn't be gone. Somebody had got it wrong.

It was just before 6 p.m. when we got home. Deidre had left, and Nigel and I tried to make sense of another tragedy. I fully expected Lace to ring me at any moment to say there had been a mistake, that she was okay. The television in our bedroom was on and we could hear the start of the National Nine News. We went in to see the headlines. I watched as my beautiful friend was shown on video, laughing and waving from on top of the aeroplane. Then it suddenly dropped a wing and headed straight for the ground. I saw Lace duck down beneath the height of the frame just as she was meant to do in an emergency. Then the plane crashed into the ground nose first. It burst into a ball of flame, and Lace was gone forever. Bob had survived and he'd run into the flames to save her. His burns eventually took his life too. I stood in the bedroom, frozen in time. I broke down, sobbing into Nigel's arms as he tried in vain to comfort me. Death was no stranger to me. But it would always hurt.

I cried so much in the period leading up to Lace's funeral that when the day arrived I had no more tears left. The church was full. Lace's sister, Amanda Porter, delivered a beautiful eulogy. She talked about Lace's life as an intricate tapestry and how, since her death, so many parts of the tapestry had been completed for her family. I think the many tributes to Lace from her friends meant that the family knew her even better now.

Lace was an avid writer. She wrote the following poem as a celebration of her love of flying.

Two Moons and Tapestry

> May my joy be yours to hold
> for because of you my wings unfold
> To explore a world of fantasy
> where two moons glide with clarity
> Onyx lake and sapphire sea.
> Where patchwork fields of tapestry
> are harrowed by harrowed men . . .
> Past whom the silent rivers wend
> painting paths for me to trace
> Safe within my sky's embrace
> because your love makes dreams come true
> I wish my wings to be yours too.

Lace had made my dream come true. She had shared her wings with me, she had taken my hand and helped me find direction in my life. I used to say she was an angel on earth. Now I believe she is a real angel with golden wings.

At the end of the funeral service, the group from Canteen let go a multitude of coloured balloons into the air. It was their way of saying goodbye. I watched the colours dance around in the wind and drift up into the sky out of sight.

A month later, Nigel and I were driving home from Sydney on the same freeway. I was thinking about Lace and some of the funny things we had done together. My pain was starting to ease by then and I was at peace with her memory.

Directly in front of us was a single wispy cloud sitting alone against a brilliant blue sky. The sun filtered through its misty hue and it developed into a rainbow of luminous prismatic colours.

'Look at that, Nigel'

'It doesn't look real, does it!' he said.

'I was just thinking about Lace. I wonder if that's her watching over us.'

I like to think so.

A few months after the funeral, I visited a helicopter flying school at Hoxton Park, a small airfield west of Sydney not far from Bankstown Airport. I wanted to learn to fly helicopters and I needed to know if my legs were going to restrict me in any way. I wouldn't know if I didn't try.

Although Kevin had let me have a fly of his helicopter, he had been in control of the tail rotor pedals that are operated by your feet.

I had contacted Chris Townsend and his wife, Elena, who owned and ran the school, Townsend Helicopters. I'd explained to Chris, who would be my instructor, that I didn't have a lot of feeling or movement in my legs, due to a spinal injury. He was encouraging and he asked me to come in and take a trial instructional flight.

The helicopter was a Robinson R22. It was so tiny it looked like a toy. It had only two seats and was quite cramped in the cabin. Where's the remote control, I wondered. Kevin's helicopter could seat up to seven people but this looked like a little bubble.

Chris and I sat in the cabin while he explained the instruments. Most of them were similar to those in the aeroplanes I had flown in the past. He then took me through the controls.

The cyclic was a pole extending up from the centre just in front of the instrument panel. It had a boom handle extending in both directions that allowed either of us to operate it at any time. This control determined the direction of flight. All I had to do was point the cyclic in the direction I wanted to go. Easy! The tail rotor pedals on the floor controlled the yaw, and the collective that sat beside my seat at my left hand made the helicopter go up and down. Pull it up to go up. Push it down to go down. The collective had a twist-grip handle. This was the throttle.

It seemed to be getting very complicated, but Chris assured me it was merely a matter of coordination. 'Like patting your head and rubbing your tummy at the same time,' he said. I never could do that!

Everything was set for the flight. Chris turned the key and she fired up straight away. He engaged the clutch, which after a few seconds began to rotate the blades. The helicopter started making horrible grinding and crunching noises before the blades began spinning around so quickly you couldn't see them.

'That sounded awful,' I said to Chris. He promised me it was normal for those noises to occur. It was just the clutch belts kicking in.

'Are you set?' Chris asked.

'Let's go for it!' I said.

We lifted into a hover. The Robinson didn't seem as stable as Kevin's larger Squirrel but it was nippy and very responsive. Chris followed the taxiway to a grass area adjacent to the main runway and again established us into a hover.

'Ready?' he asked.

'Ready!' I responded.

He tipped the nose down and we ran along beside the runway about five feet off the ground. He held the helicopter down, picking up speed. The visibility was greater than Kevin's helicopter. I could see the ground rushing along beneath my feet. It was exhilarating.

There was a huge tree coming up and we were heading straight for it. I wondered what Chris was doing, but just in time he eased back on the cyclic, popping us up over the canopy, and we climbed into the clear skies above.

'It's all yours, Allana.'

I took hold of the controls and manoeuvred around. Chris watched my feet and legs intensely, analysing my control inputs on the tail rotor pedals.

'You won't have any trouble learning to fly helicopters. Your injuries shouldn't restrict you at all,' he confirmed. I was elated. Our flight came to an end far too quickly. Our half hour felt like five minutes. I could have stayed up there all day.

Back in the office, I explained to Chris that I couldn't afford regular flying lessons yet. I intended to do the ground studies and sit the necessary exams, hoping to start my lessons next year. Elena helped me pile the stack of text books I'd need into my car. I was so motivated after my flight that I started studying that afternoon.

A few weeks later, Chris rang to see how I was going. He told me he would be running a ground school for a couple of his other students and asked if I wanted to join. The course ran for two weeks. There were only three of us in the class: a young man who eventually decided learning to fly helicopters was too much hard work, and a woman named Anne. She had begun flying and was learning in a Jetranger, a five-seat turbine helicopter. I was very jealous. Anne and I became friends. It's not often you find other women flying helicopters. So I valued that friendship greatly.

The Basic Aeronautical Knowledge course covered many subjects including meteorology, aerodynamics, engines and systems, flight rules, and a small amount of navigation. Study was a bit of a shock to the system. I had only stayed at school until Year Ten, leaving at the age of fifteen. And here I was, at twenty-seven, having to grasp the concepts of physics, a subject I had never taken at school.

One afternoon we heard the sound of a helicopter coming in to land outside Chris's hangar. It wasn't the usual sound of a Robinson. This had to be a very big helicopter. Elena came into the study room and told us it was the ABC's Squirrel. The pilot knew Chris and Elena. He introduced himself to us as Gary Ticehurst.

'You don't remember me, do you?' Gary asked.

I was a bit embarrassed and racked my brain trying to recall where I'd met Gary before.

'I'm sorry, but I don't,' I answered.

'I was at the accident site in the Burragorang Valley. I was there when you were pulled out of the aeroplane wreckage.'

Gary and I had an instant bond. It was something I felt with everyone who had been there that day.

'You're learning to fly helicopters?' he asked.

'I hope to next year, but at the moment I'm getting the study out of the way.'

Gary took me for a fly that afternoon. His helicopter was a lot different from Kevin's. We had a chance to talk about the day of the accident and I asked Gary if one day he'd take me back out to the crash site.

'Whenever you're ready, I'll take you,' he said.

At the end of the course, I sat my first exam – Basic Aeronautical Knowledge – which I passed with flying colours. This gave me a good grounding to work towards my next exam, which would be for my commercial licence. I engrossed myself in study every day. It provided distraction from the stress I was feeling about my legal compensation case now that it was about to go to trial.

The commercial subjects were a lot more involved and the level of study required was immensely greater than that needed to pass Basic Aeronautical Knowledge. I was weaving my way through a pile of text books. Sometimes the technical jargon or aerodynamic theories or mathematical equations and algorithms were so far over my head, I'd be looking down reading a page that seemed full of mumbled-jumbled words and numbers. Then I'd have to close the book and take a break for an hour. There were a few times I went over the same topics more than a dozen times before they sank in. I'd never considered myself to have a great intellect. But through sheer perseverance, I progressed, even to my own surprise. Sometimes I would think of how I used to do anything to avoid school work when I was a child. But this was different. Now I wanted to learn, and I was working towards achieving something that was very important to me.

The commercial exam lasted six hours and covered many subjects. The first two hours were on flight rules and procedures, the next three hours navigation, meteorology and air legislation, then the last hour was a general knowledge test which included aviation medicine, human performance, aerodynamics and so on. By the end I was exhausted. Although I managed to finish, I felt a bit apprehensive about the result.

A week went by while I waited for my score to arrive in the mail. The pass mark was seventy-five per cent. I couldn't stand the waiting and decided to ring the examinations section of the Department of Aviation. One of the markers answered my call. I managed to sweet talk him into giving me my result – seventy-four per cent, he said.

I couldn't believe it. I had failed by one point. He told me they'd consider a request to review my exam and I would probably be granted a pass. But I didn't want to cheat myself out of a real pass. So I went back to my studies and sat the exam again. The result – eighty-eight per cent.

Chapter 12

Taking on Goliath

Only weeks after my accident Sergeant Helen Curtain, the police officer who was at the crash site, had visited me in hospital to take my statement for a coronial inquest. After that, I asked Nigel to help me find a good solicitor. I felt that I needed to be represented in the Coroner's Court. I also knew I would have to consider my future and that there would be compensation cases to face.

Tom Goudkamp was recommended by a friend of ours. He came to see me straight away. It was only two weeks after the accident and I was still groggy from the painkillers. At my bedside, Tom recorded my account of the day. He also interviewed Nigel and my parents. He was a very compassionate man and we felt confident that my case was in the best hands. Six months later, Tom visited Nigel and I at home to prepare me for the inquest.

Wheeling into the lobby of the Coroner's Court, I noticed Steve Johnson, who had been the first man on the scene of the crash. Steve was sitting alone on a bench. I went over for a chat and I was pleased to have the chance to thank him for helping save my life. There were several more of my rescuers there and they greeted me as well. I couldn't remember all of them, but I made sure to thank everyone who was involved in my rescue. It was to be a very emotional day.

Steven Doggert was at the court with his parents. He had lost an enormous amount of weight as a direct result of his injuries. He was a shadow of the strapping young bloke who'd climbed into VH-PLD with me six months earlier.

Mr and Mrs Watson, Janine's parents, were in the lobby. As they lived in Camden, Nigel and I had seen them regularly, usually at the airport. Despite losing their daughter, Greg and Christine Watson had been incredibly supportive of me during my recovery. They had even given me a set of Janine's exercise weights to help me strengthen my arms. I must admit I was slightly uncomfortable taking such a gift from them, but appreciated it very much and I understood their need to give.

By the time everyone had arrived at the court, there was a lot of activity around me. Trying to put people and places together got a bit confusing, but I made sure to identify the families of my friends who didn't survive.

Mr and Mrs Hannah, Allan's parents, were easy to pick out. I'd met them once at Camden Airport when they'd come to see the little red bi-plane 'Oscar'. Allan was the spitting image of his dad.

Mr and Mrs Holmes, Robert's parents, were standing quietly alone, and so was Mrs Whitehurst, Peter's Mum. Mr

Whitehurst wasn't in the lobby, although I think he did attend the inquest.

For the first time, I experienced an overwhelming feeling of guilt. These people are here to find out why their loved ones died that day. Why did I survive? The chance that two people out of six could live after such an horrific disaster didn't make sense. It wasn't fair. It seemed to me that day that we all should have died, or we all should have lived. That would have been fair. I found it difficult to look at my friends' parents. Why had I been spared? I didn't know the answer to that.

During the coroner's inquiry, several people were interviewed by the police prosecutor, Sergeant Carlo Zoppo, including Steve Johnson. After lunch, the coroner, Mr Kevin Waller, asked me to take the stand and I was sworn in. My statement was read out to the court and I was cross-examined by several people. I was asked to mark on a map for the coroner the site where the plane had crashed and the general track we had been flying during the search.

It turned out that our crash site had been six kilometres outside our designated search area, 'Charlie'. I was asked if I knew why Peter and Allan had flown outside the area, but I didn't know. Each area had been allocated its own search aircraft and team of observers. I had no idea why we were in someone else's zone. I was questioned a number of times about the conversations that took place between Peter and Allan during the flight, and after the engine had begun to fail. I reminded the coroner that the aircraft wasn't equipped for headsets in the back seat, so I couldn't hear what they were saying. I was questioned about the clearing that Janine and I saw with the power wire running through it, and I was told that it hadn't been a power wire. It had been a flying fox. At the end of the questioning, I was excused and Mr Waller thanked me. He wished me well for the future.

The next morning, the Channel Nine news footage was shown to the court. Mum had come to the inquest with us that day. I didn't want her to see the tape, but she insisted. It was horrific, re-living my friends being put into body bags and hearing my own gut-wrenching screams as I was cut out of the wreckage. My pain and grief were still raw. To see those horrible scenes recorded on tape brought back a flood of emotion to me and everybody else in the room.

The mood in the room was subdued. At the end, I asked Mum if she was okay. She assured me she was.

'The tape was as I expected it to be,' she said.

I'd told Nigel in detail how horrendous the crash scene was, but even he was a little shaken by the footage. As for me, I just wanted to run away and hide. I pushed my way into the ladies' room, hoping to find brief sanctuary there, only to meet Robert Holmes' mother, who was very upset.

'Please tell me my son didn't suffer,' she said, when she saw me enter the room.

I suddenly felt responsible, as if the whole cause of the accident rested on my shoulders. I needed to be strong for Mrs Holmes. I felt her loss deeply. If only she knew. But all I could do was reassure her that Robert didn't suffer. Finally, I found a vacant cubicle and closed the door, as if shutting everyone out. I was shaking and crying, and I knew I had to regain my composure to face them all again.

The tape had shocked everyone in the courtroom. The mood in the afternoon session was one of distress, made even worse by the audio tape of Allan's radio broadcasts. I didn't blame Mr and Mrs Hannah for leaving the room before Mr Waller began the tape. But they would have been so proud of Allan's composure and his calmness during each radio update on our situation. He had been professional and efficient until the end.

The inquest into the deaths, resulting from the crash of VH-PLD, was adjourned to 23 October, 1991. The inquest had taken a total of four days to complete. The crash was due to a simple case of engine failure. Technically, it had been caused by two connecting rod bolts that failed due to fatigue crack. One of them had come loose, had punctured and then become jammed in the top of the crankcase. The oil pressure had plunged as oil sprayed onto the windscreen, until the engine had finally stopped. During the hearing, there had been a suggestion of human intervention by one expert. He tried to lay blame on the engineer who had performed the last reconditioning of the engine, saying that there was evidence he had hand-filed the bolts. This engineer burst into the courtroom, strongly denying the allegation. For a minute, it was like a scene out of a Hollywood movie.

The issue of VH-PLD flying outside its designated search area was also addressed in the coroner's finding. It had been dangerous for several reasons, one being that we might have come into conflict with the other search plane whose area it was. The reason why our pilots were not fully complying with instructions could not be determined.

The official finding was that people had died when the

aircraft in which they were travelling had suffered engine failure and crashed into wooded country.

The inquest into the crash of VH-BUO, the aeroplane we were looking for, was complicated and very controversial. In court, the case had been outlined, telling how flying instructor, Andrew Patterson, aged 19 and cadet pilot, Angeline Neal, aged 18, had gone out on a training flight at 4.40 p.m. on 21 December, 1990, in the single-engine Cessna. They had been in company with another aircraft, VH-HCE, whose occupants were Jason McLaughlin and Simon Goldschmidt.

Although informing the control tower that the purpose of the flight was for training, the four had previously agreed to make a scenic flight over the lake and to the telephone box. Jason McLaughlin, the pilot of VH-HCE, said that he had been following VH-BUO at five hundred feet when it had suddenly climbed about another one hundred feet. Jason had flown beneath BUO and lost it from sight. Jason had not attempted to contact Andrew and he'd kept flying for a minute or two. When Jason had finally tried to make radio contact with Andrew, there was no response. He'd returned to the site where he had last sighted BUO, but found nothing. He then returned to Camden and, when he'd established that BUO had not returned, he'd raised the alarm. A search had been mounted before the sun set.

Certain things didn't add up with the statements made by Jason McLaughlin and Simon Goldschmidt. One question was: Did BUO plummet from six hundred feet to hit the water in the dam? BASI inspector, Alf Tremayne, had found that BUO had not suffered an engine failure and it had impacted the water at a shallow angle of about thirty degrees. While the inquest was underway, Mr Tremayne went to the coroner with a videotape he had been given in confidence. It showed footage of planes, from the Air League camp in July, 1990, flying at a height of only fifty feet over the water near the telephone box. Andrew Patterson was one of the pilots identified on the film. The minimum height over the lake was set at five hundred feet. Separate evidence given by McLaughlin and Goldschmidt was contradictory on several points and an admission of low flying by either pilots was not forthcoming. Such an admission would have severely jeopardised their flying careers as was noted by the coroner, Mr Waller. The finding on the deaths of Andrew and Angeline was due to flying too low, flying outside their zone and misleading the tower. They simply flew too low over the water, hitting it first with the left-hand wing, then cartwheeling in.

As a result of the inquest, Kevin Waller made a recommendation that the telephone box be removed from the island which was done some weeks later.

The coronial inquest into the crash of VH-PLD left questions unanswered. Why did the engine fail? What caused the connecting bolt to crack? BASI had contacted the engine manufacturers, Teladyne Continental, only one day before the inquest was concluded. They reported that they had known of four connecting rod failures within the previous fifteen years, but none had led to a fatality.

I needed to know more. Not only for myself, but for the thousands of people flying around the world who rely on such engines.

★

The year, 1994, was supposed to see the finale in my case for compensation. With Tom Goudkhamp's help over the past two and a half years, the cause of my accident had become clearer. We had built a case against Teladyne Continental and Cessna that was set to be heard in Mobile, Alabama, in the United States in November.

In October, 1991, Coroner Kevin Waller had delivered his finding in the crash of VH-PLD. It was clearly caused by engine failure when a big end bolt had cracked due to fatigue. When the maker of the engine, Teladyne Continental, was contacted by BASI the day before the coronial inquest was completed, they were asked if they could shed any light on the cause of the big end bolt failure. A representative of Teladyne Continental informed BASI that there had been failures of these bolts in the past, but it wasn't known if they were exactly the same type and there had been no fatalities. They had, in 1985, increased the torque rating on the bolt. That would increase the clamping force and reduce the chance of failure. They had also altered the assembly to eliminate the use of a lubricant. This was also expected to reduce the chance of failure.

Mr Waller noted that if Teladyne Continental had been contacted earlier, they may have been able to assist with the inquest. He put his faith in BASI to take the necessary steps to discover just exactly what had caused the engine to fail and reduce the chances of it happening in the future.

There were many questions needing to be answered. We employed the help of an attorney, Roger Clark, in Los Angeles. He had represented an Australian in an aviation matter in the past. With Roger on our side, we began our investigations and, towards the end of 1992, it became apparent that Teladyne Continental had a case to answer. The changes to the big end bolt had been made by the manufacturer in 1985, and they had been put into practice in their factories. However, those changes had not been formally promulgated to the rest of the industry, maintaining those engines around the world.

The question of seat belt harnesses was also considered. Clearly, the single lap belt supplied by Cessna in the aircraft was inadequate. My injuries could have been greatly reduced had I been wearing a proper lap/sash belt.

The headquarters for Teladyne Continental are located in California. But unfortunately the statute of limitations for personal injury claims in that state is one year from the date of the accident. We had missed the deadline. The engine had been manufactured in Mobile, Alabama, and in this state the statute of limitations was two years. Cessna also had a factory in Alabama. We filed a suit in that state against both companies.

A second attorney was to be briefed in Mobile and Fred Killion was employed to work with us on the case. My team was expanding and, although I had the support of Nigel and the other victims of the crash, I was terrified. I was David taking on Goliath. Teladyne, one of the largest companies in America, was prepared to fight the case till the end. I was taking out more bank loans to keep the case running. We had to employ experts in many fields to supply reports. A metallurgist's report, which cost over $20,000, provided us with a manual full of information about the metal fatigue in the big end bolt.

They were very tough times, financially, for Nigel and me. Sometimes I wondered how we made it through. If I didn't win the case, we would be ruined and I'd spend the rest of my life paying off my legal bill.

For the American case, I had to subject myself to being poked and prodded by doctors again which was invasive and often distressing. I was required to re-live the whole nightmare of 22 December, 1990, over and over, to doctors and lawyers. My life was being exposed and scrutinised.

One day Nigel and I were sitting in the lounge room at home watching television. Ben was roaming in the backyard on the other side of the creek. He started barking, and he sounded more aggressive than usual. I walked out onto the decking and there was a man crouched behind a bush. He had a camera and was pointing it straight at me. Ben had bailed up the man who, when he noticed he'd been spotted, scooted away through the scrub onto the road and out of sight.

Now my privacy was being invaded. I had known my claim for compensation would be a tough fight, but I hadn't expected this. I had to keep my nerve and my strength. I had gone so far, I couldn't turn back. I had faith in Tom, Fred and Roger. They also had a lot at stake. I tried to continue life as normal, whatever normal is. I felt anxious about leaving the house though, and I kept looking behind my back wondering who was watching me. When I was at home, I would keep the blinds closed and I rarely ventured into the garden. I was becoming paranoid.

The question of how to try a case in the south of America for an accident that happened in NSW, Australia, was always going to be a difficult one to answer. The judge in Mobile ruled that he would hear the case in Alabama, but under NSW law. That meant we had to employ an Australian barrister to write a paper summarising NSW law.

My barrister in Sydney, Andrew Morrison, travelled to Mobile with Tom to brief Judge McDermott on his report. The continuing communication between Tom's office in Sydney and our attorneys in America meant that often Tom or his assistant, Patrine, would be at their desks telephoning America and sending faxes at 3 a.m. because of the time difference between the two countries. Their dedication was unprecedented in my experience.

In February, 1994, the legal representatives for Cessna and Teladyne, as well as Roger and Fred representing me, travelled to Australia to take depositions from people who had information to contribute to the case. I had spoken to my American attorneys over the telephone. Now I had the chance to meet them in Tom's office before the depositions began. Roger was just as I imagined him, in his forties and dressed in a well-tailored professional suit. Fred was an older gentleman, who spoke with a broad southern drawl. He had a friendly face and was big and cuddly. He would have made a great Santa Claus, I thought. I was pleased to have both of them on my side.

We had two rooms in Goldfields House in Sydney for the depositions to be taken, one for damages and one for liability. All my doctors, past employers, my family and friends were called in to give evidence, some describing the experience as an 'interrogation'. I felt guilty that I had to put them through this harrowing experience. Each statement had to be videotaped and taken down by a court reporter.

During my own deposition, which had been scheduled to run for an hour, the attorneys for the defendants were free to dissect my claims about my injuries and about the accident. I was prepared for an aggressive examination. But, apart from some very personal questions that made me uncomfortable, I managed to get through it without too much stress.

The last question I was asked was, 'Do you feel good with yourself, with your disability?'

I thought it was a dumb question, but I answered it anyway. 'No, not at all. I don't like being like this for one moment!'

Before Fred and Roger left to return to America, they arranged to view the wreckage of VH-PLD that had been stored in a private hangar near Camden Airport. I went along to answer any questions they might have. We met outside the building and waited for the owner to unlock the doors. I hadn't really thought much about seeing the wreckage again. I wasn't anxious or nervous. It was going to be a technical viewing for the case. That was all.

The big metal doors rumbled open and there it was. From where I was standing, I could see into the cabin and there was the back seat where I had been sitting on that fateful day. Fred and Roger went straight in and began preparing their reports. But I couldn't move.

My feet were stuck to the ground. My mind flashed back to the carnage that was around me that day. I remembered the pain, I remembered the smell, and I remembered my friends. Those images had never left me. But now, to see the aeroplane again, I was confronting my memories.

I had taught myself to re-live the event as if I were reviewing a movie I had seen, or a book I had read. This way, the characters wouldn't be real and I wouldn't have to feel the pain. But this wasn't fiction. It was real! To see PLD made it so. The metal guides that ran along the ground for the hangar doors had become a boundary to keep me away from what was real. I paced up and down the guides a few times, then I gathered what courage I had left and stepped towards what remained of PLD.

The blood-stained seat belt, which had cut into my stomach, lay intact. The roof of the cabin still revealed the havoc that had taken so many lives. I just stood and stared. Fred came over to me and said, 'I bet you wish this was all over.'

'I wish for a lot of things, Fred!' I replied.

Four months later, I was required to travel to Mobile to be examined by the two US teams of doctors, who would represent me and the defendants in court. Nigel and I would also give a further deposition each.

The city of Mobile was hot and humid. The oppressive heat was difficult for us to adjust to, having come from Australia's winter. Alabama was interesting, though. The southern accent amused us greatly and the people were very friendly. It would have been an enjoyable trip, had our purpose been a different one.

Again I had to cooperate as I was examined by psychiatrists, rehabilitation specialists, neurologists and so on. One doctor ordered a series of X-rays to be taken.

'If I have one more X-ray, I'm going to glow in the dark,' I told him. 'I've had more than sixty X-rays since the accident. They are with my attorney. Surely you can use them for your report?' I asked. He agreed.

Some of the doctors for the defendants tried to encourage me to say that I was more able-bodied than previous reports had stated. I denied this. But it made me realise the real fight hadn't even begun.

Taking my deposition in Mobile continued for hours. This time the attitude of the defendants' attorneys was aggressive. The onslaught of questions was confusing. The same questions were often asked in varying ways to try to trick me into giving the answers that the attorneys wanted to hear. During the morning session, they had focused on a hand-written note that I sent Comcare years before. Comcare had taken over my case in early 1992. They had offered me worker's compensation, because they considered me to be a Commonwealth employee on the day of the accident. The controversy in the letter stemmed from me asking Comcare to acknowledge that my claim for worker's compensation had been made with the understanding that my civil claims for damages would not be jeopardised. The defendants, Cessna and Teladyne, interpreted this as meaning I had already settled a claim for damages with the Commonwealth Government and, because of this, I would have no further claim under US law.

It was pretty exciting at lunch time as we hurriedly contacted Andrew Morrison in Australia. He was able to interpret the Australian law under which the case was being heard, assuring us that the claims by Teledyne and Cessna were incorrect. Now it was on for young and old! When I completed my deposition in the afternoon, I left the room exhausted. I was feeling like a victim again. The final trial was expected to run for more than two weeks. How ever would I cope, I thought.

Several inquiries hadn't been completed and it had been agreed that the wreckage of VH-PLD should be shipped to Mobile to be used as evidence in the courtroom. For these reasons, the date of the hearing was moved back to April, 1995. It was only another five months to wait, which shouldn't have seemed much after four years of legal hearings. But I was despondent. I just wanted it to end.

It was late in the year, 1994, as Nigel and I were preparing for Christmas again, that Tom called to say Teladyne and Cessna wanted to meet with me at a mediation hearing in Los Angeles in January. At first, I thought it would be just another tactic to make me spend more money, travelling back and forth to America. Our funds had already diminished as we tried to keep the case going. When Teladyne and Cessna had offered to pay my airfare and expenses for the trip, I knew they were serious about settling out of court. Steven, the other survivor of the accident, and the family of one of the deceased, had also filed claims through Tom. They too were to be invited by Teladyne and Cessna to attend the mediation to try to settle their claims.

Nigel wasn't able to come with me this time. We couldn't afford his air fare and he was busy with work. If the case went to trial, we'd be back in America in three months anyway. Tom and Patrine came along for the three-day hearing that lasted from Friday to Sunday.

Both parties made opening statements presenting their case before a judge, who was there to guide us to a resolution. Teladyne and Cessna had joined forces and were working as a team. During their statement to the judge, they implied that I had conspired with Peter and Allan on the day of the accident to go outside search area 'Charlie'. If we had been in our allocated search area when the engine failed, we would have been able to put the craft down in open fields. I sat at the back of the room and listened to these lies, unable to interrupt or object. It was so frustrating not being able to tell the judge that I hadn't been wearing a headset in the aeroplane. I couldn't speak to Peter and Allan, and therefore I had been unaware that we were out of our search area. I imagined how a group of jurors – normal everyday people – might absorb this rubbish as being factual. It frightened me to think they might choose one story over another. I was a foreigner in their country and I couldn't predict what prejudices they might have. Cessna and Teladyne were major employers of workers in their town. It could even be difficult to find an impartial jury.

The day's proceedings were extremely stressful. That night, I couldn't sleep and I couldn't eat. I had a bath to try to relax my body, but my muscles were so tense that my neck and back ached. Even my jaw was permanently clenched with the tension. I lay in bed feeling very alone. This was only a taste of dramas to come. I knew I wouldn't be able to survive the hearing. Somehow we had to settle out of court. I had rung Nigel earlier and told him about the day. He'd encouraged me to be strong.

'Don't let them make you weak. We can go to trial and we will win.' If only Nigel was with me, I thought. He'd understand how tough it was going to be.

On day two, we went backwards and forwards, claiming and counter claiming, on major points in the case. The judge, John K. Trotter, was very impressive, diplomatically acknowledging each party's arguments. Much of the data presented was extremely technical. I wondered how a jury would make head or tail of it, if it had to be explained to them in court. I had been listening to this talk for three years and I still didn't understand it fully.

On Saturday, the office block we were using in central Los Angeles was deserted. The phone system was shut down and we were limited to local calls only. Although I had asked to phone Nigel, I wouldn't be able to talk to him until I returned to my hotel room later that night.

I hadn't been able to eat. The strain of the two days in mediation was taking its toll, and I was feeling faint and sick. I managed to digest a few grapes from a fruit platter that Fred and Roger arranged to be sent to my room, but still I couldn't sleep. My heart continued to pound and my head throbbed. I had never experienced this level of tension before. I knew tomorrow was the last chance we would have to resolve this dispute or we'd be going to trial.

I telephoned Nigel before I left my room the next morning. I told him I probably wouldn't be able to speak to him from the mediation offices because of the restricted phones.

Nigel begged me not to agree to anything without speaking to him first.

'If that's not possible, you will have to trust me,' I said.

The judge had arranged for me and the other two plaintiffs from Australia to be in separate rooms so negotiations could be made in confidence. Judge Trotter sat with me and my attorneys alone. He told me that if the case went to trial, there was a good chance we would win. If we did win, however, I would have to expect Cessna and Teladyne to appeal the decision. At that time, there was a three-year delay into the appeals court, he said. He gave me his opinion on how much the case was worth, and he advised a range of figures from which I should consider accepting a settlement.

Figures had been going backwards and forwards between the lawyers all day. I borrowed a mobile phone off a young clerk just after lunch, and spoke to Nigel. I told him what the judge had said. But Nigel wasn't keen for me to settle.

Patrine and I were outside getting some fresh air as the third plaintiff settled their case. It was Sunday evening and it was already dark.

Now Steven and I were left.

I was made an offer that was worth consideration. But I told the attorneys for Cessna and Teladyne to settle Steven's case first. I had to know that he'd be looked after. I couldn't leave him to battle alone. I was sitting in a room waiting, while Tom and the others stayed with Steven. A little later, Roger poked his head in and told me they had reached a settlement.

'I have to speak to Steven. I have to make sure he's happy with the outcome.'

Steven and I had a moment together and we each decided that we'd had enough. Neither of us wanted to go to trial. We just wanted our lives back. Steven was pleased with the outcome of his case. That left me free to continue my own negotiations. I tried again to contact Nigel, but I couldn't. This was a big decision to make, and I had to make it on my own. I hoped he would understand.

I was tired and frustrated, but I stood my ground on a figure I would accept. I even had an emotional outburst towards my own counsel, which I regret to this day. But I needed to secure my future, financially. I needed to make sure I could look after myself and ensure that I would have the very best medical care in the years to come. Finally, we reached a compromise and we sealed the agreement with handshakes all round. It had been an extraordinary chapter in my life. Now I could close it. I shed an emotional tear, relieved that it was all over.

It wasn't until I got back to my hotel room that I was able to call Nigel. He was very angry with me for settling. We could have got so much more, if we had let the case go to trial – so much more for what, I wondered.

I felt confident that with the money I had been awarded, I could ensure my future medical expenses would be paid. Nigel and I would never have to worry again about how we were going to pay our day-to-day bills. He could never have imagined how nerve-racking the past three days had been. The trial would have been even worse. I had fought a long, hard battle and I was relieved that it was all over. I just wanted to put it all behind me and get on with my life.

Chapter 13

A New Beginning

That year, 1995, was the start of a whole new beginning for Nigel and me. Our financial future was secure. There would be no more courtrooms, no more prying doctors. And we were debt free.

We had always dreamed of owning our own hangar on Camden Airport. Now we could afford to build one. Our plans went into full swing straight away. In the meantime, I started my flying lessons. Chris and Elena had gone overseas for six months, but I soon found another school at Bankstown Airport.

I had a few instructors, starting with Steven Dines. During this initial training and through trial and error, Steven and I worked on techniques to help me control the helicopter, given the problems I had with my legs. Because my feet were fixed at ninety degrees with the calipers I had to wear, and because I couldn't feel what was happening below my knees, the heel of my shoe was getting caught on the carpet beneath the pedals. We worked out that the most successful position for my feet was up off the floor with the tail rotor pedal resting in the heel of my shoe. Footwear was very important.

The other problem was that I couldn't get feedback from the helicopter. I couldn't feel, through my legs, what the aircraft was doing, so other senses – sight and sound – took over. The delicate control inputs took some time to sort out. I couldn't feel outside forces on my legs, nor could I feel what my legs were doing. It all seemed a bit daunting at first, but I was determined to somehow make it work.

My first lessons consisted of learning to hover. We would practise over a grass area, away from the main runway of the airport. The little bit of flying straight and level that I had done had seemed easy. But hovering over one spot on the ground was like trying to balance on a big rubber ball. I kept drifting backwards and forwards, and from side to side. The more I tried to control the helicopter, the more out of control we became.

Each time, Steven would calmly take over and settle us again, stationary at five to ten metres off the ground. He made it look so simple. But when I took over, we'd go careering off course. I wondered if I'd ever get the hang of it.

'Don't worry. It'll all fall into place. You just have to keep practising,' Steven kept assuring me.

He was right. One day, for some reason, when he asked me to take the controls, I was able to keep the helicopter straight. We didn't move at all. I felt very clever and wondered why I wasn't able to do it before.

My training continued outside Bankstown's control zone. We'd fly out just beyond a reservoir where, over open fields, we would practise more advanced manoeuvres. Then we would follow a pipeline back into the airport. Another instructor, David Coxhead, had begun flying with me too. One day, we went to Hoxton Park and I was taken through the procedures to follow if the engine should fail during a hover. I knew I had handled this pretty well when David hopped out of the aircraft and told me to pick up the helicopter into a hover and taxi to the opposite end of the airport and back again. I felt free. I could go in any direction I wanted, as fast or as slow as I wanted. It was effortless and pain free, unlike my walking.

I had learned how to control the helicopter in most situations, even in emergencies. David and I had spent hours doing engine-off landings. This had taken a lot of concentration. When he'd cut the engine, I would instantly drop the collective and pull back on the cyclic, at the same time putting in a boot full of right pedal. Coordination was everything. We'd maintain sixty knots, but the helicopter felt as though it was dropping out of the sky like a brick. At about fifty feet up, I'd flare then level out, raising the collective to settle us on the ground. If it sounds difficult, it was. I'd finish our session feeling exhausted, but it was important to master autorotation because you never know when you'll have to put one into practice. I didn't have to be told that twice!

Flying a circuit was also challenging. At first, there seemed to be so much to do, so many radio calls to make. I'd get overloaded and inevitably forget something, but after a while it became second nature. I flew so many circuits that I was getting dizzy. On 6 April, 1995, with Steven flying with me, I had been in the circuit for over an hour. I came in, landing on a grass area near the helipad.

'You're ready to fly solo now, Allana,' he said.

I hadn't been expecting this. I was instantly in a panic.

'I don't think I'm ready,' I said.

'You know you don't have to do it. But I'm confident in you. You fly well.'

I sat for a moment, wondering what I was afraid of. What if something went wrong? Would I be able to handle it? I knew I would. My instructors had been my security blanket. But some day I had to fly on my own. It might as well be today.

'All right. How many circuits do you want me to do?' I asked.

'Just one. Then come back and pick me up here.'

I looked across to the empty seat beside me remembering my first circuit in an aeroplane over eight years ago. Steven waved me off as I headed for the helipad.

'Bankstown tower, helicopter Juliet Kilo Hotel is solo for circuits. Received Bravo.'

'Helicopter Juliet Kilo Hotel clear for take off.'

I was nervous but I ran through my procedures, concentrating on my flying. The helicopter felt very different without Steven beside me. It was much lighter. I was on the down-wind leg and I checked my altimeter which read nine hundred feet. I was too high. I quickly dropped the collective, bringing me down to the circuit height, which was seven hundred feet. On final approach, I could see the helipad lined up in front of me and I coasted down gently. I had flown my very first circuit – solo!

It didn't take long before I was scooting around the training area by myself. Sometimes I would drop in to Camden Airport for a quick coffee with Nigel before flying back to Bankstown.

One of the part-time instructors was John Broom, a pilot with the Westpac Rescue Helicopter Service. John briefed me for a flight to Wollongong on the south coast. I'd flown there over a month earlier with David and our track had taken us over a thick forest, which had unnerved me. I wondered if I'd ever come to terms with flying over trees. John and I set off. All was going well, until we reached the boundary of the Royal National Park. Again, when I looked down and saw the trees, I remembered the day of my accident. I couldn't stop thinking about the sound of trees hitting the wings of the aeroplane.

John kept talking to me, but I wasn't responding.

'Is everything okay?' I finally heard him say.

'I don't like being over the trees.'

John knew all about my accident from his days at Westpac Rescue.

'I want you to call up on the radio and get the area QNH,' he said.

After I had done that John had another task for me. During the next twenty minutes, he kept me so busy I didn't have time to think about the trees. This technique worked and I used it to fly by myself to Wollongong a few days later.

But my greatest challenge was to fly to Bathurst on my

own. The track took me over the Great Dividing Range and some of the most hostile terrain in the country. It was just north of my accident site. I completed the trip with confidence and knew that I had confronted my fears and won. There was no stopping me now.

It had taken almost a year to complete my training and, thankfully, there was not too much fuss from aviation medicine specialist, Dr Graham Maclarn, to pass me fit to hold a commercial licence. My flight test was set for 8 February, 1996.

My mission was to fly a pretend photographic job that would take us over the Olympic stadium site at Homebush, then to Sutherland Hospital, over to Rooty Hill, and then to Hoxton Park. The weather on the day was dismal. The cloud base was as low as twelve hundred feet. At times, there was light drizzle falling. I had to assess the conditions and decide if the flight should be cancelled or not. If this was a real photographic job, it would have been silly to make the flight because of the poor visibility. But the conditions were not unsafe. I was pumped up and rearing to go, and I decided to make the flight. I had worked out all my headings, time intervals and fuel. I felt confident as my examiner, Grant Johnson, climbed into the seat next to me.

'Make sure you're all strapped in, Mr Photographer,' I said.

'Thank you, Ms Pilot. I will,' he replied. Once we were established over the Olympic stadium, I circled a few times until my passenger told me he had completed his photographs. Then I contacted Sydney to gain clearance to fly to Sutherland.

The Best I Can Be

Sydney tower gave me a radar vector to follow. This was different to the heading I had prepared. But I complied with his instructions. Then after a few minutes, the tower changed the vector again. I was concentrating hard on the heading the tower had given me. I didn't want to stray off course. Then they changed it a third time. I hadn't planned for this, but I tried to look confident for the examiner. I knew we were being taken in the direction of Sutherland.

'Hotel India Papa track direct for Sutherland,' came the call.

'Hotel India Papa,' I replied, to confirm his instruction.

I had been directed all over the place. I didn't really know where I was. I discreetly scanned my chart, trying to match the waterway we were approaching to the river system marked on the map. I was a little left of the line I had drawn on my chart. I quickly established our position and headed straight for Sutherland.

The weather was getting worse. We were at one thousand feet and just under the cloud base. There weren't a lot of other aeroplanes flying around on this horrible day. But it had become evident that a student pilot, who didn't speak English very well, was flying in the area. Somehow, he had managed to get himself lost. The student pilot was also at one thousand feet and had flown into a restricted area in Holsworthy. The Holsworthy Military Base is where army personnel train and the site is often used for bombing practice. For this reason, the entire base is off limits to air traffic.

The air traffic controller was very frustrated as he tried to communicate with the student pilot. In the meantime, he directed me to climb to fifteen hundred feet.

'Negative tower. We have a cloud base of twelve hundred feet.' We had reached Sutherland Hospital and were told to remain at one thousand feet and circle until the problem with the disorientated pilot was resolved. Because the exact location of his aircraft was unknown, all traffic in the area was ordered to hold position. This is standard safety practice to reduce the chance of any aircraft coming into conflict with the missing plane. Two Qantas jets were being held out to sea while the problem was sorted out.

Almost ten minutes had passed. Grant and I were getting dizzy. We were relieved when we were directed to track across to Rooty Hill. I established my heading and hoped it would be the last time Sydney tower would alter my plans.

'Hotel India Papa, divert to Picnic Point,' came the controller's voice again. I couldn't believe it. I quickly examined my map and found Picnic Point, altering our track – again!

We did finally make it to Rooty Hill, then flew direct to Hoxton Park Airfield where Grant put me through my paces with autorotation and other emergencies. I showed him how I could land on a slope and take off and land with limited power. We continued for about half an hour before flying back to Bankstown.

I was stuffed. Grant hadn't said much during the flight test. As I shut the helicopter down, I was thinking to myself that my slope landings hadn't been very good and I was a bit lost flying to Sutherland. I hoped I hadn't failed. Grant took my flight plan off my lap and hopped out of the aircraft. He disappeared towards the back of the helicopter out of sight. I wondered what he was doing. A few seconds later, he pressed my flight plan up against the window. Across it, he had written in big bold letters, PASSED!

'I'll see you inside,' he said.

It had taken me a year and now I was a commercial helicopter pilot. It sounded good! It felt great! I stayed sitting under the bubble, absorbing the feeling of achievement. I had come far and I'd had to jump over many hurdles. But I'd done it!

Before I went inside, I called Nigel from my mobile phone. He was excited to hear that I'd passed. I also rang my friend, Kevin Weldon. Kevin was so proud of me. He'd offered to let me use his helicopter to continue training and get my Squirrel endorsement. I was so motivated to keep learning that I accepted his offer – after the National Aerobatic Championships which were coming up again.

During that year, Nigel and I had been pursuing our own interests, me with my helicopter flying and Nigel often away performing at air shows around Australia or overseas. He was also determined to win the next Australian Aerobatic Championships. Nigel knew he was well prepared and flying confidently.

When Nige had first started flying aerobatics, just after my accident, I had asked him what he hoped to achieve.

'I'm going to be Australian champion one day,' he'd said.

It had been a dream back then. But he'd dedicated himself to aerobatics, bringing out coaches from Russia to help train him over the past three years. His commitment was immense and complete. By 1996, Nigel was the one to beat.

The competition was held at Griffith and ran for three

days. Nigel and another five pilots were in training full time for weeks leading up to the championships. For months prior, we had eaten, slept and breathed aerobatics.

After the flying each day, we'd wait in the Griffith Aero Club hall until the judges had posted the results for each category. Nigel led for the first two days and he looked certain to take the championships. After every competitor had flown on the last day, we waited in anticipation. The room was full of people. Most of them hovered around the notice board where the scores would be placed. I couldn't stand the tension. I stood on the opposite end of the room with Nigel in my sights. Liz Cook, the head judge, reached up and put the results on the board. People were almost clambering over each other to get a glimpse.

It didn't take long before Nigel was being patted on the back. There were handshakes and congratulations all round. I caught his eye from across the room and clapped my hands in recognition of his win. There were tears rolling down my face. This was Nigel's moment of glory, but I knew his thoughts would be with Allan as mine were. It was a win for him too.

Nigel's triumph moved him towards deciding whether to continue competing on the next level which would be the world competition to be held in Oklahoma City. There would be an Australian team of up to six pilots attending. The expense of shipping the aircraft to the States and the cost of training over there for a month or two before the competition would have to be met by each competitor. It was a big decision to make. And, after some deliberation, Nigel decided to enter.

The Best I Can Be

During the months leading up to this Nigel and I had been experiencing conflicts that were difficult for each of us to manage. These personal issues were based on our differing career paths, individual dreams that no longer merged as one, our own expectations of life that clashed in many areas and the changing roles we were playing in each other's lives. We were drifting apart at a great rate.

Amongst all this turmoil, Nigel's children moved to Indonesia with their mother. This caused an enormous amount of stress for Nigel and it compounded the tensions at home.

At this time, Nigel and I decided to sell our mountain house and move closer to Camden. Our new hangar was up and running. Nigel spent most of his time at the airport and the forty-minute drive home to the mountains was a drag. Initially we found it difficult to locate a house that would cater to my needs. It had to be on a level block with preferably no stairs. After months of looking, we found the perfect home in Cobbitty. It was bigger than we needed, but it overlooked the Camden Valley and the airport. We could even see our new hangar from the house. It was perfect! I was hopeful that making this new home together would help our relationship.

Nigel's daughter, Kylie, who was now sixteen, was very unhappy living in Jakarta. She wanted desperately to come and live with us in Cobbitty. This was a big decision for us to make. But her letters were so heart wrenching that although Nigel and my relationship was rocky, I felt having Kylie live with us should be Nigel's decision to make. I didn't want to deny her happiness or the safe environment of living in Australia, so at Christmas, 1996, she moved into our new home.

In the meantime, I had absorbed myself in flying. I contacted Kevin who had arranged for me to learn to fly the Squirrel with his instructor and chief pilot, Roger Corbin. I'd met Roger earlier in the year at the school at Bankstown. He had just finished working as a pilot for Westpac Rescue at Prince Henry Hospital. Before we went flying, I was shown over the helicopter and the pre-flight inspections were explained.

The Squirrel is a very big helicopter and some of the checks meant climbing on top near the blades.

'I can't climb up there,' I said to Roger.

I was a bit embarrassed. I didn't want to appear defeatist before we had even started. But I knew there was no way I could do it.

'Can you climb a ladder?' he asked.

'Not very well. But I'll give it a go.'

Because the rungs of ladders don't support the full length of my foot, I find them very difficult to use. Roger explained the inspections on the blades while I watched from the ground. Then he set up a ladder next to the engine cowl so I could climb up and see clearly inside. This seemed to work okay. I held onto the helicopter for added support.

The systems in the gas turbine helicopter were very complicated. It took a while to become familiar with the different instruments and cockpit layout. My first attempt to pick the helicopter up into a hover was a bit shaky too. It felt very twitchy close to the ground. The controls were very light. They were operated by hydraulics, which is similar to power steering on a car. My endorsement training was expected to take ten hours to complete and was well and truly on schedule.

The last thing I needed to master before Roger gave me my endorsement, were emergency procedures. Autorotation was similar to those in the Robinson, although the inertia in the big blades made the trip down to the ground a lot slower. I also had to learn how to fly and land the helicopter without hydraulics. This was a bit scary at first. Roger would turn the hydraulics off mid flight. Then after a few seconds, the controls became suddenly very heavy, requiring an enormous effort to move them even centimetres. Luckily, my upper body is so strong from having to carry my body weight around on my arms all day. I managed the collective and the cyclic pretty well and in forward flight, the helicopter stayed straight so I didn't have to work my legs on the pedals too much.

Slowing the helicopter in to land ... fifty knots ... forty-five knots ... forty knots. At this stage, the aircraft started to yaw to the left, requiring right pedal input to keep it straight. I pushed down with all my might, but I simply didn't have the strength in my legs. Roger took over, putting us safely on the ground. I wasn't put off at all. I'd just have to try again and work harder this time, which is what we did. Each attempt we made, the same thing happened. When we slowed down below fifty knots the yaw to the left began. But my legs didn't have the power to counter it by pushing the right pedal in. Without the hydraulics, the controls were too heavy.

'I can't give you your endorsement until you can do this,' Roger told me.

Our next lesson wasn't scheduled for a week. I went back to the gym every day and worked hard, building up the power in my legs. Even a little bit more strength would make the difference, I thought. I was keen to see if my hard work had paid off. But on my first attempt, the same thing happened. Roger took over again, landing us safely.

'You're not going to be able to do this. I can't give you the endorsement,' he said.

'Don't give up that easily. There has to be a way,' I told him.

If I'd given up that easily over the past six years, I'd be sitting in a wheelchair somewhere knitting.

'Can you push your leg forward and lock it in straight?' Roger asked.

'I don't know, why?'

'I have an idea!' he said. We took off again and established eight hundred feet, then turned the hydraulics off. We flew the circuit and lined up on the final approach, maintaining sixty knots.

'Now push your right leg down on the pedal all the way and hold it there,' Roger instructed.

The helicopter yawed dramatically to the right, but he assured me it didn't matter. As I slowed the aircraft down ... fifty knots ... forty-five knots ... forty knots, the nose of the helicopter began turning to the left. My leg was locked in place with the right pedal fully engaged. As we slowed to a crawl, the helicopter continued to nose further to the left and was almost straight now, allowing me to make a controlled landing. I don't know who was more excited, Roger or me. It wasn't the conventional way of landing without hydraulics, but it worked.

'Congratulations, you've completed your endorsement training,' he said.

'Let's practise some confined areas before we go back to Bankstown,' Roger suggested.

We flew to an area known as Little Africa. This was a small clearing surrounded by trees in the shape of Africa, hence the name. I'd flown in and out of here many times during my training and I felt confident as I took the Squirrel in to land.

'We'll do a few more approaches,' Roger said.

Each time, he gave me more safety tips and, as I landed for the third time, I felt happy with my flying.

'Now what do you want me to do?' I asked.

'I want you to fly that same circuit on your own,' he said as he unbuckled his seat belt and began to climb out of the helicopter.

'What are you doing!'

I panicked. Kevin's insurance didn't allow me to fly the Squirrel solo until I had four hundred hours on that type of helicopter.

'The helicopter's not covered if I break it,' I said.

'I have faith in you. You won't break it,' Roger assured me.

'I can't do this, Roger.'

'Yes, you can,' he said as he defiantly closed the door behind him. He sat stubbornly cross-legged on the grass nearby.

I remembered feeling this way when I flew my very first circuit in a helicopter. I wondered what I was afraid of back then, but this was different. If I stuffed up and damaged it in any way, Roger would be responsible.

'I have faith in you,' he'd said.

I hoped I wouldn't let him down. I took a deep breath and tried to stay as calm as possible, running through all the emergency procedures in my mind, just in case anything went wrong.

I popped up into the hover and raised the collective further, flying up over the trees. Being in command of such a complex machine was exciting. I flew the circuit confidently and, as I turned onto final approach, I could see Roger still sitting on the grass. He hadn't moved at all. I bet he was more nervous than me though.

Once I was safely back on the ground, Roger climbed on board. I thanked him for believing in me and not quitting when my hydraulic off landings seemed impossible. He'd taken a big risk allowing me to fly the Squirrel solo but it gave me confidence and my ego had had the biggest boost.

Kevin was thrilled to hear I'd completed my training on the Squirrel, although I didn't tell him about my solo adventure. Whenever it was convenient, Kevin allowed me to fly the Squirrel, which was usually up and down the coast between Sydney and Coolangatta with Roger or himself. I managed to clock up many hours but I am still working towards the four hundred I need for insurance purposes to fly it solo. Gary Ticehurst and I had talked many times about flying out to the crash site. This was something I simply had to do. I didn't quite know why. I had come to terms with what I had experienced that day. I had accepted my injuries and the loss of my friends. It wasn't a matter of putting the accident behind me. That would never be possible. But I knew to just fly out there would somehow fill a gap in my life, and make me complete.

That day came one Sunday afternoon. I had agreed to meet Gary at his base at the ABC television station, where he'd just finished polishing the helicopter. Gary had the coordinates for the accident site in his office.

'Come and I'll show you through the studios on the way,' he suggested.

We were going up in the lift to the offices and when the door opened, there were a few men standing waiting to go down.

'Allana!' said one of them, looking surprised to see me. His face was familiar. After a few minutes of small talk, 'How have you been?' and so on, I had to ask where I knew him from.

'You sold me my house in the Blue Mountains,' he said. The memory came flooding back to me. I remembered the house in detail and even what I was wearing the day he'd bought it – a tailored grey business jacket, my little black woollen mini skirt, with sheer black stockings and high stiletto shoes with the little diamantes that ran down the heel.

My mind was flicking between the comparisons of Allana back then and Allana now. I couldn't help being amazed that I'd met up with Bruce again on this significant day. But I also felt a bit bewildered as to why my recollection of the purchase of his home, over seven years earlier, was as clear to me as if it had happened yesterday. I indulged in a moment of recollection, absorbed in the way it felt to be whole, beautiful and able-bodied back then. I had taken so much for granted that day. If only I could have known my fate!

Gary and I returned to the helicopter and climbed on board. He'd put the dual controls in so I could fly it. I was surprisingly calm about flying over the Burragorang Valley again. Even as we approached the mountain range, which we'd been flying over on the day of the accident, my only thought was – isn't it a beautiful day! We passed over the clearing that Janine and I had spotted. I could see the flying fox clearly running into the river nearby. I remembered the last words I heard Janine speak, 'No, Peter, there are wires.'

As I examined the area, I saw it was clearly impossible to land there anyway. The sky was clear, just as it had been 22 December, 1990, and the surrounding terrain had remained unchanged. We tracked towards the south and retraced VH-PLD's flight path all the way to the valley floor where the aeroplane had ultimately crashed.

The site itself was insignificant. It was an area amongst a blanket of trees that all looked the same. There was nothing at all to reveal the tragedy that had occurred. I imagined bushwalkers traipsing through, unaware of the four lives that had been lost on this spot. The earth was unscarred. It didn't seem fair to me, and it left me feeling deprived of the justification that I suddenly realised I was searching for out there.

In the vast monotony of the Burragorang Valley, I had found no answers to the question, 'Why did this have to happen?' I knew now that the void in my life that needed to be filled with meaning and understanding, would never be satisfied with any more than, 'It just happened, that's all.'

It was October, 1996. Nigel had sold an aeroplane to a client of ours. The plane was in America and had to be shipped to Australia in a forty-foot container. We did our sums and discovered that an R22 helicopter would also fit in the container with the aeroplane. Nigel knew how frustrated I was, not having an aircraft to fly. At least if I had my own helicopter, I could fly it whenever I wanted.

Nigel phoned some of our contacts in Florida to try to find a suitable machine to buy. We only had a few weeks to locate an aircraft and have it delivered to Miami, Florida, before the shipment was due to leave. There were a few good buys in America at the time, but the best was in Arizona. We employed an engineer to give us a report on its condition. Ninety-five per cent inside and out, he said. That was good for a second-hand machine, so I went ahead and bought it. We then arranged for a pilot to ferry it to Miami.

What a Christmas present! The container arrived at our new hangar late in December. It was nerve-racking watching it being loaded off the truck and onto the ground. I watched as the container doors opened. And there it was! It had survived the long trip intact and was my very own helicopter. It was hard to believe. Nigel and a few helpers carefully dragged it out, placing it on the floor in the hangar. The rotor blades were off, but I still sat in the cockpit imagining what it was going to be like to fly her. The helicopter was transported to Bankstown Airport later in the day to be assembled and put on the Australian register. But it wouldn't be ready to fly until early January.

Sadly Nigel's and my personal problems didn't improve. In fact, they reached an unbearable point, where I needed to assess the basis of our marriage, and why he hadn't left me straight after my accident, when he'd said he wanted to.

I felt that I had no control at all over any aspect of my life. I didn't feel Nigel and I were living a life together, we were on separate paths and conflicted on many issues. I felt like a stranger in my own house and dreaded going home each evening. We were not partners any more. I had many dreams and desires but I was a bird with clipped wings. I'd worked so hard to get back on my feet but I knew there was more I needed to achieve. I only wished Nigel could have nurtured and encouraged this passion and shared in my enthusiasm. This was not to be.

By March, I simply couldn't stand the ongoing stress, the tension between us. I had to escape and give myself time to think clearly about my future. Nigel's daughter was still living with us, and I thought it was easier if I left the house, instead of disrupting their lives.

This was one of the most difficult times of my life. I arranged to rent a unit in Cronulla for six months. I had to leave my dream home and all I took with me was a bag of clothes, an old toaster and some cutlery. I had to start building my life again from scratch. I bought a bed to sleep on, and I rented the basics – fridge, television, washing machine etc. The first night in my new home, I was sitting in a big empty room eating takeaway, and feeling very lost. I was down to the bare essentials. Despite the hardship of my situation, I can now look back on this as a time of growth for me.

I moved my helicopter into a hangar at Bankstown and kept my flying up as much as I could. I was working on several deals with the helicopter. I was on my own now and I needed to establish a future for myself. The business Nigel and I had built up over the past eight years would be his. My future was again very uncertain, but I did know I needed to support myself. I was working hard on a contract involving the helicopter. I was trying to negotiate deals and portray a professional image, but all I had was a mobile phone – no computer, no fax, not even a landline phone. I was on my own and going nowhere fast!

Chapter 14

My Greatest Adventure

The dream of one day flying around Australia was still on my mind. I was at an airshow in Maitland one weekend when I met up with Grant Shoreland and Jamie Campbell, friends of mine who also flew helicopters. The conversation turned to flying around Australia which was something Jamie and Grant had each been wanting to do, independent of the other. It was very exciting to find we shared the same dream. If I was going to do such a trip, I knew I'd have to take someone along to help with things like climbing up the helicopter to re-fuel. The thought of three helicopters flying together was much more exciting than doing it alone.

We began to plan our journey, agreeing to leave in early June. The timing was perfect. I hadn't been able to secure any flying work and my personal life was in a lot of turmoil. This adventure would be just what the doctor ordered.

Another friend of Grant's heard about the trip and decided to join us. Then there were four. Jim Wickham, and his wife, Jenny, were lovely people. I was glad to have another woman along.

Grant had been on many flying safaris around Australia in the past, including a lot of the places we'd plotted on our maps. His knowledge was invaluable. I had managed to secure some sponsorship, including Air BP, who very generously agreed to pay for our fuel. And Konica provided camera gear and film. Dick Smith, the first man to fly a helicopter solo around the world, was extremely supportive.

Six weeks before we were scheduled to leave, we had a group meeting at Grant's place to make final arrangements. Many of the destinations along our track were remote and desolate so survival and first-aid equipment were essential. We needed life jackets and camping gear, too. That wouldn't leave much room in our small luggage compartments for personal items. There was much to do, but we were very excited. It would be the trip of a lifetime. We would fly to Luskintyre in the Hunter Valley on 6 June and leave as a quartet of helicopters from there.

I had made arrangements to start and finish my journey at the Westpac Helicopter Rescue base at Prince Henry Hospital. It was fitting. These were the people who had saved my life seven years earlier, and this was where I had been nursed back to health.

There had been increasing media interest in our trip and, when I arrived at the Westpac base, several camera crews were waiting. My friend, Gary Ticehurst, was also there with the ABC helicopter. I was so pleased to see him. The rescue team had come to see me off, including Stewart Bailey who had been at the accident site in 1990. The crew helped me pre-flight the helicopter and secure my bag to the passenger side floor. With the equipment I needed to take, there was barely enough room for me.

The media attention was overwhelming. I was asked a lot of questions about the trip.

'We'll just keep Australia on our left, the water on our right and fly right around the whole country,' I told them.

Professor Jones, my spinal specialist, was with me, and was being interviewed by the news crews. I could see a young girl in a wheelchair being pushed across the oval where we were standing.

'This is Lisa,' the professor told me. Lisa had become quadriplegic – requiring a respirator to help her breathe – after a car accident in her home town of Bathurst. I was taken by surprise. She'd been inspired by my story, enough to come all the way across the hospital grounds to see me. I remembered meeting people like Janine Shepherd, the author of *Never Tell Me Never*, who had helped motivate me when I was recovering. I realised I had the same opportunity to help other people with problems in their lives.

It was almost 11.30 a.m. when I climbed into VH-ELF and started her engine. To fly the coastline of Australia would take us up to eight weeks.

'I'll see you all in a few months,' I called out as I closed the door.

Everybody was waving. I waved back and climbed overhead, flying towards the bright blue ocean. White foaming waves were pounding into the cliffs along the coastline. I'd be used to this sight by the end of my journey.

I was trembling from the adrenaline pumping through

The Best I Can Be

my body. This is it. I was off on my life's greatest adventure. What would the next eight weeks hold for me? I'd be in the air for over one hundred and sixty hours. I hoped I wouldn't have any mechanical problems. I hoped I wouldn't get sick along the way. We were planning to camp in the Kimberley. I hoped I wouldn't get taken by a crocodile. There were sure to be testing times ahead. But I was ready to face the challenge. What an achievement it will be when I make it back to Sydney.

At Luskintyre, I was soon joined by the three other helicopters which flew to the field in formation about an hour later. Nigel also flew up. Although we'd been separated for three months, we were still friends and we had been trying to work through our problems.

The Luskintigers put on a barbecue in the evening to send the 'Robinsons Around Australia' off in style. In the morning, we were anxious to get going. Nigel helped me pack my gear away, then we said goodbye.

'Have a good time and don't bump into anything or anybody,' he said.

Grant's passenger was his son, Grant Jnr. Jamie's passenger was Stewart who I'd met last year on another flying trip. I was the only pilot flying solo so I offered to take any excess gear from the others. The floor next to me, all the way to the top of the instrument panel, was piled high with bags, and my spare seat was full of equipment.

Our first leg of this mammoth journey seemed ridiculously short, only twenty-five minutes to Digger Bourke's place. Digger was one of the Luskintyre group, and he wanted us to drop into his place for breakfast.

'You can land in my neighbour's backyard,' he said.

We kept in contact by radio. It was exhilarating, flying through the crisp morning air, the four helicopters staying close to each other. I could see Jenny already taking photos. She put her camera down and waved to me.

'Good morning, ELF,' she said over the radio.

The sky was covered with a thick blanket of cloud. In the distance around us were scattered rain showers, although our path to Digger's was clear. The mountainous terrain below looked green and lush, the canopy of trees almost tropical. I remembered being afraid of flying over trees once. I'd come a long way since then.

We created quite a stir in the little village of Stroud. I'd never landed in anyone's backyard before. It was as much a novelty for the neighbours who came out to meet us, curious to know why four helicopters had landed at their back doors.

'We've just come for breakfast,' we told them.

Our final destination today would be a place called Gwingana, a conference centre owned by Kevin Weldon and located in the hills west of Coolangatta, four hours' flight away. Leaving Digger's, we tracked towards the coast. Once we were established over water, we could drop down and fly lower which is much more fun.

'Last one down's a rotten egg,' Jamie called. The four helicopters snaked along the beaches, waving to unsuspecting sunbathers who gingerly waved back, curious at the sight of the four flying tadpoles heading north.

Each helicopter had a flying range of three hours, which was not enough to make it all the way to Coolangatta. We planned to stop at Coffs Harbour to have lunch and re-fuel. There were people everywhere at Coffs. The sight of four helicopters landing together certainly captured interest. When I walked into the club house to pay my fuel bill, a woman approached me.

'You must be Allana,' she said, 'I saw you on the news last night.' She introduced herself as Carol Durkin, president of the Women Pilots' Association. 'You're a great inspiration to our young members learning to fly,' she said.

I was a little bit shy about the attention, but I thanked her for her words of encouragement.

Clearer skies welcomed us back into the air.

'Look at the dolphins,' Jim called over the radio.

'Where?' asked Grant.

'Just to my left. Where are you, ELF?' Jim asked.

'I'm right behind you.'

'Did you see the dolphins?'

'I did. They're playing in the surf.'

Although we were talking to each other on the radio, we had to keep on our toes to ensure we knew where each helicopter was at all times, to make sure we didn't get too close and have a mid air collision. It was a weird feeling if you were leading the group, not to be able to see the other helicopters. We quickly built up the necessary trust and watched out for each other. Our first day had been perfect!

We woke to blue skies, but there was a strong breeze blowing. There was no hurry to get airborne, and it was midday before we climbed our helicopters skywards. We'd be staying with Grant's brother, Grahame, in Noosa for the next two nights. There was a vacant block next to

Grahame's place where we could land the helicopters. There were a few power wires and trees to watch out for on approach, but we made it in safely.

We'd been told there was a shipwreck just north of Noosa. One of the locals was famous for taking an ice-cream truck out there each day. We decided it would be a good place to stop for breakfast the next day. Sure enough, there he was. A young family was getting into their car and about to leave, but when they saw us fly in and land on the beach, they stayed to find out what we were doing. The ice-cream vendor was a great Australian character. Yum Yum, he called himself. He'd been taking his Streets truck and souvenirs to the site of the shipwreck for many years. Rain, hail or shine, you'll find him there. I had a hot dog for breakfast and Grant Jnr indulged in the same, followed by an ice-cream chaser. Bad move before a day's flying!

Our next leg was to a town called Emu Park on the coast near Rockhampton. The conditions were blustery and unpleasant. I could see Grant climbing. It looked like he was at about two thousand feet.

'Where are you going, Grant?' I called.

'I'm just trying to find some smoother air,' he answered.

'Your passenger isn't well? He's peering into a sick bag. It must have been that ice-cream!'

Half an hour later, we landed on a sandbar near a settlement called Seven Seventeen to bury the bag. Poor Grant Jnr was looking very green. We stopped a few times that day for the same reason. This earned Grant Jnr his new name of 'Chuka'.

The local police at Emu Park agreed to allow us to land

the helicopters in their compound, a small grass area right in the middle of town. The approach was tricky. Power wires and a fence framed our landing site and a small building off to one side also needed to be avoided. One by one, the helicopters landed. The townsfolk must have thought they were being invaded. Cars drove in from every direction and stopped to greet us. We felt like celebrities, and we enjoyed the attention we were getting wherever we went.

Often I'd hear, 'There's a girl flying that one.'

It is rare to see a woman flying a helicopter. But when I got out and hobbled away with my walking sticks, I'd leave people open mouthed and speechless. I wondered what they'd be thinking.

Every day offered new experiences. It was exciting being constantly on the move. My flying skills were improving with each leg. Before now, the only places I'd ever landed were at airports. I was enjoying the challenge of landing in tight spots with so many obstacles to watch out for.

We were heading towards the Whitsunday group of islands. I thought of Nigel and remembered our honeymoon. I could even see Thomas Island. What an adventure that had been. The surrounding mountains rose dramatically from the ground. Some looked almost volcanic, like a scene from the movie, *Jurassic Park*. As we flew closer, the wind picked up and before long we were pounded by unforgiving turbulence. One minute I was flying along, then bang! A wind current would hit with such force it would shoot me higher into the air. My altimeter would be winding up, rising quickly. A few seconds later another would hit, sending me plummeting towards the earth, losing height at a great rate of knots. All I could do was ride wave after wave. I positioned myself in the downwind side of Grant so I could watch what his helicopter was doing. Every time he was thrown around, I would brace myself to inevitably fly through the same furious gusts moments later.

We were all tired. The intense concentration required to fly in this sort of weather was draining. Besides, we were very hungry and ready for a break. We landed near a caravan park that was nestled in a pretty bay to have a bite to eat.

I was relieved to escape the treacherous flying conditions and find smooth air, although there were rain showers up ahead. It didn't matter. In fact, this was a good chance to give the helicopters a bit of a rinse. After flying through the sea air along the coast, salt builds up on the airframe and blades. If it's not washed off regularly, it can cause corrosion. Whenever there was a bit of rain around, we'd call it our 'fly-through helicopter wash'.

Little drops spread quickly over the bubble, fanning out around me. A few made their way through a gap in the door and sprayed into my face. The sun shone brilliantly beyond the veil of water that soon cleared, popping the helicopter out into the warmth.

I could see a rainbow developing to my left. It glowed so brightly and, as its arc formed, it reached right into the cockpit. I couldn't believe what I was seeing. It was as if I could reach right in front of my face and touch it. I had experienced some strange phenomena before, but this was magical. I wondered if I was dreaming. I was trying to decide whether to share this spectacle with the others, but I was worried they'd think I was mad.

Jamie's voice came over the radio. 'You won't believe this, guys, but a rainbow has come into my cockpit and has ended in my map bag.'

Each of the four helicopters had a rainbow of its own.

Over the days that followed, we edged closer to the tip of Australia, continuously hugging the coast and waving to people scattered along the beach. We took our time to have a look around Hinchinbrook Island with its many cascading waterfalls and lush vegetation. Beyond there, we found our first pair of whales, porpoising through the water in perfect unison.

Before we departed Cairns, we said goodbye to 'Chuka', who had to get back to school. We waved the Qantas plane off knowing there was a very reluctant passenger on board. Stewart, originally invited on the trip by Grant, would now be Grant's passenger.

Accommodation was scarce at the base of Cape York Peninsula. Grant had heard about a cattle station, in a place called Silver Plains, which provided bed and breakfast-type lodging. The man Grant spoke to sounded a bit vague, saying he lived at the station on his own. He had a couple of single beds and one spare double room. We could stay if we wished, but the girls would have to do the cooking. It sounded like a good deal, but we were a little apprehensive. It looked like tonight could be an adventure in itself.

Silver Plains was a pleasant surprise. Our host, Des, had the ranch-style homestead spotlessly clean. Even the resident goanna came out to make us welcome.

It had been nine days since we'd left Sydney. We'd been lucky with the weather and all the helicopters were running well. Des gave us directions to a unique group of waterfalls that weren't far off our track north. The next morning we found them exactly where he'd said they'd be. There wasn't enough room for four helicopters to land so we found another spot further up the river to have a swim. I circled around while the others settled in amongst the low scrub that was making it difficult to land. Stewart jumped out of the helicopter as Grant shut down. He ran across and cleared a few branches in an area just big enough for ELF to fit. I was very pleased to be down without hitting my blades on any of the obstacles. This was great flying experience.

Before I had time to shut down, Grant and Jim were in the water, splashing around and enjoying the relief from the oppressive heat and humidity.

'There are heaps of crocs up in those rivers. You'd wanna be careful,' Des had told us.

There was no way I was getting in the water. I'd had visions of having to outrun a crocodile, an obviously impossible feat. Des had told me the crocs could only run in a straight line.

'If you see one coming, just hobble ninety degrees to the direction he's travelling,' he'd said. 'They can't climb either, so make your way up the first tree you find.'

This was something I couldn't do either. All these little hints were running through my head as I took charge of the billy and prepared cuppa soup for our lunches – always keeping an eye on the surrounding bush.

The tip of Australia was only half an hour away. We could see an occasional vehicle travelling along the dusty road that led to the top. 'Road' is a generous word for those corrugated dirt tracks. They would be murder to travel on.

'Australia is getting very narrow,' Grant commented.

We could see water on either side of this part of the country, and it continued to close in. I found myself becoming very emotional. I'd flown all the way to the most northern tip of our beautiful land. This was an achievement I had only dreamed of.

I made sure to land briefly on the helipad at Pajinka Wilderness Lodge, the same one Paul had taken Nigel and me to in Kevin's helicopter years earlier. I sat quietly for a moment, remembering how I'd told Kevin, 'I'll fly myself around Australia one day!' They were easy words to say back then. Now here I was really doing it.

The countryside flying south down the Cape York Peninsula was very flat and uninteresting. Thankfully, it was less than three hours to our destination at Weipa and the Albatross Hotel where Nigel and I had stayed with Kevin.

Today was going to be a big day. All the way to Normanton at the base of the Gulf of Carpentaria. Our total flight time would be almost six hours. That's a long time to sit in the same position and maintain the high level of concentration needed. We met early to take advantage of the cool morning air although, under the bubble of the helicopter, it was still like sitting in a sauna. The small air vents didn't do much to circulate any air. We made sure to take plenty of water on board to avoid dehydration. We were also becoming very tanned, despite slapping on the sunscreen.

Our track headed south along the beach. There was a fifteen-knot headwind that would slow us down. After a few hours, my back and knees were aching. I tried to shuffle around and change my position to ease the cramping pain that was beginning to agitate me.

'Let's take a break,' I suggested.

'I was just thinking the same thing,' Grant replied. 'There's a homestead marked on the map at the head of a river about ten miles ahead.'

'Let's aim for that,' Jim said. The site we'd picked looked like a shantytown with lean-to buildings scattered around. There were farmyard animals, remnants of old vehicles and piles of junk everywhere. We picked an area, clear of rubble, to land. However, the grass came up to the bottom of the door on the helicopter. A young woman named Janine and her three-year-old daughter greeted us, looking a bit cautious at first. But after we explained we were only tourists, she invited us in for a cup of tea. There were a few sites similar to this along the rivers, mainly accommodating squatters, who had set up very basic homes and lived off the land, although Janine did have cable television and a fax machine. It was certainly an eye-opening experience to see how some people lived.

Almost two hours further down the coast, we landed at another squatter's dwelling. These people had only been living on the river for a week. They invited us in and offered us welcome cool drinks. They had just retrieved a huge catch of mud crabs from the many traps along the riverbank.

'Take some with you,' they generously offered.

Despite their initial refusal to take any money, we reached a compromise and paid forty dollars for six enormous crabs. Fortunately my helicopter was piled full of gear and I couldn't fit the hessian bag full of muddies. Jamie was elected to take the crawly passengers. I was relieved. I'd had visions of one escaping mid flight and sightseeing around the cabin.

The scene below us began to change during the last leg before reaching Normanton. The ground, flat as far as you could see, was like an artist's canvas where intricate patterns were sketched into the light sand as a result of the tidal waters. Some of the pictures were as clear as if a master artist had magically brushed the delicate branches of an autumn tree, or outlined the skeletal remains of a giant prehistoric animal. An intricate river system weaved its way ahead of us, dramatically framing the many pictures. Like a serpent, the blue water snaked around, sometimes crossing over itself until it narrowed and spread like little fingers into the sand, finally petering out to nothing.

We'd made a booking to stay the night at the Normanton Pub, and we arranged to land the helicopters in a vacant block across the road. The sun was getting low on the horizon when the township finally came into sight. Everyone was tired. It had been a big day's flying. We lined up one after another and made our approach to land.

'Watch out for the power wires,' Grant called. I could see the poles that ran around the boundary of the grass area we were aiming for. But, no matter how hard I strained, I simply could not pick out the wires between them. I slowed down until ELF was almost stationary, hovering high above the poles, then inched slowly forward. It wasn't until I was right on top of the wires that they became visible. This gave me quite a fright. I'd heard so many horror stories of people being killed by flying straight into power wires. I could see how easy it would be.

We arrived at our next destination, Escott Station near Burketown, just on lunch time the next day. We'd be staying here for two days' rest, and we hoped to find somewhere nearby to try to catch a barramundi. Jamie stayed behind and relaxed while the rest of us flew west. Fifteen minutes later, we landed near the bend of a river to try our luck. Two hours and not a bite. Not even a nibble. After speaking with some of the fishing guides at the station that night, we learnt that the barramundi was very illusive in these areas. Some people spent weeks fishing the local rivers and never caught a thing. At that point, we made a pact that we would catch a barramundi before the end of the trip.

Escott Station was fantastic. We had our own bungalow with all facilities. The kitchen was fully equipped. We put it to good use and prepared our feast of mud crabs.

We'd made good friends at Escott Station, but we were keen to continue our progress through the Gulf of Carpentaria. We were given coordinates for a site only half an hour's flight away where there were two World War II aeroplane wrecks. They were almost on our track and were easily found. The surrounding area was heavily wooded and unsuitable for landing so the four helicopters joined in an anti-clockwise circuit, flying around the wrecks. I find these tragic sites very sad. We knew several people had died here. Unlike my own crash site, the remnants would remain, untouched, as a memorial to the deceased. At least I was able to imagine what the pilots and crew must have been through. There had been no survivors.

We didn't stay long before heading inland to a camping ground at Cape Crawford. It felt weird not being able to see the ocean, but the ever-changing landscape below was equally captivating. There was nothing but a blanket of greenery as far as you could see. Then round, smooth boulders were pushing their way up through the earth. This lead to a strange escarpment where enormous towering forms had eroded out of the reddish-coloured rocks and stood grandly pointing to the sky. Some were so lifelike they appeared to be celestial figures intentionally carved into the rocks, their sphinx-like faces peering down like sentries to a holy shrine. This was a strange and spooky place, enough for me to mark it on my map with the intention of finding out more about it.

One of the best things about the Robinson R22 helicopters is that they don't require a large area to land, so each time we flew to our next accommodation, we would try to park right at the site. Cape Crawford was located on the Carpentaria Highway. As we flew overhead, we could see the caravan park was full. There were several suitable spots to land, but there were too many people around and we decided it wasn't safe. There was a helipad next door but a Jetranger was already there and the many scattered fuel drums made this a potentially dangerous landing spot. The four of us were circling around for a few minutes. I decided to land on the dirt airstrip across the road. The others followed. The fine dust, swirling around and engulfing ELF, blinded me momentarily. I landed quickly so as not to make too much mess, although my helicopter was already coated with the fine red powder. We walked across the road, passing many of the campers as we made our way to reception.

'We thought we were being invaded,' one woman called out in delight.

'Where have you all come from in the helicopters?' another asked.

Our arrival had certainly made an impact. After collecting the keys to our cabins, we were encouraged to join a group in the bar of the adjoining roadhouse. There were candles down the length of the bar. The waitress looked like Morticia Adams, complete with the slinky long black dress and hair. At the end of the bar sat two scruffy old men, looking like typical outback Australian characters. They would surely be interesting to talk to so I propped myself up on the vacant stool next to them. They had long wiry hair and leathery skin, the result of the harsh Australian outback.

'Hullo,' I said to the man sitting closest.

He looked friendly enough but he didn't respond. Next thing he bashed his fist down on the timber counter.

'Got ya!' he cried.

It gave me a bit of a fright and I quickly asked, 'What was it?'

'It's those damned cockroaches,' he said.

I can't stand crawly things and I was pleased he'd taken care of the problem. But again he slammed his open hand down, almost spilling his freshly poured beer.

'Got yaaaa!' he said again.

This time I could see that he was swiping at invisible cockroaches.

'Okay!' I said, swivelling around in my chair, looking towards another group of men sitting in the corner. They were watching, amused to see my reaction to the man whose idiosyncrasies they knew well.

'You're one of the helicopter pilots, I'm told,' one of them said.

'Yes I am. I'm Allana.' I reached out and shook his hand.

'I'm Michael. I fly the Jetranger parked next door.'

Thank goodness I had a normal person to talk to.

'What do you do with the helicopter all the way out here?' I asked.

'I mainly do tourist flights out to the lost city,' he explained.

The lost city! It sounded so mysterious. As Michael explained the lost city rock formation to me, I realised it had been the eerie place we'd flown over on the way here. Michael was taking some people out in the morning. I told him I'd suggest to my friends that we fly out and meet him there. At that moment, I noticed the two scruffy fellows next to me, each picking up a candle off the bar. They held them below their faces and proceeded to chant in harmony a queer rendition of a religious song. I couldn't take my eyes off them and I wished Stewart had been here with the video camera. No one would believe this, I thought. At the end, I showed my obvious delight and encouraged them to do it again. Instead, they went back to chasing cockroaches across the bar.

My overwhelming curiosity about these two people was obvious. Michael told me that they were brothers and their job was to trek into the far-reaching outback to check the telephone lines. Sometimes they would be away for weeks at a time. I wondered if it was the isolation and remoteness that had affected them.

Before we took off the next morning, we had a round-table discussion about the day's flight. We'd be camping on Centre Island, north of Borroloola tonight, a flight of less than an hour. We decided to backtrack to the lost city. Grant and Jamie had met a man named Noel, the manager of a cattle station, who'd told them there were hot springs on the property. He'd invited us to fly across and have a swim.

Michael had landed the Jetranger at the lost city by the time we arrived. There weren't many clear places to put down, and the tortured rocky ground made it even more challenging. Everyone made it in safely, although we had landed a considerable distance apart.

'Coooeeee,' I heard echoing around the natural sandstone pillars.

'Coooeeee,' I called back.

Grant, Stewart, Jamie, Jim, Jenny and I converged to the one spot, deep within the maze, by following the resounding calls. The grandeur of this place felt very spiritual. Again, we were captivated, marvelling at the wonders of nature.

Airborne again, we flew to Bohemia Downs Station, nestled at the base of a mountainous ridge. We could see two natural spring waterfalls feeding into a crystal clear pond about half a mile from the homestead. Noel had said one spring had hot water, the other cold. Where they mixed together at the bottom, the water was warm like a bath. From there, the water ran into a larger pool, creating a lush and tranquil oasis. It had sounded like a bit of a tall tale. But we were about to experience another wondrous phenomenon of nature.

We were introduced to Harry, the Aboriginal elder of the tribe that owned the land.

'Are there any crocodiles around here, Harry?' I asked.

I realised that I tended to ask this question a lot!

'Only little ones,' he said.

'Have you seen any up at the spring?'

'All the time!' he said.

That was it for me. There was no way I was going into the water, although I did want to have a look.

We were taken along a bumpy track in Noel's 4WD, high up towards the mountain. The dense foliage opened to reveal one of the most beautiful places I'd ever seen. The rocky cliff face rose from the emerald green water that glistened as a soft breeze disturbed its mirror-like surface. Tropical ferns blended in harmony with our unique Australian eucalypts, framing the inviting pond. The scene looked more like the expensive set of a Hollywood movie.

Without hesitation, the others waded into the deep natural bath.

'It's so warm and fresh,' they were saying.

Despite some spirited coaxing, I remained on the shore. My fear of the water was something I had not been able to overcome. I'm comfortable in a swimming pool. But the thought of being in an uncontrolled environment where creatures live under the surface of the water was something

I could not come to terms with. It had become worse since my accident. I'd had horrible thoughts of little critters nibbling at my legs without me knowing. I had a nightmare once that I was in the ocean and a shark came along and bit one of my legs off. But because I couldn't feel them, I wasn't aware this had happened until I tried to get out of the water.

The group swam off around the corner and out of sight. My curiosity got the better of me. I walked towards the water's edge, squatting down so I could reach in and feel how warm it was. I wished I'd had the courage to venture in. Instead, I took the opportunity to scoop up some water in my hands and wash my face and arms. Then I remembered Harry telling me he'd seen plenty of crocodiles in this area.

'Only little ones,' he'd said. I didn't care how little they were. I quickly stood up and returned to the safety of the vehicle nearby. What a coward!

We flew to Borroloola to refuel the helicopters and buy groceries for our camping adventure on Centre Island. We'd been told of an abandoned weather station on the southern end of the island where there was supposedly a freshwater tank as well as basic facilities.

The station was a great spot. The main building was one big room with a dozen beds and mattresses. And there was even a barbecue area. Jim didn't waste time, dragging out his fishing rod and throwing in a line as the sun sank low on the horizon. Stewart and Grant had collected enough firewood to last a week and we already had the barbecue well alight.

Grant took charge of the cooking. We had a selection of tinned stew, baked beans and a beef and vegetable mix on the menu for tonight. All was serene. We'd found chairs and we were sitting around the barbecue talking about our eventful day when all of a sudden, 'CABOOM!' The explosion was in the fireplace. Nobody knew what had happened until suddenly we were being showered with Irish stew. Grant had placed the tins of food on the hotplate and failed to puncture the lids. He quickly pulled them off the heat, fearful of losing them all. I was laughing so hard that I lost all the strength in my legs, I couldn't even stand up to go and help. Everyone was picking bits of carrot and beef off themselves.

The next day we headed for Nhulunbuy where our hosts, Don and Kay Miller at the Nhulunbuy Resort Hotel, had given us permission to land on the grass next to their swimming pool.

As routine, we circled the town a few times and located the hotel that was right on the water. The grass area looked very small and there were a few obstacles to avoid. I had a concrete fence behind me and a large palm tree in front. I snuck down, trying to leave plenty of room for Jamie, who was on final approach behind me. As I moved forwards a little, descending slowly, I was more concerned with the concrete wall I couldn't see rather than the large branches of the palm tree that were uncomfortably close to me and straight ahead. A few leaves went flying as my blades cut through one of the fronds that protruded further than the others.

'Woops, sorry,' I said to myself.

Another branch caught the tips of my blades and sent

a shower of spindly leaves flying into the air.

'Sorry again,' I said.

'Doing some pruning are we, ELF?' Grant said over the radio. He could see the mess I was making. I knew hitting the leaves wouldn't damage the helicopter, but the concrete wall would. After we were safely settled, I apologised to the owners for the mess I'd made.

Don and Kay were extremely keen to hear our stories. We showed them on a map where we'd be flying the next day. You've got to stop at Arafura Swamp, it's right on your track, they told us. Apparently airboats operate from the station and are used to venture into the swamp to collect crocodile eggs. They often take tourists out in the boats. We were keen to try it.

The swamp area was clearly marked on our maps and was very extensive. As we ventured closer, we could see the ground becoming marshy and the vegetation changed into a pastiche of vibrant green shades in swirling designs. Patches of soggy ground merged into a brilliant azure blue river that sliced through the earth like a snake, creating a carnival of colour in a world that simply had to be imaginary. Nothing I'd seen before in my life could be compared with the Arafura Swamp. It was a scene from prehistoric times.

We landed next to the homestead and were met by two men who ran the facility and encouraged us to stay for a cup of tea. Jim hadn't stopped talking about the possibility of riding in the airboat. When we asked about it, we were told our timing was off. It was unserviceable and they were waiting for a part to arrive so the engine could be fixed. We were disappointed, but we got the chance to look through the egg hatchery and incubator to see the one-day-old crocodiles. Jenny held one of the tiny critters. It was hard to imagine this little guy, who fitted in the palm of Jenny's hand, would grow up to be such a monstrous creature.

We were able to buy a drum of fuel to give us extra flying time to have a look around the swamp. Airborne, we went in separate directions, each following our own part of the waterway. As I meandered along at about fifty feet above the terrain I could see the water alive with fish that leapt out as the surface was disturbed by the downwash from my blades. Towering palm trees lined the banks where, through this dense foliage, I saw the occasional crocodile scurry into the safety of the water. I pushed the collective forward, picking up speed, then climbed up to get an overview of the area. From this vantage point, I could see the three other helicopters lined abreast above another section of the river.

I dived down, heading in their direction, and picked up another waterway. As I followed a tight corner, a mass of large water birds launched into the air right in front of me. My heart skipped a beat. They were upon me before I had time to climb or turn out of the way.

'Oh, shit!' I called out. I struggled not to close my eyes, but stared ahead waiting for the inevitable collision. There were birds flying in every direction, some were so close I could almost see the shocked looks on their faces. I'm sure my own expression was the same. But, as quickly as they had appeared, my path ahead suddenly cleared. How I didn't hit one of them, I'll never know.

I caught up with the others and joined the end of the queue. Jim was leading as I watched him fly through a similar blanket of feathers.

'Wow, did you see that!' he exclaimed.

'I just had the same thing happen, Jim. Did you hit any of them?'

'No! I don't know how, but I didn't hit a single one,' he replied.

We needed to get going so we climbed up to one thousand feet and set our heading for Jabiru where we'd be staying overnight. The flat plains were soon far behind us and the earth began to rise up. The surface of these hills was mainly solid rock, craggy and tortured in places. The harsh remoteness of the environment was confronting. I wouldn't want to be flying out here by myself. To my right, a section of the rock shelf looked to have a crack right through it that extended towards the direction we were travelling. I turned towards it and established myself over the top. It was as if the earth itself had come apart. The fracture was so deep, I couldn't even see the bottom.

Further along, more cracks opened into a deep valley that cradled the dazzling white sand and fresh blue water of the Alligator River. It seemed nature had a surprise for us around every corner. When we thought we'd seen the most beautiful place, one that could never be rivalled, we'd find even more wondrous regions to discover. Sheer cliffs and flat top mountains towered above us on either side, eventually leading us to the escarpment and more flat boggy plains.

The Kakadu National Park is a favourite destination for tourists, which was obvious by the crowds of people staying at the caravan park we'd booked into. It was a shock. Up until now, our journey had taken us to quiet sleepy towns or faraway homesteads. We found this tourist trap almost suffocating and we couldn't wait to escape back into the secluded wilderness.

Our next stop was Darwin where we'd stay for three days while Jamie's and my helicopter had one-hundred hourly inspections.

Chapter 15

Going Home

We said goodbye to Stewart at Darwin as he went back to his home at Yarrawonga in Victoria. He'd been very helpful to me over the past weeks – refuelling my helicopter, carrying my bags and helping me whenever he could. I couldn't thank him enough and was sad to see him go. Grant had another friend, Greg, who joined our group. He was friendly and outgoing and we took to him instantly.

The coastline welcomed us back. Once we were clear of the Darwin Control Zone, we descended and chased each other along the sands playing dogfights. This helped to relieve the frustration we'd felt after being stuck on the ground for three days.

Our accommodation for the night was at a motel/roadhouse with a caravan park behind it. There was a small adjoining paddock where we had gained permission to leave the helicopters overnight. As I came in to land, I kept a careful look out around me for unsuspected obstacles. There was a green hose amongst the grass. I steered clear of this. The field was generally open and an appropriate place to land, although the dried-out weeds and thistles were quite long in places. I was surprised to see a small herd of goats appear to my left. They were running along the fence line and came to a halt, huddling together in the corner furthest away. I was even more surprised when moments later a turkey came bounding along in full stride, comically waddling in front of me.

An audience of spectators hung over the timber fence that led into the park and, again, their curiosity meant answering a familiar repertoire of questions.

We were standing in the office collecting our room keys when the phone rang. The manager of the motel answered it, then handed me the phone. On the other end, was a very upset lady who owned the paddock where we'd left the helicopters. I was so embarrassed. We'd landed in the wrong place. She'd ventured outside to tend to her animals and found her new garden art was made up of four little helicopters – woops! I couldn't apologise enough and assured her it was a great mistake. I explained how we had believed her land to be the area we'd pre-arranged to use and hoped we hadn't caused her or the animals any distress. She was so nice that she said we could leave them where they were. And, she added, she would transfer the goats into an adjoining field so they wouldn't chew the helicopters.

Later today, we'd be flying over an area known as the Bungle Bungles. I knew this was a unique rocky outcrop, but I didn't know much more. We were now into Western

Australia. I had just flown off map number ten – it would take twenty-two maps to complete the Australian coastline. Every change of map was a cause to celebrate.

'There goes another one,' I said over the radio.

Along the next leg, we passed the famous Argyle Diamond Mine tucked into the base of a mountain that was slowly being cut away. From here, the scenery changed again. The earth portrayed a tortured past as if it had been compressed and sections had ruptured, sending splintered slabs high into the air, like a concertina. I followed a contoured slope upward, my altimeter rising steadily towards the peak that appeared to end abruptly in the distance. I couldn't see what was beyond as I was only five hundred feet over the ground. I soon made it to the edge, where the ground dropped away suddenly and the sheer cliff pointed straight down for what looked like another thousand feet.

It was unexpected and the shock took my breath away. My heart was thumping deep in my chest and a short burst of adrenaline made me start laughing out aloud to myself. All of a sudden, I felt very small amidst the stupendous spectacle below.

High winds churned around the many ridges and slopes making our ride uncomfortably rough. We'd flown through severe turbulence before and I knew all I could do was hold on, maintaining control as best I could yet resisting the urge to over-compensate for the relentless jarring bumps. To over-control in these conditions could be fatal. Some months later, I had the opportunity to meet the designer and manufacturer of the R22, Frank Robinson, and he told me that less experienced pilots had found themselves in trouble doing this.

The tension in Jamie's voice was obvious.

'I don't like this at all,' he said, before maintaining radio silence as he concentrated intensely on his flying.

Although extremely stressful, this ordeal passed in time to become a very exciting memory of a tremendous challenge. Once the conditions had eased, I was left feeling victorious and very confident.

We continued to the area which was marked on our maps as the Bungle Bungle Range. This outcrop of large rusty-coloured mounds looked like it was home to giant bee-like creatures who had built their nests side by side, each one with a smoothly contoured surface in varying hive-inspired forms. Changing colours were highlighted in horizontal layers of rock, making the entire area look like a lunar surface plonked smack bang in the middle of the Australian outback. I imagined early explorers discovering this place and wondered what they must have thought.

Our adventure continued the next day. We were deep in the heart of the Kimberley which we all expected to be the highlight of the trip. Several days had been set aside so we could zigzag throughout the many deep river gorges and canyons. This is where we knew we'd have the best chance to catch a barra and, given we were camping out tonight, we hoped they would be on the menu.

The plan was to find a fishing hole. There were plenty to choose from. We finally ended up landing on a craggy rock shelf that was raised twenty metres above the water but, despite patiently waiting it out for a few hours, there was not a single fish caught. At times we could see schools of large black fish swimming by which made it even more frustrating that we could not hook one. Back in the air, we followed our river to a waterfall and decided to land at the top next to a sandy riverbank to set up camp for the night.

Our five days of flying and fishing in the Kimberley were magnificent. And yes, we did catch a barra, although he almost got away. From the air, the water hole had looked perfect. Jim landed first, then the other two settled, while I hovered over the knobbly ground trying to find an even surface. Ever so gently, I placed ELF down. But before lowering the collective completely, I swayed my body forwards and backwards, side to side, so I could make sure I was securely on even ground and wouldn't tip over. The helicopter teetered like a seesaw. It felt like I could topple over at any moment. I picked her up off the ground again and moved across slightly, although the uneven surface was consistent all over. When I landed, I could see the front of my skid suspended in the air, but this time at least I was stable.

Jim, Grant and I had cast our lines deep into the centre of the pond, while Jamie found a shady spot to read a book and Greg wandered around with his video camera. Jenny had walked upstream a little further. We noticed the tide was changing and had begun to run out.

'You should see all the fish swimming down towards you,' Jenny called out.

At that second my line screamed and the rod arched over, pointing towards a rocky outcrop visible just beneath the surface of the water.

'Jesus Christ! Whatever it is – it's big!' Grant yelled.

'Don't let him snag you. Keep him away from the rocks!'

Jenny came running over as Greg kept the camera rolling. 'It's got to be a barramundi,' I screamed.

I kept pressure on the line, slowly reeling it in. But a few seconds later it become snagged.

'Oh, bugger!'

I let out some slack, hoping the fish would run again, helping me to release it. But it wasn't going to help me. Despite my pulling and yanking, it was not going to budge. Jenny took my rod and walked down the bank, continuing the tug of war.

Immediately Grant's reel began whizzing and his flimsy fishing rod bent over so hard I was sure it would break. The atmosphere was electric. We were sure to have fish for dinner tonight. Jim handed me his line so he could help Grant, who was winning the battle to land the huge fish that had identified itself by flipping high out of the water – barramundi!

'Almost there, only a few feet to go.' Jim was so keen to help Grant land the fish he was almost in the water himself.

At the same time, Jenny unsnagged the line from my fishing rod which still had the fish hooked to it. Then Jim's line, which I was holding, took off. Everything was happening at once.

Grant's prize catch was exhausted. He'd put up a great fight but it was almost as though he'd accepted defeat. The boys dragged him up towards the edge of the overhanging rock. But just as Jim reached over to lift him out of the water, the hook dislodged itself, whipping out of the fish's mouth and impaling itself deep into Jim's hand. Despite the pain, Jim's only concern was the fish. He jumped into the water and grabbed hold of the barra which, having sensed the opportunity to escape, began thrashing around trying to swim away. Jim managed to trap it in a crevice between two rocks before Grant quickly threw it up onto dry land away from the water.

Poor Jim was in so much pain.

'Jenny, help!' he called out.

'Hang on, Jim, I'll just land this fish and then I'll fix your hand,' she said.

'I taught her well. The fish always comes first,' Jim said, looking up at me.

The three fish were out of the water and it was time to attend to Jim. The large hook was deeply imbedded. We agreed the best method to release it was to cut off the barb that projected backwards from the tip of the hook, then pull it out.

We had lost so many lures and hooks over the week that we didn't have many left. And out in the middle of nowhere, there wasn't a convenient tackle shop to replenish our stock. Jim was more concerned about running out of fishing supplies than his injury, and he told Grant to pull the hook out backwards.

'Oh, no! Oh, yuk!' We were all horrified.

'You're not really going to do it?' I asked.

Without hesitation Grant took hold of the hook with a pair of pliers and quickly ripped it out. We each felt the pain and cringed. This was the first time our medical kit had been used but, despite plenty of blood, the drama was over.

Although we carried camping gear, we usually stayed at outback homesteads during our trek around the Kimberley. Many of these stations provide bed and breakfast lodging. Sometimes the accommodation was very basic, but if there was a hot shower and anything resembling a bed, we didn't care.

One stop was at Beverly Springs, appropriately named because of its natural water springs. It was an incredible oasis where the surrounding wildlife roamed free, close to the house. Dozens of fancy lyrebirds dotted the landscape, including a pure white bird which was so used to visitors that it allowed us to walk right up to it.

After dinner I prepared for my shower. I was pleased to hear there was plenty of hot water and I was looking forward to washing away a day's worth of dirt and sweat. I still wasn't used to the humidity in the top part of Australia, and by the end of each day I'd feel disgusting and sticky. The bathroom was a big room with the shower in the corner. It didn't have a door or a curtain. Towards the light, I could see one wall was covered by strange little blobs. It wasn't until I got closer that I realised they were hundreds of tiny frogs. I wasn't thrilled to be sharing my shower with these guys, but I assured myself it would be okay as long as they stayed on the wall.

Breathtaking gorges extend throughout the Kimberley, each one guiding its own river system, creating cascading waterfalls and large ponds. Tidal changes alter these spots very quickly, as I was to find out.

We'd landed right next to a river where the water was running from one pool into another, gently trickling over slimy rocks. We were planning to spend most of the day fishing. Jim and Grant landed their machines on an elevated rock shelf, but I landed on slightly sloping ground just near the water's edge. We'd been down for almost an hour when I noticed the water had reversed and was running back in the opposite direction. A little while later, I observed the water line creeping closer to my ELF. I decided to move her to higher ground. By the time I'd shut down and walked back to the original site, it was almost under water.

The Kimberley region is an Australian treasure and a place I know I'll return to. Next time, hopefully, I can plan to stay a little longer.

I'd arranged for the group to stay with friends of mine, David Ritherdon and his new wife, Jill, who owned and ran an accommodation lodge in the town of Derby. David was one of the builders who helped with renovations to the house in the Blue Mountains after my accident. He had moved to Derby some years before so it was great to have a chance to catch up.

Instead of flying direct to Broome, we hugged the coast, flying in a northerly direction towards Cape Leveque. This area was made famous some years earlier when an American woman tourist who was sailing in the region decided to take a swim in a sheltered alcove and was taken by a crocodile.

Broome was a town we stayed at for two nights. We tried to ensure there were scattered recreation days along our journey to give everybody a chance to replenish supplies and rest and by the time we arrived, the break was well deserved. Greg left the group in Broome to return home to his printing business. Again it was sad to lose a member of the crew. Greg had always been there to help me carry my luggage or refuel the helicopter and I appreciated his kindness very much.

Grant had another mate who would do the leg from Broome to Perth with us. His name was Rusty. A real character, he had a thick crop of red hair and was once a gun shearer. Rusty had developed back problems from years of bending over shearing sheep, and he could no longer do that sort of work.

Grant introduced me to Rusty. His first words were, 'Hullo, isn't it a yummy day!' I liked him instantly.

It took us six days to fly down the west coast from Broome to Perth. Each day we'd clock up an average of just over four hours in the air. I didn't know much about the coastline along this stretch. There were to be some surprises.

We stayed overnight at Port Headland, then flew to Karratha Airport to get fuel. I had just finished shutting ELF down and climbed outside, when I saw a man walking across the tarmac. He had a familiar stride and as he came closer I realised it was David Coxhead, one of my first helicopter flying instructors. David had moved to Karratha just before I completed my training. He was thrilled to see me taking on such a tremendous challenge.

Heading south again, we saw an enormous pure white mountain in the distance. It glowed brilliantly against the blue sky. I thought I was seeing a mirage at first because, from a distance, it looked like a giant iceberg. Nobody knew what to make of it until we noticed we were approaching

Taxada Saltworks marked on our maps. Our iceberg was a mountain of salt.

The next section of coastline was along the Zuytdorp Cliffs, which displayed some of the most ruggedly beautiful scenery I had ever seen. The sheer rock face ran vertically into the angry sea, which swirled and lashed and frothed at its base. The earth had simply broken away in jagged pieces revealing horizontal layers of different shaded sandstone. The cliffs were so high that in one section they rose more than 240 metres from the level of the sea. That meant that when we were flying along over the water we were looking up at the top of the escarpment towering over us.

Strategically placed were tourist lookouts. However, there were many sections where the cliff face had been eroded, undercut below the top, and the overhang reached three to six metres at times. I'm sure tourists have stood on these lookouts unaware that the presumably stable platform was a vulnerable piece of earth hanging suspended in the air.

It was here we spotted gigantic whales, usually travelling in pairs not far from the coast. And just off Kalbarri, where we landed for the night, were a pod of dozens of dolphins.

The next day we reached Perth where we would stay for three days' rest. It was a great relief. Over the past two days I'd been feeling unwell, although I put it down to being tired. Before leaving the airport for my hotel, I was able to arrange to have my helicopter detailed, and I took my G.P.S. (global positioning satellite) to be fixed. The G.P.S. had being playing up most of the trip. It hadn't worked properly

The Best I Can Be

since Cairns so I was forced to rely on the old fashioned method of navigating by map crawling, which I enjoy anyway. Let's face it. We were virtually following the coast all the way around the country. You'd have to be pretty dumb to get lost.

Once settled in my hotel room, I went to bed and practically stayed there for two days, recovering from what turned out to be a flu virus. In the meantime, the rest of the group played tourist around Perth.

We met early on the third day, ready to go although the weather was atrocious – low cloud, rain and very cold. The airport was closed due to the weather conditions, but Grant and I were keen to go and so was Grant's new crew member, Ellis. He couldn't believe his first day flying could be canned and we'd be stuck on the ground all day. We knew if we could get a clearance to fly directly to the coast, we could establish ourselves over the water and creep along under the weather. We called the control tower on the phone and were given a special clearance to leave.

As soon as I hopped into the helicopter the windows fogged up, making it almost impossible to see outside. Fortunately ELF was equipped with a heater that helped to defog the windscreen. However, it wasn't until I was airborne and had established over sixty knots that the rain drops washed off the bubble, allowing me to see ahead clearly. Thankfully the weather began to break and, although there were still passing showers, it looked to be getting much better. It took us over an hour to reach Bunbury where we knew we could get fuel.

Not long after becoming airborne from there, the

weather conditions began to deteriorate once again. There were areas where we'd be flying into what looked like a wall of heavy rain. Fierce turbulence lashed at us requiring an enormous level of concentration to simply fly straight and maintain a constant height. Jim and Jenny had flown past me and warned of heavier rain ahead. It hit suddenly, pounding on the bubble. The noise was deafening although I was more worried about the potential damage to my blades from the heavy drops. I slowed down to about fifty knots and flew at thirty feet over the water, trying to stay below the cloud base.

The jagged coastline was swamped by rabid foaming waves that were being whipped up by the wind. The spectacular display below me revealed the power of nature in full flight. It was very humbling.

We'd planned to drop into Margaret River, slightly inland. But once we reached a position adjacent to the town, we could see black clouds over the land to our left. We decided to continue our track above the water until we reached Augusta.

Flying in these challenging conditions, when you have to creep beneath the cloud base, is quite safe in a helicopter along a coastline because if the visibility or rain become too severe, it's easy to land on the beach. Flying over water is also safe because you are assured of a clear passage ahead. However, to fly in the same conditions over land, where difficult-to-see power wires, communication towers or hills and trees can be very dangerous, is to be avoided.

The little air strip at Augusta was near the coast. At the time the four helicopters flew in, the wind was still gusting to thirty-five knots. It was freezing cold and the rain was coming down almost horizontally. Some of the local pilots looked on, saying we were mad to be flying in such atrocious conditions. For a moment, I stood thinking about the past few hours. Although I was exhausted and frozen, I'd had so much fun.

Before leaving Augusta the next day, we dropped in on Cape Leeuwin lighthouse to take some photographs. Then we headed for Albany, a few hours away, for fuel. We asked one of the workers at Albany Airport if there was anywhere in town we could land and have some lunch.

'You should go out to Whaleworld and land there,' he suggested.

Whaleworld is a museum on the coast at Albany. It used to be a whaling station and was established in 1952 to process humpback and sperm whales. The whaling ceased in 1978, which was a very good move. The museum is interesting because of its original machinery and nostalgic photographs, but I couldn't help feeling an overwhelming sadness. Those beautiful creatures, so like the ones we'd seen playing innocently in their ocean home, had been brutally slaughtered for many years.

When we left the museum, the sun was out. There were a few clouds around and it was very cold. Although we were flying in a group, often one or more of the four helicopters would go off, fly inland slightly, move ahead of the group or lag behind. But if there was something spectacular to see, we'd regroup for a look.

Grant and I were flying along together with the other two helicopters well ahead. There was a little green island coming up in the distance that rose out of the blue water like a round ball. It sat alone, barren. But while there were no trees or shrubs, there was a cover of short grass.

'Go and land on top of that island, ELF, and I'll get a photo. It'll look great,' Grant suggested.

'Good idea. I'll fly ahead.'

It wasn't until I was below fifty feet that I noticed the entire island was covered with strange, smoothly rounded rocks that glistened in the sun. They were the same shape and generally the same size. However, there were one or two smaller ones.

'This island is covered with the weirdest rocks. You should come down and have a look,' I said to Grant.

Just as I had made the broadcast, the rocks began to scatter, splaying out in every direction below me as I hovered a few feet off the ground.

'Hey, Grant, they're not rocks, they're seals.'

Jamie and Jim heard our conversation and immediately turned around to join us over the island. The seals were very shy. Most of them had run straight to the water's edge and jumped into the safety of the ocean. But there were a few dozen left who were just as curious about us as we were about them.

We found a place to land. Jim was braver than the rest of us. He tried to get close to one female only to be chased away by her mate. I've never seen Jim run so fast. In one group, there was a mother with a little baby. They were so beautiful with their big eyes and whiskered faces that we decided not to stay on the island too long for fear of upsetting them.

It had been an eventful day and late in the afternoon we approached a little place called Hopetoun. We'd arranged to land in a small clearing and stay at the local pub for the night. The hotel was easily sighted. However, there were children playing in the park where we were supposed to land.

'I'm not happy with this, guys. I don't want to land near the children,' I said.

'I agree,' Grant replied.

We continued circling while we decided what to do. Just at that moment, the publican came running out of the front door of the pub, holding up a big sign saying Footy Oval. We flew to the middle of town and landed on the football field.

The long stretch across the Great Australian Bight was often harsh. On one leg we flew inland across the Nullarbor Plain to a roadhouse where we'd shipped a drum of fuel. It was late in the afternoon. Low in the sky was a spectrum of blue shades following the natural curvature of the earth. The colours were reflected off the carpet of trees below which also followed the contours of the land. There was not a mountain or a hill in sight. This stark unchanging region had a beauty all of its own. To be flying through its infinite expanse was liberating.

I couldn't help thinking how day-to-day life back in Sydney would often get me down. I was thinking of this and looking around at the land stretching in all directions. It was all the same. As far as the eye could see, there was nothing. Yet it was stunningly beautiful. I felt freed of all my worries back home. I was happy to just be out in the open, enjoying our marvellous country. It puts life in perspective, doesn't it!

The Nullarbor was consistently flat. Sometimes we'd track along the highway. Then, if we were bored, we'd alter our track to the right and head off to the rugged coastal cliffs.

Eucla was our next stop for fuel and lunch. The roadhouse had its own airstrip and regularly serviced fuel for passing fliers. We were sitting inside the diner, almost finished our lunch, when just outside the window we saw a strange dusty grey motor bike with a side car pull up. It looked like something straight out of the movie, *Mad Max*, where futuristic desert vehicles were the normal mode of transport. A tall, scruffy-looking bloke stepped off the bike. He was wearing a yellow jacket with strange blue/green canvas gloves that stayed attached to the handle bars when he pulled his hands away.

'Get a load of this,' I said to the others.

The man took off his jacket and had a long driza-bone underneath. When he removed his helmet and the scarf that was wrapped around his mouth, we saw he had a long red beard that went halfway down his chest. The sidecar was piled high full of gear. Amongst it a woman was squeezing her way out of the canvas cover, attached to the bike, which had enclosed her like a pod. We watched on, amazed at this curious sight. The couple had parked next to a picnic table to have their lunch. The man walked to the back of the bike and lifted the lid of a large square box which looked like a fridge. He dragged out a pile of supplies and laid them on the table. Then the two of them sat contentedly, eating in the sun.

Where were they going and what were they doing? Before we flew off, we went outside and introduced ourselves. Harry and Jane were the loveliest couple. Harry was once a gun shearer, a term I now understood. Like Rusty, he had also developed back problems and now only worked as a general hand in the sheds. Jane was a wool classer and they were heading to a shearing shed east of the Nullarbor to work. Their lives were regulated by the seasons as they moved from one sheep property to another.

'Where are you lot headed?' Harry asked.

I don't think they believed us when we said there were four helicopters waiting behind the roadhouse, ready to take us back to the Nullarbor and eventually home to Sydney. We told them of our adventures, but still they were a bit sceptical. Harry and Jane packed away their gear ready to hit the road again.

'You head off and we'll get airborne and catch up with you,' we suggested. It wasn't long before they had a four-helicopter escort formatting above them. Jane leaned out through a gap in the canvas door and took a few photos. Jenny did the same from the air. When we reached the roadhouse on the Nullarbor, we were checking into our rooms at the adjoining motel when the bike arrived.

'That was great,' Harry said. 'Why don't you fly over to the shearing shed in the morning for breakfast?'

I'd never seen a sheep being shorn before. We were thrilled with the invitation. Harry drew us a quick map on a scrap of paper, showing us where they'd be and we agreed to fly over early.

We were up at dawn and airborne at 7 a.m. There was

a low cover of fog across the ground that shone a golden lustre in the morning light. From above, the wispy layer was like a transparent veil. But looking across towards the horizon, it became a dense cloud, making me feel we were flying high above the heavens. The four helicopters flew direct to the coast where we'd meet the sheer sandstone cliffs we'd been following yesterday. It was as if we'd flown to the edge of the world. As the fog met the vertical drop, it cascaded into the ocean like a waterfall. I couldn't help but feel invigorated and I made sure to absorb every sight and every smell of this particular morning. Its simple beauty made me come alive. I was thankful just to be here.

Our directions to the sheep property took us inland across sweeping green fields. We knew we had to be close to the area shown on our map, but there were several stations in close proximity. It could have been any one of them. We'd been flying around for a few minutes when away in the distance we saw Harry riding his bike around in circles, creating a small cloud of dust for us to see. Jim spotted it first. Although I didn't know what to expect from our morning's diversion, this was going to be a new experience for me.

The shed was small with about a dozen sheep yards adjoining it. There was an open verandah along its length where enormous bales of wool were stacked. We brought production to a standstill as the workers stood outside, watching us come in to land. I don't know who was more excited, out team visiting a real life shearing shed, or their team having four real life helicopters drop in for breakfast. Either way, it became one of the highlights of our trip.

We were sitting on the wool bales, outside in the warm sun, enjoying a cup of tea and chocolate cake and talking to the gang, when all of a sudden a siren rang. Without hesitation, everyone flew into their work leaving six bamboozled helicopter crew standing alone. Comical music blared in the background while three young shearers focused, undistracted, on their tasks. We walked inside, dodging the frenzied activity around us. Harry stood in the internal yards managing a herd of forty sheep. From here, the shearer would step towards a gate and push the counter that was used to tally his work for the day. Then he'd grab one of the woolly victims, dragging it towards a sling that was used to lean against in an attempt to support the shearer's back. The sheep were submissive and, despite the odd close shave that often drew blood, they didn't appear too worried about being contorted out of shape, pulled and yanked. Once stripped of their warm coats, they were released naked to run down a ramp into the crisp air outside. The cheerful and often cheeky music kept the workers motivated. We found it infectious and sang along with the group to silly songs with words like, 'my ding-a-ling, my ding-a-ling, I want you to play with my ding-a-ling.'

Once the sheep had been shorn, the fleece was collected and thrown on a table to have any dirt pulled off. Then it was classed and thrown into an appropriate pile to be made into a bale. Every few minutes a guy would run around the shearers with a special broom, collecting all the stray bits of wool left behind. One time, his broom dropped onto the floor and the three shearers cheered.

'What's that all about?' I asked Jane.

'That means the sweeper has to buy the shearers a round of drinks tonight.'

I could have happily stayed there for the day. It felt very Australian to be watching such a traditional activity in action. But, eventually, we had to get back on the track.

We stopped for fuel at Ceduna where Grant spent most of his time on the phone. He was running his business while on the trip, and it was becoming a bit too difficult.

We made Port Lincoln by the end of the day. Grant was becoming even more stressed about his work commitments. Finally, he decided he would have to leave the group the next morning to fly home. If he left early enough, he could make it all the way in one day.

It was sad to see him go. It would have been special to finish the trip as a group. But we understood Grant and his helicopter had to leave – so then there were three.

It was strange without Grant, but onward we went to the top of the Spencer Gulf and Port Augusta in South Australia, then down the other side into the Barossa Valley, one of our most famous wine producing areas. Earlier that day, we'd contacted Barossa Helicopters and arranged to land at their helipad in a little town called Lyndoch, where we would stay the night. The valley was spectacular and a welcome diversion from the coastline. Some of the picture book villages looked so inviting that I wished we had time to stay for a couple of days.

Our journey was coming to an end very quickly, and we all felt it. We'd be staying at Jim and Jenny's house in two days' time and, within four or five days, I'd be home. I was feeling a bit depressed now, knowing I'd be facing the realities of day to day life again soon. I felt very apprehensive about going home. Nigel and I were going to try to save our marriage once more. The agreement was for me to move back into our home when I returned. It had been almost six months since our separation. However, we still hadn't resolved many of the issues that had caused us to break up in the first place. Finally, I decided to ignore these emotions and deal with the problems when I got home. For now, I still had five days to explore Australia before flying into Sydney.

Jim and Jenny would make it home today. I wondered how they were feeling. I expected they would be excited at beating such a great challenge, but sad that it had come to an end. They were both quiet this day, which was very understandable. We had been away so long and had become great friends. Before the trip began, I had wondered how the group would get along. Jamie, Grant, Jim, Jenny and I hadn't known each other well. All we'd had in common was a love of flying and a passionate desire to circumnavigate our country. I am amazed how well we worked together. For me, to have the support of such a caring group was the only way I could have made the journey. Everyone had been there for me, often providing emotional support. And, whenever there was anything that needed doing which I physically couldn't handle, they were there to help. Their friendships mean the world to me.

The last leg that day took us along Victoria's Great Ocean Road where we took plenty of photographs of the Twelve Apostles, before flying into a heavy rain shower. It was here that I flew off map number twenty-one and onto map number twenty-two, the last in the set. Then it would be back to number one again which would take me into Sydney.

Map twenty-two was significant. Before I'd left Sydney, I'd been in the hangar at Camden preparing my charts. I laid the twenty-two maps out on the ground to form Australia. I stood in the middle and suddenly realised how enormous the task ahead was. I looked at map one and I couldn't wait for the day the trip would begin. Then I looked at map twenty-two and wondered if I'd make it all the way around.

Jamie and I followed Jim as he led us to his property. The district was made up of open paddocks with many horse properties. We landed in a field near Jim and Jenny's house. It seemed a non-event. Jenny checked her horses and the garden. Jim opened the house up, and they both filed through six weeks of mail. Nothing had really changed. It was as if they had never left.

'Let's keep going tomorrow, Jenny, and fly with Jamie to the Hunter Valley where we left as a group,' Jim suggested.

Jenny agreed. They weren't ready to end the adventure yet. I wouldn't have been surprised if they'd decided to keep going and fly around again.

There was no hurry in the morning. We flew a few minutes over a hill to an airstrip at Tyabb, where I knew a few people. During our stay, we indulged in many cups of tea and aviation chatter, before leaving to catch up with Grant at his home in Orbost. We would stay there tonight.

The sky was blanketed by cloud and it was very cold. I was thankful to have my heater running full blast in the helicopter but even then I was still shivering. We had travelled half an hour down the coast when I realised I was becoming uncomfortable. I regretted drinking all that tea. I hated the thought of holding up the group, but I kept a lookout for somewhere to land.

Jim's voice came over the radio at this point. 'I've got to land on the beach for a comfort stop,' he said.

'Same here,' I replied.

I was glad we weren't just stopping for me, but I would have liked to find somewhere a little more private. Up ahead, I could see a car park on top of a hill above the beach. There was a small round building next to it, which I hoped was an amenities block. And it was, thank goodness! There was one car in the lot and I could see a man on the beach fishing. There was no one else in sight so I decided to land as discreetly as I could, run in to use the toilet, then take off again and nobody would ever know. Jim had already landed below on the beach. Jamie continued to circle overhead, making my little excursion more conspicuous. I had just touched down and rolled off the throttle when up behind me on the left drove a park ranger's 4WD. I knew I'd landed in a national park, which is only allowed with prior permission or in an emergency. At the time, I considered my predicament kind of urgent. The ranger strode up to my passenger door, opening it.

'So what's going on, then?' he asked.

'I'm sorry. I didn't mean to cause a fuss but I really needed to land and use the public facilities,' I answered.

'You just landed to go to the toilet?' he asked.

'Yes,' I replied.

The ranger turned to his assistant and told him there was nothing to worry about. I could see he was amused.

My face must have been as red as a beetroot from embarrassment, but my first consideration was comfort so I quickly raced across to the amenities block. On my way, I noticed a few more cars arriving and I couldn't believe all the attention, just when I didn't want it. By the time I came out, a crowd had gathered and there were more cars. Some tourists were taking photos of ELF sitting in the car park. When they asked me why had I landed here, I felt it best to tell the truth and make light of it. I know I made everyone's day. I flew off thinking I could have done without that experience. But, when you've got to go – you've got to go.

We headed south for Wilson's Promontory which is the most southern tip of Australia and known for its horrendous weather conditions. Jim dives for abalone in this area and he understood how treacherous it could get.

'Do you want to cut the corner?' he asked us.

'No, let's fly all the way around the point so we can say we've flown around the most northern, southern, eastern and western parts of Australia,' Jamie replied.

The weather didn't look good. Having local knowledge is always an advantage. Jamie really wanted to do it, so – one in, all in. It was somehow appropriate that this last part of the trip would provide us with the very worst flying conditions. I have never experienced turbulence like it. The rain didn't bother me so much, but the wind did. There were times when I swear my little ELF was going to be flipped right over by the angry gusts. I was used to turbulence now, but this was frightening. It was so bad that I was hoping the helicopters would hold together. I tried to climb to see if it was calmer higher up, but there was no relief. The only thing we could do was to focus, stay calm, not panic and just fly on. We didn't say much to each other during the forty-minute ordeal. It was like the final test, and we survived it. But I was glad to be on the ground an hour later for a fuel stop and a rest.

Grant and his wife, Roz, were waiting for us when we flew into Orbost late in the afternoon. They had a large property so we could land next to the house. We went out for dinner that night and Ellis met us at the restaurant. This was the last time we'd be together as a group, so I took the opportunity to raise a toast, thanking all the crew for helping me. I told them I could not have made the journey without their help. I needed them to know how much I had appreciated their friendship. I fought back my tears. This achievement had meant more to me than I think any of them realised. I'd always known I could never have done it alone. If it hadn't been for my friends, the journey that in many ways changed my life, would never have happened.

Jim and Jamie planned to fly past Sydney and back to the Hunter Valley. But I chose to make my final landing at Wollongong, south of Sydney. I needed to end my journey where it had begun, at the Westpac Rescue base and Prince Henry Hospital. And I wanted to land there feeling fresh and with a clear head, not after a long day's flying. Mum and Dad would be waiting for me at the hospital, and so would Derek and Leanne. I had missed everyone so much and I was starting to look forward to the finale. A hot shower, a good sleep, then a short flight from Wollongong to Sydney would allow me to savour the moment.

We turned the corner at the border into New South Wales and headed north. The weather was kind and the southern New South Wales beaches I had loved so much as a child were as beautiful as ever. Groups of people, walking on the white sand, waved to us as we passed. As I waved back, it felt as though I was waving goodbye. To fly around the entire coast of Australia was an achievement I could be very proud of, but I didn't want the dream to end.

'Let's go around again,' I said, as we made our approach to Wollongong.

'It's very tempting,' Jamie replied.

The three helicopters landed at the airfield which basked in sunshine. Jim and Jamie refuelled and helped me do the same. Then Jamie tied down the blades on ELF and Jim and Jenny helped me drag out my luggage and put the bubble cover on. This was the last time we'd be playing out this ritual. It was very sad. Before they left, I thanked them again for their help and gave each of them a big hug.

As the helicopters took off, I waved goodbye, feeling happy and sad at the same time. What an adventure we'd had!

After I paid my fuel bill, I called a cab that took me to the Novotel Hotel on North Wollongong Beach where I was able to have a shower and prepare for the final leg tomorrow. I remember lying in bed that night, thinking about my life. Where it had been, what had happened to me, where I was going and what I would do from here. I had expected that this journey would give me some direction in my life or, magically, give me answers to my questions. I'd played the final scene on approach into Prince Henry Hospital through my head time and again during the past months. I'd imagined having a revolutionary, almost spiritual, experience similar to an apparition where I would finally find the answers. Suddenly I would understand why my life had been so tragic. Why I'd been left paraplegic. And finally, I'd know where my life was headed.

But this wasn't going to happen. I knew that now. I didn't know exactly how I'd feel when I completed my journey tomorrow. I didn't know what to expect when I saw Nigel. And I wondered if he'd even be at Prince Henry Hospital to see me land in the morning. But I hoped he would be. I didn't know where our marriage was going, or if it was over. The thought of moving back to my home in Cobbitty frightened me. But after eight years of marriage, we needed to try to hold it together. It deserved a second chance.

My friend, Bruce Tarrant from Westpac Rescue, and the reporters and cameramen are wishing me good luck as I climb into the cockpit. It feels strange knowing I have only thirty minutes left to fly and I've done it. I've flown right around Australia!

I turn the key and start the engine. ELF makes her usual grinding and crunching noises as the clutch belts tighten and the blades begin whizzing around above my head. I do my pre take-off checks for the last time, then slowly raise the collective, floating me into the air. Everyone is waving to me as I taxi towards the runway and climb away, flying directly towards the coast. The final leg. I did it! I really did it!

I'm thinking about my accident and my injuries. I don't know why they had to happen to me but, despite my difficulties, I really am a whole person. I can achieve anything I put my mind to. I've proven that!

I'm flying high over the water, waving to people on the beach. I'm thinking about Laurie, who showed me how to fly. He shared his passion and gave me wings. I wonder if he's watching me now, I wonder if he knows what I've achieved.

I'm thinking about Allan, who really did live for flying. I admired his dedication, and I remember watching him in his last aerobatic competition. I see his abilities in Nigel. I think he still lives for flying through him.

I'm thinking about Peter, who was my favourite instructor. Sometimes I can hear him calmly giving me instructions: 'Watch your airspeed – that's good. Level your wings – perfect.' Peter lost his life, but he saved mine. He is my hero.

I'm thinking about Janine, who I know would have had a brilliant flying career. In everyone's opinion, she was a natural. Her life was cut way too short.

I'm thinking about Robert, who on the day of the accident, put his own safety second to another. He was a hero that day, too. I hope his mum and dad are at peace with his memory at last.

And I'm thinking about my beautiful friend, Lace, who shared her wings with me and showed me how to fly higher than I ever dreamed. She is always in my thoughts and she'll always be in my heart.

They're all gone now, but a piece of each of them will forever fly with me.

So how do I feel? I feel different to the girl who left the

helicopter base at Prince Henry Hospital almost seven weeks ago. I feel strong. I know I can do anything. I have no boundaries. I know I'll have many more challenges ahead in my life. Now I can approach them with greater strength.

'Helicopter Echo Lima Foxtrot, this is Sierra Victor November.'

'Sierra Victor November, go ahead.'

'Welcome home, Allana. This is Channel Seven. What's your present position?'

'I'm abeam Corrimal 500 tracking northbound.'

'We're heading south and would like to get some shots as you come in.'

Before long, the news helicopter appears on my left and the reporter on board conducts a mid air interview before flying off ahead. I'm approaching Cronulla and can see the tower where my rented unit is. I know I'll be moving from there soon.

'Helicopter Echo Lima Foxtrot, this is helicopter November Tango Victor.'

I know that voice so well. It's my friend Gary Ticehurst in the ABC chopper. I get a lump in my throat. To have him here as I make my approach towards Prince Henry Hospital means so much to me. Gary was with me on the day of the accident. He has been with me throughout my training and now, in my finest hour, it's appropriate that he's here with me again.

'November Tango Victor, go ahead.'

'Welcome home, mate, we've got you sighted and if you slow down, we'll fly in on your right and take some shots.'

'Come on over, Gary, I'm glad you're here.'

The other helicopter continues ahead and lands at the hospital at the front of the Westpac base. Gary and I fly a few orbits just out to sea, then right on 11 am, it is time for me to land.

'In you go, kid. I'm right behind you,' Gary broadcasts.

My landing site at the Westpac Rescue base is right on the coast. I approach from the east and descend slowly. I can see Mum and Dad, Derek and Leanne and my niece, Deniele. I can see Nigel's car and I know he must be down there somewhere too. The whole experience is surreal. Uplifted by the people around me and by the people in my thoughts, I realise they are my strength. I am able to achieve and I have my inner strength, because of the people who love me. I think about a fable I once heard that tells of birds who have a competition to see who can fly the highest. The eagle knows he is the biggest and the strongest. He will surely win. The eagle flaps his wings and climbs higher and higher until the world looks round and he knows no other bird can fly higher. But little does he know that a tiny wren has climbed upon his back. As the eagle begins to fly back to earth, the wren takes to the air and flies higher and higher than the eagle, winning the competition.

Through the support of my family and my friends, I have achieved more than I ever thought possible. They are my eagle.

I land on the cushioning grass and take a deep breath, relishing my accomplishment. A small group of Westpac crew members are lined up at the front of the hangar, and there are several television cameras and reporters waiting for me to shut down. This feeling of elation is one I'll never forget. The moment my blades are stationary, my brother Derek leads a group of people who come hastily towards me.

Derek embraces me. 'Congratulations, Sis,' he says.

There are people crowded around. There are cameras and microphones being pushed towards me. The questions come, but at first I can't speak. I try to, but I'm choked.

'How does it feel to be home?'

At last, I gather my composure.

'It feels terrific.'

I realise my life will never be the same ever again. I have the entire world at my feet. I've welcomed it into my life and it, in turn, has embraced me. I have so much of myself that I want to give back for the support I've received over the years, sometimes from complete strangers. I've asked God so many times to give me a reason, a purpose, for all that I've been through. And now I think I know.

I can see Nigel in the distance through the crowd in front of me. He's leaning against his bright red ute. I wonder why he doesn't come over to me. A few moments later, I catch a glimpse of a red vehicle leaving. It's Nigel. I watch him driving away out of the hospital gate. I guess he, too, realises that our lives have changed forever. I know he loves me, but Nigel didn't ever want to share me with the rest of the world. I've grown up. I'm independent now. I'm not his twenty-year-old little girl any more, and he chooses to walk away.

I see him disappear and I hear the roar of the car engine fade, wishing he could have shared my happiness, but knowing it is the end. My heart is filled with sadness. If only he'd raced up and embraced me, if only he'd told me, well done! Or, you did it! Or, something.

Cameramen and reporters still mingle around. There are people everywhere, but I feel very alone. I look towards the south and see my helicopter sitting on the grass and I smile, not wanting to spoil my moment of achievement.

Right then, a beautiful rainbow develops over the horizon, embracing the helicopter. I cannot believe what I'm seeing. I wonder if it's a sign of my friends smiling down on me. Maybe they're saying, well done. Or, maybe they're applauding. I don't really know.

I've been followed by rainbows before and this one gives me a feeling of peace. Now I know I'll never be alone!

No bird soars too high if he
soars with his own wings.
— WILLIAM BLAKE